P9-DZY-964

TELL THE NEXT GENERATION

TELL THE NEXT GENERATION

Homilies and Near Homilies

WALTER J. BURGHARDT, S.J.

PAULIST PRESS
New York/Ramsey

Grateful acknowledgement is herein made to publishers indicated for their kind permission to quote from the following works:

An excerpt from "A Kind of Loving" by Rod McKuen is reprinted from his volume *Listen To The Warm* by permission of Random House, Inc; copyright, 1967 by Rod McKuen.

An excerpt from "After Christmas: A Passage from a Christmas Oratoria" by W. H. Auden is reprinted from *W. H. Auden: Collected Poems*, edited by Edward Mendelson, by permission of Random House, Inc; copyright, 1944, by W. H. Auden.

An excerpt from *The Velveteen Rabbit or How Toys Become Real* by Margery Williams is reprinted by permission of Doubleday and Company, Inc.

Copyright © 1980 by
Walter J. Burghardt, S.J.

All rights reserved. No part of this book may be reproduced or transmitted in any form or by any means, electronic or mechanical, including photocopying, recording or by any information storage and retrieval system without permission in writing from the Publisher.

Library of Congress
Catalog Card Number: 79-91895

ISBN: 0-8091-2252-9

Published by Paulist Press
Editorial Office: 1865 Broadway, New York, N.Y. 10023
Business Office: 545 Island Road, Ramsey, N.J. 07446

Printed and bound in the
United States of America

TABLE OF CONTENTS

SACRAMENTS AND SACRED COMMITMENT

ANNIVERSARIES AND ANNUAL EVENTS

HUMAN AND CHRISTIAN LIVING

HUMAN AND CHRISTIAN DYING

". . . tell the next generation
that this is God. . . ."
(Ps. 48:13–14)

PREFACE

Two books of sermons have preceded the present selection: *All Lost in Wonder* (1960) and *Saints and Sanctity* (1965). Since then, in large measure due to the Second Vatican Council (1962–65), the homily has been startlingly highlighted within Roman Catholicism. For the first time in my memory, the homiletic word is recognized on a broad scale by priests and people as integral to the liturgy itself—not merely mandated by law, not just an introduction to the *real* liturgy, a prologue to Offertory, Consecration, and Communion. Moreover, the intimate link between liturgy and Scripture has triggered a return to the Bible for homiletic inspiration and content.

Regrettably, there is another side to the picture. The word from the pews is that our pulpit performance is hardly proportionate to our fresh inspiration. Why this is so, I make bold to suggest in the address that serves as Prologue to this volume. No need to repeat or defend those reasons here. The causes may be argued; the effect, a general homiletic inadequacy, seems beyond challenge.

And still I am not discouraged. I suspect that homiletics may be paralleling, even participating in, the evolution of the new liturgy. The liturgical *books* have been reformed; but the reform to which the books point, where liturgy actually expresses and effectively molds the faith of a community, is in its infancy. Similarly, the homily has been restored to its older dignity, is set forth by experts as itself a form of liturgical prayer; but the implementation of this reform in the life of the parish has only begun. Nor will the process be swift; it cannot be. For homiletic reform makes demands not only on the vocal chords of a priest and on his power to project, but on his imagination and his prayer life, on his openness to people and his willingness to undergo a lifetime of continuing education.

My primary purpose in publishing *Tell the Next Generation* is to help the reform along in a small but perhaps not insubstantial way. That is partly why each item is preceded by a brief introduction that places the piece in context and suggests the problem a priest might face in addressing the situation in question.

Not all the addresses in this volume can claim to be homilies in the proper sense; hence the subtitle *Homilies and Near Homilies*. I am brash enough to think that the nonhomilies *could* have been preached within a liturgical event, given different circumstances; hence their inclusion here.

Finally, it may not be impertinent to hope that this will not prove to be a book "for clerics only." After all, it is the laity to whom homilies are ordinarily preached. I pray earnestly, therefore, that my brothers and sisters who did not sit before me when these words were spoken may draw profit from them, some human and Christian warmth, even if the type is cold.

Walter J. Burghardt, S.J.

INTRODUCTION

THE WORD MADE FLESH TODAY

A book based on the power of the spoken and written word should reveal how the author looks at words, should suggest the background out of which his own word-weaving is born. A book that is in large measure a collection of occasional homilies ought to explain how the author sees the homiletic word as distinguished from other "words." A book that claims to link the word to human living might well indicate how a speaker, a homilist in particular, can translate the eternal word into flesh-colored syllables that will speak to today's man and woman.

These three facets of the word form the three sections of this introductory address, "The Word Made Flesh Today." It was originally fashioned for the Sixth Annual Conference (1977) of the Notre Dame Center for Pastoral Liturgy. The Conference theme was "Liturgical Ministry in America," and the address here reproduced fitted into the sessions on the need for word in the Christian community—indeed, the human community. It represents an effort to put together, in coherent fashion, ideas that have gradually taken shape in my thinking, writing, and speaking through four decades.

This address, then, is introductory. I intend it as framework for most of the talks included in this volume, to make them more understandable. This may tell you, better than a biography, where I come from and who I am.

Some years ago, at old Woodstock College in Maryland, I was plagued by a bothersome rhetorical problem. I had just about finished an Easter homily, but I was dissatisfied. So I walked down the corridor to the room of my learned colleague and dear friend John Courtney Murray. I told him: "John, I need your help. This Easter sermon here—I have my usual three points, and I have my conclusion. But I don't have an introduction." I was thinking, of course, in terms of a startling opening story, an attention-grabber. Murray looked at me for a moment, then said quietly and simply: "Walter, why don't you just tell them what you're going to talk about?"

That day I learned a lasting rhetorical lesson. An intelligent audience will forgive a preacher for not playing Bob Hope, if he lets them in on the subject of his sermon. And you will forgive this theologian for not tickling your palates with pâté de foie gras, if I give you a clear idea of the main course.

So then, my topic is the liturgical word we call "preaching." I have titled my talk "The Word Made Flesh Today." Three stages to that title: the Word ... made flesh ... today. (1) What is "word"? (2) What kind of word is it that is enfleshed in the liturgi-

3

cal homily? (3) How can the homiletic word be enfleshed today, be incarnated for this believing people? The Word . . . made flesh . . . today.

I

I come to you a weaver of words. Ever since I can remember, I have been seduced by syllables. In grade school my brother and I began the great American novel; to no one's surprise, it aborted. In high school I delighted in debate—either side of any question. But it was the Jesuit juniorate that genuinely focused my verbal future; for there I reveled in the rhythms of the Greeks and Romans, waltzed to English word masters.

I wept to the prophetic plaints of Aeschylus' Cassandra, laughed to the mocking irony of Aristophanes, even croaked to the music of his frogs: "Brekekekex, ko-ax, ko-ax." I agonized with gentle Sophocles over the incest of Oedipus, joined the closing chorus: "wait to see life's ending ere thou count one mortal blest."[1] I thrilled to Demosthenes assailing Athenian peace-at-any-price, was turned on by his classic description of panic in Athens that begins *Hespera men gar ēn* ("evening had already fallen").[2] In imagination I invaded Plato's cave and its prisoners, stared transfixed at the fire and the shadows of reality on the wall.[3] Time and again I wept at Socrates' parting words: "I go to die, and you to live; but which of us goes to the better lot, is known to none but God."[4] For all his verbiage, Cicero's command of the idiom could still excite me—whether castigating the conspirator Catiline or analyzing old age. I memorized vast sections of Homer, particularly organ sounds like *polyphloisboio thalassēs*, the shore of "the loud-resounding sea";[5] found a foreshadowing of the Christ-event in Vergil's *Fourth Eclogue*: "magnus ab integro saeclorum nascitur ordo;/ iam redit et Virgo. . . . "[6] I wrote Latin odes in imitation of Horace's "integer vitae,"[7] his "carpe diem" (live today!),[8] his "nunc est bibendum" (it's cocktail time).[9] And many a night I fell asleep, chastely, in the Lesbian arms of Sappho.

On the English scene, Shakespeare's artistry was ceaseless delight. Henry V roaming the camp at night, musing on the burdens of kings: "What infinite heart's ease/ Must kings neglect, that private men enjoy!"[10] Romeo forsaking his very name for Juliet: "Call me but love, and I'll be new baptiz'd."[11] Hamlet's "native hue of resolution . . . sicklied o'er with the pale cast of thought."[12] Shylock's ageless cry of the Jew: "If you prick us, do we not bleed?"[13] There was more than Avon's bard, of course. With Francis

Thompson, I fled the Hound of Heaven's "majestic speed, deliberate instancy." I resonated to Gerard Manley Hopkins comparing the Blessed Virgin to the air we breathe:

> If I have understood,
> She holds high motherhood
> Towards all our ghostly good
> And plays in grace her part
> About man's beating heart,
> Laying, like air's fine flood,
> The deathdance in his blood;
> Yet no part but what will
> Be Christ our Saviour still.[14]

With Cyrano in his last hour, I watched the Venetian-red leaves fall to the ground:

> Yes—they know how to die. A little way
> From the branch to the earth, a little fear
> Of mingling with the common dust—and yet
> They go down gracefully—a fall that seems
> Like flying.[15]

With Carl Sandburg, I experienced Chicago as the "hog butcher of the world"; went "down to the seas again" with John Masefield; sang an ode to Shelley's west wind, "thou breath of Autumn's being"; looked with Keats into Chapman's Homer; blew bugles with Tennyson to "set the wild echoes flying"; heard the revolutionary rustling of Whitman's *Leaves of Grass*.

Newman's periodic sentences entranced me, and sermons such as "The Second Spring" revealed how fact and reason could be infused with imagination and intuition. The paradoxes of Chesterton, that huge man with sombrero, swordstick, and cape, captured my fancy—from the incredible insights into Aquinas to the tantalizing, perhaps debatable "There is a Catholic way of teaching everything, even the alphabet, if only to teach it in such a way as at the same time to teach that those who learn it must not look down on those who don't."

There was all this, and much more. But it was in theology at rural Woodstock that words took flesh, that what might have been dilettante seduction became Christian life and death. For in theology the word took on unexpected meaning. In the Old Testament, I discovered, the word is wondrously alive. As John L. McKenzie was to phrase it years later, the spoken word for the Israelites was a distinct reality charged with power. It has power because it emerges from a source of power which, in releasing it, must in a way release itself. The basic concept of the word is the word-thing. The power of the word . . . posits the reality which it signifies. But in so doing it also posits the reality which speaks the word. No one can speak without revealing himself; and the reality which he posits is identified with himself. Thus the word is dianoetic as well as dynamic. It confers intelligibility upon the thing, and it discloses the character of the person who utters the word.[16]

That is why *God's* word is particularly powerful.

In the New Testament, I discovered, the word as a distinct reality charged with power is fulfilled to perfection. God not only expresses Himself in human syllables; He expresses Himself in a Word that is itself a Person. The same personal Word God utters from eternity, He uttered on a midnight clear—to us. "In Jesus Christ is fulfilled the word as a distinct being; as a dynamic creative entity; as that which gives form and intelligibility to the reality which it signifies; as the self-revelation of God; as a point of personal encounter between God and man."[17]

The word, I learned from St. James, is a perilous thing. "We use it to bless the Lord and Father, but we also use it to curse men who are made in God's image" (Jas 3:9). And still, in St. Paul's eyes, the word is an indispensable thing. "How are men to call upon him in whom they have not believed? And how are they to believe in him of whom they have never heard? And how are they to hear without a preacher?" (Rom 10:14).

Words, I learned from experience, can be weapons, and words can be healing. Words can unite in friendship or sever in enmity. Words can unlock who I am or mask me from others. Two words, "Sieg Heil," bloodied the face of Europe; three words, "Here I stand," divided the body of Christendom. Words have made slaves and freed slaves, have declared war and imposed peace. Words sentence to death ("You shall be hanged by the neck") and words restore to life ("Your sins are forgiven you"). Words declare a marriage dead, and words covenant a life together in love. Words charm and repel, amuse and anger, reveal and conceal, chill and warm. Words clarify and words obscure. A word from Washington rained down atomic hell on Hiroshima; words from an altar change bread and wine into the body and blood of Christ.

With all this, I feel no guilt in being a weaver of words. A word is real; a word is sacred; a word is powerful; a word is . . . I.

II

This leads to the second level of my argument; for our "word" here is not just any word, it is a liturgical word. If your experience goes back to mid-century, you remember how little the "liturgy of the word" once mattered. A brief but pungent proof: you could miss the whole liturgy of the word without having to confess it. Gloria and Credo, Epistle and Gospel and homily—you could come in out of the cold after all these were said and done, and still "hear Mass," still fulfil your obligation. No manual of morality did more than rap your knuckles lightly.

Why? Because the sole stress was on the sacrifice. One word alone was all-important: the consecratory word. Here was *the* Real Presence; here was the efficacious word, objectively infallible, utterly trustworthy, limpidly clear. No worry about the person, about reader or preacher, songstress or danseuse. No need for lips to be touched by live coals; enough that they whispered distinctly "This is my body." The back of the priest was more symbolic than his face; for the true priest was the hidden priest, the Christ of the sacrifice.

Today's liturgical attitude is refreshingly different, more balanced. In Vatican II's wake, there is fresh stress on the whole word as a locus where God transpires, comes to light. Music, readings, homily, dance—God is there (or can be there), a real presence.[18] My focus is on one of those four liturgical "words," the word that is homily.[19]

What is the liturgical homily, the homiletic word? If you prefer chaste Roman rhetoric, you have an official definition from the Congregation of Rites in 1964: "an unfolding either of some facet of the readings of Sacred Scripture or of some other text taken from the Ordinary or from the Proper of the Mass of the day, taking into consideration either the mystery being celebrated or the special needs of the listeners."[20] From this text, two concerns ought to dominate the homily and its preparation: liturgy and people—this liturgy and this people. This liturgy, because in the Lectionary and the Missal we find the substance of what is to be preached: in the words of Vatican II, "the proclamation of God's wonderful works in the history of salvation"—a proclamation that "should draw its content mainly from scriptural and liturgical sources."[21] This people, because in the liturgy "God's wonderful works" are not just read, not just remembered; they are re-presented, made effectively present. In the words of the Council fathers, "the mystery of Christ . . . is made present and active within us."[22]

The first concern, this liturgical event, the mystery, is the background for the second concern, this people, "the mystery made present." Because it is the indispensable background for the proclamation, for the word made flesh today, I devote to it this second main point. And I suggest that here four critical demands have fashioned four problems which prevent today's homily from being any better than yesterday's sermon: fear of Sacred Scripture, ignorance of contemporary theology, unawareness of liturgical prayer, and lack of proper preparation. A word on each.

First, fear of Scripture. For all too many priests, the Bible is a no-no; they don't dare touch it. "The exegetes have taken away my Lord, and I know not where they have laid him." What Jesus himself said, the words the Word proclaimed, the exegetes have hidden like Easter eggs, and the faithful in their paschal finery run around in circles trying to find them. And what do we come up with? What the *early Church* thought Jesus said or meant, or would have said if. . . . Miracles are out, the Magi barely in. Was Jesus virginally conceived, or is virginal conception a physical way of expressing a spiritual reality? Did Jesus "physically" rise from the rock, or doesn't the question make any sense any more? And—more bad news—stop looking for some specifically Christian content to morality that leaps out of the Bible; that, some moralists say, is highly dubious.

And the Old Testament? Forget it! Oust it from the rectory! It no longer announces Christ. Mary is not in Genesis 3:15, Jesus not in Isaiah 7:14; the priest is no longer prefigured in Melchizedek, the Mass in Malachi. The Song of Songs is secular eroticism and would be banned in Boston; the prophets preached social justice.

Scripture is indeed a mystery, if only because it is God's plan hidden in God from eternity. But it is a mystery revealed. The word of God that is Scripture is a unique, incomparable way in which God speaks to us, reveals Himself, challenges us, graces us. Here we come to know Christ as nowhere else. That is why St. Jerome could say "Ignorance of Scripture is ignorance of Christ." Difficult as it is, Scripture is still the single most important source for any Christian preacher. Not even dogma supplants Scripture in dignity or content. As Vatican II confessed, the magisterium "is not above the word of God, but serves it. . . ."[23]

Let me be blunt. I have no special competence in Scripture that gives me a head start over the parish priest. We have the same sources: meditation on the word and recourse to the commentaries. Prayer and sweat. When I preached for the golden jubilee of

John Quasten's ordination, the liturgical readings emphasized wisdom. They forced me back on biblical dictionaries, on Kittel and Léon-Dufour. It was there I discovered who the wise man is, and what he does that is so wise, and how he comes to be wise. When I preached to the Catholic University community on Holy Thursday, I was faced with the frustrating foot-washing Gospel. As so often, I turned to Raymond Brown's commentary on John. From mild sweat came bright light: *two* interpretations of the foot-washing in Johannine circles—and both exciting. Indeed Brown destroyed some old seminary simplicities; but, like most genuine scholars, he uprooted only to plant more richly.[24]

A second obstacle is ignorance of theology. Theology is indispensable for the word because it is the Church's ceaseless effort to understand the word. Once again, an obvious problem: where do you look? Mid-century theology may have been boring, but you could trust seminary professors to do what Pius XII expected of theologians: "show how the doctrines taught by the living magisterium are found explicitly or implicitly in Scripture and in divine tradition."[25] For that you look in vain: the manuals have vanished, and each theologian has his or her theology—from Baum to Tracy, from Reuther to Rahner, from Curran to McCormick. Theologians question everything, from the first sin to the Second Coming, from abortion to bestiality. Is there any help for the homilist?

Frankly, I see nothing but band-aid remedies until we fill a neuralgic priestly need: continuing education of the clergy. The Church's search for understanding did not grind to a halt when I took my last theology exam; nor is the meaning of God's word preserved immobile in a Vatican capsule. Our basic Christian words, the words we preach, must be constantly recaptured, rethought: God, Christ, and Spirit; sin and redemption; church and sacraments; justice and love; death and resurrection. Books like Dulles' *Models of the Church*, periodic reports like McCormick's "Moral Notes"—these can help. But until the clergy can read theology with understanding and a critical eye, liturgical homiletics will continue to be impoverished.

A third obstacle: unawareness of prayer—liturgical prayer. John Gallen's thesis is well known: "What the contemporary reform of the Church's liturgy needs most in this moment of its history is the discovery of liturgy as prayer."[26] Liturgical prayer, like all prayer, is a response. The God of mystery touches me, touches the worshiping community, with His presence. The initiative comes from God—not present coldly, abstractly, distantly, but laying hold of me, laying hold of the believing community, at the very core of our being. Prayer is our response to this kind of presence, to the thrilling action of God within us.

But what manner of prayer is the liturgical response? On your answer depends in large measure the kind of homily you construct. For me, prayer is fundamentally and ultimately "sacrifice of praise." Not that I downgrade conversion, petition, thanksgiving. I claim that all three are subsumed ritually in a glorious doxology: Glory to God. . . . In the liturgy I celebrate God. Oh, I do not minimize man or woman. I simply claim that liturgy will be a humanizing experience to the extent that, in playing before God, the human person becomes increasingly image of God. To become human is to praise God.[27]

The point is, the homily is liturgy. In Jungmann's strong sentence, the homily "should emanate from the consciousness that although it is freely created by the liturgist, it is liturgy itself."[28] And the liturgy is prayer. Conclusion? The homily is prayer. The logic is impeccable; only the meaning is debatable. When you proclaim "God's wonderful works," when you help re-present the mystery that is Christ, when with human words you touch the Christ-event to this particular people, what manner of prayer is this? Is it prayer at all?

An examination of conscience, then, to humble the homilist: What is your theology of prayer? Of liturgical prayer? Of homiletic prayer? Do you have one?

The fourth obstacle is the kind of devil that cannot be overcome even by prayer and fasting. To me, the unprepared homilist is a menace. I do not minimize divine inspiration; I simply suggest it is rarely allotted to the lazy. Here I resonate to a story told me two years ago at Belmont Abbey by the famed Baptist biblicist and preacher Dale Moody. A student in his Spirit course at the Louisville seminary wasn't meeting the professor's expectations. So Dr. Moody called him in and (in a delightful drawl I cannot imitate) said: "Son, you're not doin' all that well in my course on the Holy Spirit. You been studyin'?" "Dr. Moody," the young man replied, "I don't have to *study* about the Spirit; I'm *led* by the Spirit." "Son," Moody asked, "that Spirit ever lead you to the library? If He doesn't soon, you're in deep trouble."

The homilist is in deep trouble if the Spirit does not lead him—lead him to the chapel indeed, but lead him to the library as well.

Implicit in these four obstacles is the major thrust of this second point: the mystery must be preached—God's wonderful works in the story of salvation. From the Spirit of God moving over the waters and a loving God toiling over clay, through the first sin and the first death, through covenant after covenant to the final covenant in God's blood, down to today's "signs of the times," the word must take flesh. Despite the difficulties, God's wonderful works must be preached, especially as they surge up from Scripture and the liturgy. If they are poorly proclaimed, the liturgy will be less effective in making God's works effectively present.

III

This leads to the third level of my argument. I have spoken of the word, and of the word made flesh in the liturgical homily. Now the crucial issue: how can the word be made flesh today? So far, the power of the word and the need for the word. Now, how do you incarnate the word for this people? How can the mystery be made present, not for the Jews of 27 or the Gentiles of 57, but for this congregation in 1977?

Here two realities come together in striking fashion: the insight of the theologian and the hunger of the people. In a typically perceptive article, Yves Congar has addressed the problem of liturgical preaching.[29] He locates three links between word and worship. First, Christian worship is an anamnesis: it is an actualizing memory, an active re-presentation, "of the acts by which God intervened to make a covenant with us and to save us," so that these acts "keep their operative value for the believers of all ages, who make them actual again in the Spirit when they celebrate these acts in faith and thanksgiving."[30] But the liturgy's insights "are more or less veiled"; liturgical texts and forms tend to be immobilized, with rare exceptions are the same for all, whatever their condition; the connection between the Church's sacraments and Christ's pasch is not instantly recognizable. What the homily does is extend the immemorial symbols to a particular time and place, a particular people.[31] The old is expressed anew; it must be, to come alive, to keep alive, to make alive.

Second, worship is a witness to faith—faith being "my response to God's action communicated to me through his Word."[32] The sacraments, Aquinas insisted, are sacraments of faith. In what sense? Because, Vatican II explains, the sacraments "not only presuppose faith, but by words and objects they also nourish, strengthen, and express it."[33] But the peril of liturgy is that it can be impersonal. The homily personalizes what the rite expresses in a common and general way. It should rouse the faith of this people more personally than is possible for liturgical symbols and ritual actions.[34]

Third, Christian worship is a spiritual sacrifice: it consists basically in accepting gratefully God's Eucharistic gift and in uniting to it the spiritual offering of our concrete existence, our total life. The specific function of the homily is not only to explain the liturgical mystery, but to bring the faithful into the mystery "by throwing light on their life so that they can unite it to this mystery. When this happens, the sermon is truly a Word which prompts a response."[35] Says Congar in a startling sentence: "I could quote a whole series of ancient texts, all saying more or less that if in one country Mass was celebrated for thirty years without preaching and in another there was preaching for thirty years without the Mass, people would be more Christian in the country where there was preaching."[36]

Theological insight is reinforced by people hunger. Our people are hurting. Not merely the millions consciously squirming in the pews, but the uncounted Christians who are hungry and do not know why. To deepen their Christian living, at times to make it endurable, the homily should throw light on their life in such a way that they can link human living to the paschal mystery. It is not primarily a matter of facts, biblical and theological information. They hurt because, on the one hand, the ritual does not express their faith experience, the symbols do not symbolize, God's wonderful works are just too wonder-full, and, on the other hand, the homilist who should bring liturgy and life together apparently does not know how. He does not speak to their hungers.

What to do? My pressing plea will force you back to my first point; my recommendation revolves around words. That first point was not a *tour de force*, not narcissistic autobiography. We homilists will not link worship to life unless we become translators. What that involves staggered me recently when I read a remarkable article on justice as a culture problem by that fine Fordham sociologist Joseph Fitzpatrick. In part he wrote:

> ... I don't know whether you've read Father André Dupeyrat's wonderful little book, *Savage Papua*. Among the Papuans the pig is a sacred animal. The women may nurse the pigs at their breast if there is no sow around to nurse them. In our Scriptures the sacred animal is the lamb. "Behold the lamb of God." This

meant absolutely nothing to the Papuans. In order to communicate to the Papuans what "Lamb of God" meant among the Hebrews, Dupeyrat would have to say "Christ is the pig of God." Jesus a pig! In New York? Imagine my going into the pulpit in New York and saying "Glory to God and praise, and to the Lord Jesus who is the pig of God." Yet if I want to communicate to the Papuans the meaning that is communicated to us and to the Hebrews and to the religious tradition of the West, I have to learn what their meanings are.

This is not easy to take. There is no intrinsic relation between the Lamb and the Savior. He was born among the people for whom the lamb was the source of food and the source of clothing, the great economic basis of their life and their society. And the pig was a scavenger. In the parable of the Prodigal, the son is described as reaching a hopeless state of degradation—he was feeding pigs. The most wonderful thing a Papuan can do is to feed pigs. Note how these basic economic realities become symbols. Religious meanings become projected in them and they become the context in which our psychological and emotional response to them as religious symbols eventually gets put in place. Then if you take the symbol away and put another in its place, our religious experience starts to turn upside down.[37]

The Papuan pig is not only instructive for missionaries; it is a paradigm for every preacher. In preaching, I must translate.[38] God's definitive revelation was indeed given through the divine Word, but it "uses human words that were already current and loaded with overtones from the surrounding world."[39] When that revelation is translated into dogma or interpreted by theology, it is not yet the preacher's word: it is jargon-infested and culture-conditioned. One example. Years ago a reviewer commended Ronald Knox's sermon style with a sentence something like this: Knox never uses expressions like "Holy Mother Church," which some preachers use as casually and as carelessly as sailors use obscenities, to conceal their inability for sustained communication.

My constant question must be: What do these words say to this congregation? Karl Rahner put it concisely: "The preacher should be able to hear his own sermon with the ears of his actual audience."[40] John Courtney Murray expressed the same idea more captivatingly: "I do not know what I have said until I understand what you have heard." What does this audience hear when I say "church"? Institution? Community? Sacrament? Herald? Servant? Does their experience of "church" conjure up the qualities of love and tenderness I associate with my physical mother? And "holy" has taken on triumphalistic overtones for Christians who see themselves, their community, and especially Rome as sickeningly sinful.

Take a more likely example, the monosyllable that makes the world go round: love. Here, if anywhere, the committed Christian confronts confusion. On the one hand, the whole Christian "thing" is love, or it is hoax. On this, God's own word rings loud and clear: God *is* Love; whatever exists, man or mountain, blue marlin or robin redbreast, stems from love divine; out of love God gave His only Son to earth and cross; on the twin command of love rest the law and the prophets; love towers above faith and hope; unless I love my brothers and sisters, I cannot claim to love God.

On the other hand, the word "love" is frightfully mangled, manipulated. Dr. James Shannon put it vividly to a Christian Family Movement seminar: we use love to describe "the motive for the voluntary death of Jesus Christ on Calvary, the subject matter of hard pornographic movies, the bond of affection between Flower Children at Woodstock, the intimate union of a husband and a wife, and the unbuttoned promiscuity of Fire Island on a weekend."[41] And so he suggested a moratorium on the word "love"; during the moratorium, experiment with other words, words that say precisely what we mean. I would add: let not the liturgist sell short those who just sing about love—where the naked syllables ("When you say love, you've said it all") are admittedly inadequate, but the beat, the rhythm, the music makes for meaning.

Admit it: the homiletic movement from Scripture through theology and prayer to the present liturgical moment is a frightening function, a dismaying task. It is not simply a matter of escaping the malapropism—not imitating the acting mayor of New York City who assured a Harlem audience: "My face may be white, but my heart is as black as yours." What is time-consuming and soul-searing in each homily's preparation is that I must (1) grasp the genuine meaning of a word as it emerged from the mouth of Jeremiah or the pen of Paul or the contemplation of a Johannine community, (2) touch it to the paschal mystery celebrated by the Church, and (3) transform it so that the word takes on the personal and cultural clothes of this moment, of these believers. Here is the agony of preparation, here its occasional ecstasy.

I am not boasting when I confess that I consume four hours in preparation for every minute in the pulpit. Some of it goes into research, sheer information. In preaching on the Bread of Life, for example, it was important for me to discover that Jesus' discourse in John 6 is colored by two themes; scholars call them the sapiential and the sacramental. Jesus feeds us with his word and he feeds us with his flesh; the "bread from heaven" which "gives life to the world" (Jn 6:33) is God's revelation and Christ's flesh. Some of those hours are spent in mulling, over days at times—what this scriptural data might have to say to a community living the paschal mystery today—until a promising central idea bursts forth. Ah yes: in today's context of human hungers, talk about the Bread of Life will sound awfully empty, suspiciously hollow, unless we who feed on the Eucharistic Christ are ourselves eucharists for the life of the world. It is a question of real presence. If I am to be a eucharist for the life of the world, my feeding on the flesh of Christ must take me from church to world. I must begin to be present to others, present where they are, present in ways that respond to their needs, to their hungers. *I* must be present—not merely my money or my mind—somewhat hidden at times but always totally committed because as a Christian, as a Christ, my life is love and only love can bring life.

From that point my hours are given over to . . . words. Precisely here is a preacher's crucifixion. A word is not an entry in Webster; it is colored by living experience. The Eucharist is indeed a bread that gives life; but when *you* hear the word "life," you hear something quite different from the 200,000 skin-and-bones starving who "live" in the streets of Calcutta, build tiny fires to cook scraps of food, defecate at curbstones, curl up against a wall to sleep—perhaps to die. Yes, a word is real, is sacred, is powerful, but inevitably a word is . . . I. This makes a double demand on a preacher: I must sense what my people hear, and I must say what I mean.

But clarity is not enough. A homily is not a catechism or a manual of dogma or a textbook in theology. The word flings forth a challenge; it is a summons to decision; God wants a reply. In Semmelroth's words, "in the word of preaching the flood of historical redemptive events is grasped and brought before man for his decision. Again and again men are addressed in preaching and moved to fashion their lives in accordance with what is said."[42] But really, are they so moved? God's grace is indeed all-powerful, but it dashes against two powerful Catholic adversaries: a homilist dead below the larynx, and a minimal vocabulary dominated by abstract nouns ending in -tion. If I am to persuade, my whole person should be aflame with what I proclaim. If I am to move, the words I utter must be chosen with care and love, with sweat and fire. That is why, before I set pen to paper, I listen to Beethoven or Tchaikovsky, Vivaldi or Mary Lou Williams, Edith Piaf or the theme from "Doctor Zhivago"; I read poetry aloud, Shakespeare or Hopkins, T. S. Eliot or e. e. cummings—something to turn me on, so that the end result will not sound like a Roman rescript or a laundry list. To challenge, the word must come alive.

Ultimately, *I* am the word, the word that is heard. And—I say it fearfully—it is not a clever rhetorician the people need, but a holy homilist. Holy in what sense? Because aware that I am only *a* word, not *the* word: if God does not speak through me, I am "a noisy gong, a clanging cymbal" (1 Cor 13:1). Because my homily is a prayer: in preparation and pulpit, I stand before God in praise of Him, not of my own rhetorical perfection. Because aware of my own weakness: I too need the word I preach, I too need forgiveness, I too am vulnerable, I am a *wounded* healer. Because, like my hearers, I too ceaselessly murmur: "I believe, Lord, help my unbelief." Because I am in love: with the things of God, with the people of God, with God Himself. Because the hungers of God's family are my hungers: when they bleed, I weep. Unless some of this breaks through, the word may indeed be proclaimed, but it will hardly be heard. The word is . . . I.

My brothers and sisters in Christ: The word can be made flesh today. But only on condition that we take the word seriously, handle it sacredly. Every word: the scriptural word, the sacramental word, the secular word, the homiletic word. For all our pulpit problems, I am not disheartened. I take heart from two disparate sources: the Christian faithful and four lines of verse. In thirty-six years of priestly preaching, not once have I encountered an unresponsive congregation, not once a believing community that could not be stirred. And on those occasions when I have been most acutely aware of a chasm, of a gulf that yawns between the audience and myself, between their experience and mine, I draw Christian hope from Rod McKuen:

> I make words for people I've not met,
> those who will not turn to follow after me.
> It is for me a kind of loving.
> A kind of loving, for me.[43]

THE LITURGICAL
YEAR

1
THE ABSENCE OF CHRIST
For a homilist uninspired by the readings

Early in 1968 I was asked to preach at a Sunday liturgy for Georgetown University students, within a series of Lenten sermons by guest preachers. What precisely to talk about took much mulling. Our country was at war; campuses were aflame, literally and figuratively. And still I hesitated to look in those directions. It was not simply that, in my twenty-second year of teaching seminarians at Woodstock College in Maryland, I lived at a safe remove from fire bombs and bloody protests. Rather, I was persuaded that our young men and women of intelligence were growing up in a climate where a crisis even more basic than war and injustice confronted them, a crisis that might well lie at the root of most others. In 1968, what could a man or woman believe?

The question was far from academic; it arose from a pervasive doubt and cynicism, and it touched men and women wherever they lived, in everyday existence. Where do you find God? Where discover the face of Christ? I was convinced that theology and Teilhard had something pertinent to offer college students, might point them Godward, Christward.

As I read this sermon a decade later, it seems that the same questions are being asked. We are no longer at war; it is hard to muster a covey of collegians for dramatic confrontation. But the 1968 question has not vanished; the search for the Transcendent still agonizes us. Where do you look for God and His Christ?

Today is an age of crises. I mean an age of critical issues that agonize the human heart. There is the crisis of war: how much blood may a human being shed for justice' sake? There is the crisis of race: where dare a human being draw the color line? There is the crisis of sex: what may two human beings do in the name of love? There is the crisis of poverty: how long must two fifths of the world go hungry? There is the crisis of religion: at what point does a form of worship become heresy or idolatry?

War and peace, white and black, man and woman, rich and poor, Catholic and Protestant—these are indeed critical issues. But I submit that at this moment in history there is a crisis more crucial, more basic, than any of these. The most critical issue of all is not bombs, not skin, not morals, not food, not even church. It is the crisis of God. What can a human being believe? In the twentieth century, is belief still possible? And if it is, how do the man and woman of today touch God? How does God touch them?

Interior to the crisis of God is the crisis of Christ. Not merely, *what* is he? How can the human mind grasp "God-man," divinity and humanity made one in the womb of a virgin? More critically, *where* is he? How can the whole person lay hold of him? Can I honestly say of him "There he is," as I can say of you "There you are"? Is he really present, or is it more honest to admit his "real absence"?

This afternoon I shall do three things briefly: (1) analyze the absence of Christ, (2) project the presence of Christ, (3) suggest the task of the intelligent Christian confronted by this paradox. More simply: I shall say, Christ is *not* here; I shall say, Christ *is* here; and I shall ask, where do you go from there?

I

First then, there is a genuine sense in which *Christ is not here.* He is not here as he was in Palestine. I do not see him as Mary did, bundled in straw. I do not reach for him as Peter did, walking on the waters. I do not speak to him as Dismas did, bleeding on the wood. I do not grasp him as Magdalene did, risen from the rock. I do not see the smile part his lips; I do not hear the thunder or the music of his voice; I do not trace his wounds with my finger. In that sense Christ is indeed absent.

More than that: a whole generation of Christians has grown up, is still growing up—young men and women who do not sense the presence of Christ where I do—not at all or not so easily. There are youthful Christians who do not discover Christ in *nature*, do not experience him in the things they see and hear and touch, are insensitive to the insight of a poet like Plunkett:

I see his blood upon the rose,
And in the stars the glory of his eyes,
His body gleams amid eternal snows,
His tears fall from the skies.[1]

Many a young Christian fails to find Christ in the *preached word*: I mean, in the proclamation of Scripture or the declamation of a preacher. A centuries-old Semitic text is ripped from context and flung into twentieth-century Washington, five minutes of unrelated moralizing are mingled with a spate of parochial announcements— and in some miraculous fashion the Lord is supposed to transpire. Understandably he does not.

Many a contemporary Christian fails to touch Christ in the *liturgy*, whether in the liturgical assembly or in the communion of his flesh and blood. It may be that too often the gathered people of God are strangers, faces in a crowd, to all appearances joyless and loveless. It may be that for the sophisticated Catholic transubstantiation is too hard to swallow. Whatever the reason, too few Christians can sing as lyrically as Aquinas:

> Godhead here in hiding, whom I do adore
> Masked by these bare shadows, shape and nothing more,
> See, Lord, at thy service low lies here a heart
> Lost, all lost in wonder at the God thou art.[2]

Too few Christians find Christ in their *fellow man*. It is not that they find little to love in the poor and the black, in the slave and the starved, in the maim and the lame and the blind. Quite the contrary: the remarkable thing about today's young is their yearning to serve their brothers and sisters, the way they can live and love, cry and die. But is it not man that emerges from all this? In what save some poetic sense is this Christ? What do the words of Christ really mean: "As long as you did it to one of these, you did it to me"? "Give him a cup of cold water, and you give it to me"? Somehow what emerges from the streets of Selma and the shacks of Appalachia, from the vineyards of Delano and the paddy fields of Vietnam, is not the face of the risen Christ but the features of crucified man.

II

So then, there is a genuine problem here: the absence of Christ. He does not seem to be here. Neither from nature nor from the spoken word, neither from liturgy nor from living man, does the Lord of the living leap forth. Encounter with Christ is not easy. Is the experience even possible? The question leads logically into my second point. I say the experience is possible, because *Christ is here*. The absence is only apparent, the presence is real.

To grasp the paradox, I suggest that two remarkable sentences from Teilhard de Chardin's *The Divine Milieu* can be wonderfully helpful. The language is difficult, but the insight is glorious.

> If we may alter a hallowed expression, we could say that the great mystery of Christianity is not exactly the appearance, but

the transparence, of God in the universe. Yes, Lord, not only the ray that strikes the surface, but the ray that penetrates, not only Your Epiphany, Jesus, but Your Diaphany.[3]

The point is: God's self-manifestation, Christ's disclosure of himself, does not modify the apparent order of things. Rain remains rain: precipitation has not been displaced by the tears of Jesus. The words of Scripture and of the preacher are still man-made symbols, feeble attempts to express an idea or vision that defies expression. The Eucharistic species contain after consecration the selfsame chemical constitution as before. And man remains man, with his hates and his loves, his laughter and his tears, his agony and his ecstasy.

In other words, what strikes the eye, the ear, the flesh, remains the same: a raindrop, a word, a loaf of bread, a human being. The new thing lies on a deeper level. It is, Teilhard says, like some translucent material: put a light within it and you illuminate the whole. So too, he says,

> the world appears to the Christian mystic bathed in an inward light which intensifies its relief, its structure and its depth. This light is not the superficial glimmer which can be realised in coarse enjoyment. Nor is it the violent flash which destroys objects and blinds our eyes. It is the calm and powerful radiance engendered by the synthesis of all the elements of the world in Jesus.[4]

The idea is deep and dense and difficult, but at bottom it simply expresses in breath-taking accents the omnipresence of Christ: he is everywhere. This is the thrilling Christian fact. With the coming of God in flesh, all creation was transformed, because it was given a new direction: Christward. St. Paul saw it—that breathless section in Romans, "We know that all of creation has been groaning together in travail until now" (Rom 8:22): nature itself shares the stress, the anxiety, the pain we ourselves feel as we wait for the promised redemption. The early Christian Fathers sensed it: for them, the world is so truly one whole that when the Son of God broke into it, simply everything took on a new dignity. Poets have glimpsed it: for Gerard Manley Hopkins, "The world is charged with the grandeur of God." And even if "all wears man's smudge and shares man's smell,"

> . . . for all this, nature is never spent;
> There lives the dearest freshness deep down things. . .

Because the Holy Ghost over the bent
World broods with warm breast and with ah! bright wings.[5]

Teilhard grasped it with unparalleled richness—so much so that he could salute matter "charged with creative power, ocean turbulent with the Spirit, clay molded and animated by the Word Incarnate."

This is not an unchristian pantheism; it is an effort to take the Incarnation seriously. Since Bethlehem, not only man but all reality has been charged with the presence of Christ. But do not look for the *face* of Christ—this is sheer imagination. It is his energizing *activity* that charges the rainbow and the atom: with him and in him and through him the world is moving *toward* him.

Similarly for Scripture and the preached word. Christ is indeed there. But not an epiphany, a revelation from outside, on the surface of things: the face of Christ on the printed page, my lips suddenly the lips of Christ. This is not magic: read the Bible, and Christ will talk to you; listen to Burghardt, and your darkest doubts will disappear. There *is* something divinely dynamic about the word of God: it comes from Him and it speaks of Him; His breath warms the cold syllables. But there is no *real* presence of Christ in the word of God without your response to it. And this response is impossible unless Christ is already present within you: I mean, active in you, energizing you. Remember the chilling words of Christ to those Jews who did not believe him when he spoke the truth to them: "He who is *of God* hears the words of God. The reason why you do not hear them is that you are *not of God*" (Jn 9:47).

In like manner for the liturgy. Christ is indeed here. In your gathering together: "Where two or three are gathered *in my name*, there am I in the midst of them." Beneath the consecrated species: "This *is* my body; this *is* my blood." But once again, there is no automatic epiphany of Christ on the face of your classmate or your fascinating date, in the texture of the bread or the sparkle of the wine. The Christ who is in them becomes translucent through the Christ who is *in you*—through the faith and hope and love which themselves bear eloquent witness to the potent presence of Christ within you.

So too for your brothers and sisters—those who share your commitment to Christ and those who reject it, those for whom life is intoxicating laughter and those for whom life is a burden almost too heavy to endure. Christ is indeed there, in all of them, in each of them. As Vatican II put it, "by His incarnation the Son of God has united Himself in some fashion with every man."[6] Christ is there. But not some surface epiphany—the face of Christ suddenly superimposed on LBJ or Martin Luther King. The Christ in every man will become translucent, will come through to you, on one condition: that your faith and your love are strong enough to light up the Christ who is profoundly there—there by his love, by his concern, by his ceaseless activity, there in every human yearning for bread or peace, for justice or freedom, for life or love.

III

Apparent absence, real presence. My third point: where do you go from there? First, a twin realization. On the one hand, the search for Christ is extraordinarily difficult, because so much depends on my faith and my love. On the other hand, encounter with Christ is possible, simply because he surrounds me, to be encountered everywhere and in everyone, ready to reveal himself to faith and to love. Here Teilhard is superb:

> In our hands, in the hands of all of us, the world and life (*our world, our life*) are placed like a Host, ready to be charged with the divine influence, that is to say with a real Presence of the Incarnate Word. The mystery will be accomplished. But on one condition: which is that *we shall believe* that *this* has the will and the power to become for us the action—that is to say the prolongation of the Body of Christ. If we believe, then everything is illuminated and takes shape around us: chance is seen to be order, success assumes an incorruptible plenitude, suffering becomes a visit and a caress of God. . . .[7]

Secondly, if you commit yourself intelligently to this search, you will find yourself increasingly sensitive to four tangible aspects of your relationship to God in Christ: (1) You will find yourself absorbed by a *living* presence, a divine activity more real than your physical surroundings. (2) You will be aware of a *holy* presence that fills you with awe and fear, the while it warms and draws you—what Mouroux called "a kind of rhythm between hope and fear, each mutually supporting and generating the other." (3) You will know an inexpressible *loneliness*; for in the presence of Love, you will still be far from Love, agonizingly aware that to find yourself you must lose yourself, to grasp God you must risk all. (4) Even within sorrow you will sense a profound *joy*, strong and unshakable, a joy that will not be imprisoned but must burst forth to be shared with others.[8]

This will be real presence, because this will be shared love.

2
DON'T BE AFRAID
Advent for the medical profession

Again a distinctive challenge. The time: a weekday in Advent 1974. The situation: a special liturgy for the medical personnel of Georgetown University Hospital in the nation's capital. The obvious problem: what does Christ's advent, his coming, say specifically to the medical profession?

One approach seemed uncommonly promising: start not with the doctors but with the people to whom they minister. Common to most hospital patients is a touchingly human emotion: they are afraid. For various reasons, as I try to explain. And what makes the Incarnation ceaselessly pertinent is that the Son of God took flesh to touch not only our sins but our fears, to taste and share them, to make possible a love that enables us to live, if not without fear, at least with fear.

The challenge to a Christian doctor is the challenge at the heart of his profession, of his apostolate. A dozen times each day Christ "comes" to each doctor, comes with very human fears, comes to a man or woman in a white coat who, like Christ, is a healer. Christ meets Christ; yes, fear meets fear; love lightens fear, at times casts out fear.

Paradoxically, even the doctor may learn from his/her fearful Christ not to be afraid.

About seven years ago, something unforgettable took place in a Phoenix hospital. A sixteen-year-old girl lay close to death. She knew she was going to die, knew she would die in a matter of days. A day or so before she died, a dear friend, a priest, came into her hospital room; it was the last time he would see her. He was dreadfully distressed, and the pain was there on his face for all to see. Janet looked up into his anguished eyes, and very simply she said: "Father, don't be afraid. . . . Don't . . . be . . . afraid."

I

My brothers and sisters in Christ: Your Christian apostolate in medicine has to do with people who are afraid. From the cavity in a tooth to the cancer in a breast, people who come to you are afraid. And there are at least three good reasons why they are afraid—why *I* am afraid. I am afraid because it may hurt; I am afraid because I am alone; I am afraid because I may die. Any one, or all three.

(1) I am afraid because it may hurt—or already does. Pain is inseparable from human existence: agony of body and anguish of spirit. Most of it I bear without you. But there are moments or months when you are intimately part of my hurt. I come to you because I have to, or because I trust you. But even when I trust you, I hurt, and I am afraid you may add to my hurt—you may lay bare the flesh that festers or the self I do not want to face.

(2) I am afraid because I am alone. There is something chillingly lonely about sickness. I am brought face to face with myself, my helplessness, my insufficiency. That body or mind which, when well, others reached out to, that same body or mind, when broken, others are ill at ease with; I am set apart. And there is something chillingly lonely about a hospital. There are indeed warm bodies around, a swarm of personnel; but I almost lose my identity, my singularity, my uniqueness as a person: I become a room number, a disease, a blood type, a wrist tag. Many years ago, I counted the people who entered my hospital room, beginning with the new-linens' dropper at 6 a.m. I stopped counting at 5:30; there had been 29, and I knew . . . none. I was chillingly lonely.

(3) I am afraid because I may die. In all genuine illness I face to some extent the ultimate mystery: death. And I do not want to die. Because I love life, this life; because there is so much life right here, now, in me and in you. Or because there are very few persons who do not, at some time, share the agonizing concern of my dear friend with Hodgkin's disease. About 35, three young children—she has fought this disease for eleven years through every debilitating treatment, every promising experiment, known to medical science—fought it with a faith in man and God that brings tears to my eyes: a cure would be found; if not, God would work His wonders in her. And now—now it is likely that in 18 months she will be dead. Man has failed, and God will not intervene. And so she phoned, after hearing a highly questionable homily on the problems of resurrection—phoned to ask in heartsick accents: "What will happen when I die? Will I, will this body of mine, really come alive?"

II

Now what has all this to do with Advent? Quite a bit, really. Advent (*adventus*) centers on a coming—the coming of Christ: Christ has come and Christ will come again. The reason why he came is symbolized in today's first reading (Gn 3:8–10). The first human person, shaped by God's loving hands, cowers and quivers among the trees in a garden. God calls to him: "Where are you?" And he can only respond pathetically: "I heard the sound of you in the garden, and I was afraid, because I was naked; and I hid myself."

What sin has spawned is rupture—alienation on four levels. (1) Sin severs man from God. In the words of the prodigal, "I am no longer worthy to be called your child" (Lk 15:18). (2) Sin severs man within, sin is schizophrenia. In the words of St. Paul, "I do not understand my own actions: I do not do what I want, I do the very thing I hate" (Rom 7:15). (3) Sin severs man from man: we shed the blood of our brothers and sisters. "Cain rose up against his brother Abel and killed him" (Gn 4:8)—in Ireland, in the Middle East, in the District of Columbia. (4) Sin severs man from earth: we enslave the earth, rape it, and the earth now threatens to destroy us. Little wonder we are afraid; for we are naked to our enemies, strangers even to our God, strangers to ourselves.

For this Christ came. He *is* Reconciliation, the possibility of a peace the world cannot give. It is summed up in today's third reading (Jn 14:25–27): "Peace I leave with you, my peace I give to you. Not as the world gives do I give to you. Let not your hearts be troubled, neither let them be afraid." In Bethlehem God confronted with His own flesh the foundations of our fear, began the fourfold task of reconciliation: He made it possible for me to live at peace with my God, with myself, with my brothers and sisters, even with a hostile earth. I can live unafraid—it is possible—through Jesus Christ, our Lord.

But to live at peace, to live unafraid, is not something automatic, magic from the wand of Christ. Fear will disappear from my existence to the extent that love lays hold of me. Today's second reading (1 Jn 4:16–18) is crucial here: "There is no fear in love, but perfect love casts out fear." I will live at peace with God and myself, with human persons and inhuman things, in the measure that I can reach out to them, hand and heart, can touch them in love. There is no other way to cast out fear, all fear, to live unafraid.

III

So far, two of my three points: (1) People who come to you are afraid: because they hurt, because they are alone, because they may die. (2) God took flesh, our flesh, to touch that fear, to taste it, to share it, to make possible the love that lightens fear, the perfect love that casts out fear. But, third and last, what has this to do with you? By all means, let a loving Christ cast out fear! It may even help textbook medicine.

No, my brothers and sisters. The heart of the matter is this: the Christ who once came in flesh, the flesh he took from Mary, comes to you again in flesh, the flesh of the frightened, the flesh that comes to you trembling with fear. Here is your Advent, your Christmas. Do not look for Christ in a stable, in a feeding trough, in straw: he is not there! In your life, with your commitment, Christ will come to you in frightened flesh, or he may not really come to you at all.

Don't misunderstand me. Christ will come to you on Christmas as he comes to you today, in this mystery of his love—cradled in your hand, pillowed on your tongue. And Christ will always be present in response to your love: "If anyone loves me . . . my Father will love him, and we will come to him and make our home with him" (Jn 14:23).

The point is: in your specific apostolate, Christ comes to you in a special way. He comes to you in people, in every new Bethlehem and each fresh Calvary, in holy innocents and crucified sinners. This is not pious poetry. It was Christ himself who told us how he will ultimately judge our Christianness. On the last day he will say to the just: "I was hungry and you gave me food, I was thirsty and you gave me drink, I was a stranger and you welcomed me, I was naked and you clothed me, I was sick and you visited me, I was in prison and you came to me." And the just will be puzzled: "Lord, when did we see you hungry and feed you, or thirsty and give you drink? When did we see you a stranger and welcome you, or naked and clothe you? When did we see you sick or in prison and visit you?" And the Lord will respond: "I tell you, as long as you did it to one of these, as long as you did it to the least of my brothers and sisters, you did it to me" (Mt 25:35–40).

You know, you are incredibly fortunate. You have a perpetual Advent, a ceaseless Christmas. Christ comes to you every day, dozens of times a day. He comes to you afraid. Afraid because he hurts: "My soul is sorrowful, even to death" (Mt 26:38). Afraid because he is alone: "My God, my God, why have you forsaken me?" (Mt 27:46). Afraid because he may die: "If it be possible, let this cup pass from me" (Mt 26:39).

Christ comes to you, as fearful as when he sweated blood in Gethsemane. How you respond will measure the depth or shallowness of your Advent—not only your Christmas but your very Christianness. You can address yourself with professional skill to a growth or an abscess, to a thermometer or a bathroom bowl—and you will do well. Or you can address yourself to a person, address yourself to Christ in Gethsemane. It's dreadfully difficult; for time is your enemy, and a crucified Christ can be repulsive, can turn you off. But there Christ is, and there is no other way of being Christian save to reach out to his fears—honestly yes, but with infinite compassion. To cast out all his fear is rarely possible; after all, it calls for "perfect love." But the love that you have, this love you can touch to his fear—each one of you. It is not so much a matter of words, of reaching out with rhetoric; it is *you* Christ needs—your willingness to give not simply what you have but who you are.

The paradox of such love is that, in reaching out to Christ, to Christ afraid, you play a Christ-role yourself, you become Christlike, the healing Christ. And in this way you realize the profound purpose of Christian community: Christ touches Christ in love. And it may well be that in the touching your own fears will be touched: through this fearful Christ whom you touch in love, *you* may come to a more profound peace with God, within yourself, with other human persons, and with the things of earth that you use as instruments for your healing. Someone may say to *you* from a hospital bed: "Don't be afraid."

My Christmas prayer for each of you: May Christ touch Christ in love!

3
WHAT ARE YOU WAITING FOR?
Advent without pretending

Each December, in mid-Advent, before the students take off for the Christmas holidays, Georgetown University offers its Candlelight Advent Liturgy. The liturgy proper is preceded by an appropriate artistic performance presented by the University's Liturgical Arts Community. On December 13, 1978, that gifted and enthusiastic community—comprising the Dahlgren Chapel Choir, the Chamber Ensemble, the Chapel Dancers, the Drama Group, and Visual Arts—offered a moving rendition of Parts 1 and 2 of Bach's Christmas Oratorio.

The liturgy itself took up the familiar Advent theme: waiting. But if the theme is familiar, its meaning is hardly transparent. The problem is encapsulated in the very title of my homily: what are you waiting for? Different people indeed give different answers. The expected Christian answer is: we are waiting for Christ. But, come to think of it, that answer is less than illuminating. Christ has already come in the flesh we wear; he will not come that way again. His final coming, "on the clouds of heaven," though unpredictable, was not anticipated for December 25, 1978. His Eucharistic coming, though linked inescapably to the first Christmas, is a daily, ceaseless advent: we are not Christmas Christians.

What, then, are we waiting for?

This evening I want to do three things: (1) state a *fact*; (2) raise a *problem* to which the fact gives rise; (3) suggest a *solution* to the problem.

I

First, the fact. You see, one word sums up Advent: waiting. From beginning to end the liturgy revolves round a tireless refrain: be ready and waiting. Today's reading from Romans reminds you that "the night is far gone, the day is just about here" (Rom 13:12). The Gospel warns you to "be ready, for the Son of Man is coming at an hour you do not expect" (Mt 24:44). Next Sunday Isaiah will tell the Jews in exile not to be afraid: "your God . . . will come" (Isa 35:4). John the Baptist will question Jesus from behind prison bars: "Are you he-who-is-to-come, or shall we look for another?" (Mt 11:3). Is our anxious waiting over, or must we wait some more?

30

James, the Church's leader in Jerusalem, will urge Christian converts to be patient. How long? Till the Lord comes. Till then, be patient—like a farmer, through winter and spring rains (Jas 5:7 ff.).

II

But this simple fact raises a real problem: what are you waiting for? You . . . not the Jews in Babylon or the Christians in Jerusalem or the Baptist in chains. Isaiah and his people knew what they were waiting for: a God who would lead them out of Babylon. The Baptist knew what he was waiting for: a fiery social reformer, Elijah come to earth again. James knew what he was waiting for: an imminent, final coming of the Lord, throned on the clouds of heaven.

But unless your "thing" is biblical studies, your Advent problem is not Isaiah, not John the Baptist, not James of Jerusalem. Your Advent problem is . . . you. What are *you* waiting for? Another way of phrasing it: what do you want for Christmas?

What *in fact* you are waiting for, you alone really know. There are always some Christians who are waiting simply for the whole thing to end. Like Lent, so Advent: it's a bore—a liturgical bore, a scholastic bore, a penitential bore. Advent has all the irritation that attends waiting—a small boil coming to a head. Do not open till Christmas.

What in fact you are waiting for, you alone really know. But what *should* you be waiting for? The liturgy trumpets it ceaselessly: you should be waiting for the Lord, for the coming of a saving Christ. "Your God will come and save you" (Isa 35:4).

But isn't this a form of charades, of play-acting? We make believe that Christ has not yet come, and all the while every bell tower and TV channel, every department store and cash register, jingles that he has come. And not only the "world." The New Testament and theological reflection assure us that the Son of God did touch our earth in Bethlehem; that Jesus is here, in our midst, because we are gathered in his name; that in a few short moments he will be sacramentally present on this table; that the Christ we offer here in the Calvary of the Mass will give himself to us as food; that day in and day out he is present within our whole person, because if we love him, he and his Father come to us and make their home within us. He has come; he is here; he lives with us and within us. What is there to wait for?

The answer, I suggest, comes in a third point: *how* are you waiting for the Lord?

III

You see, there are various ways of waiting. A poor old fellow on a bench in Lafayette Park; a Georgetown student in National Airport; a pregnant woman in a maternity ward. Each is waiting, but oh what a difference! The old fellow doesn't expect very much; he'll be happy if someone, anyone, comes along—someone to talk to, to make the time pass till supper. He'll be satisfied if he's not mugged, if his tired legs will take him from a cold bench to a cold-water flat.

Georgetown at the airport, after exams! In one sense you are only waiting for a silver bird. But there's an excitement here; the plane *means* something. It's all the difference between school and home, between D.C. and San Juan, between being stranded on a cold campus and being warmed in love by family or by a Caribbean sun. The waiting has meaning; it's filled with tension and anticipation; it's exciting!

The mother-to-be, about to give birth. Tension, anticipation, excitement, of course. But two facts are uncommonly true here, peculiarly pertinent to our Advent waiting. First, "he who is to come" has been there all along. The problem is, the child has been a hidden presence, a bit unreal, at times not quite believable. But at a certain moment the child actually transpires, comes to light, is held in loving arms, is uniquely here. Then there is joy and rapture, peace and calm. Second, there is a remarkable co-operation: something is happening to her, whether she feels it or not, *and* she is helping to make it happen. Nine months ago it began to happen; now she helps bring it to completion. And so she not only dreams; she cries and gasps and prays, she pushes and sweats and bleeds. And through the agony of it all, "he who is to come" comes.

Such, I suggest, ought your Advent to be. Not the boredom of a park bench; not only the anticipation of an airport; rather, a bringing to light. I doubt that any of you are totally alienated from the Lord; you would hardly be here if you were. Christ is here—not only among you but within you. His life lives in you like an embryo, moves in you like a fetus. But there's the rub. Like an embryo: you don't experience him. Like a fetus: more uncomfortable than exhilarating. Advent is a form of parturition: its function is to bring a living Lord to life in your living. Christmas for you is not a given day, December 25. Christmas is when the Child actually transpires, comes to life, is held in your loving embrace, is uniquely yours. Christmas is when Christ becomes real to you. Then you will "rejoice," for the Lord will be awfully "near" (cf. Phil 4:4–5).

But for Christ to become real, you have to help make it happen. Oh yes, he is taking shape within you whether you feel him or not. But he is more likely to come to light, you are more likely to experience him, if you cry and gasp and pray, if you push and sweat and bleed. One concrete test is suggested by Isaiah and Matthew: you can tell that your Savior has come if the eyes of the blind are opened and the ears of the deaf are cleared; if the lame leap like stags and the tongues of the dumb sing; if the dead are raised to life and the poor have good news preached to them.

I am suggesting that your Savior may come to light, may transpire, if the faith you speak is a justice you do. You need not fly to El Salvador to find the oppressed and the burdened and the brokenhearted. They surround you, they dot D.C., they cover your campus. Bring food and drink, bring life and light, bring love or a song, bring good news, bring yourself to those whose hearts or bodies are heavy, and you will bring Christ to them. And paradoxically, in revealing Christ to them, you may unveil him to yourself. Coming to life in them, he may come to light for you.

A sympathetic Jew has told us gently but firmly: "We [Jews] must . . . question, in the light of the Bible, whether the message of the Old Testament which the New Testament claims has been fulfilled, has in fact been fulfilled in history, in the history lived and suffered by us and our ancestors. And here, my dear Christian readers, we give a negative reply. We can see no kingdom and no peace and no redemption."[1] Does your faith-life reveal to anyone that Christ's kingdom is in the making? Does your Christian existence pass to another the peace of Christ? Does it redeem anyone from enslavement? Does anyone see in you the one who is to come, or must everyone who touches you wait for another?

4
TO THOSE WHO HAVE SEEN THE CHILD
Christmas as a Christian constant

*For a homilist, Christmas is at once a joy and a trial. A joy be-
cause on Christmas, as on Easter, it's hard to "miss." The people
in the pews, regular churchgoers and twice-a-year Christians alike,
are benevolent: in the spirit of the season, almost anything except a
lecture on birth control is accepted as a gift. A trial because most of
the congregation have fixed ideas on what Christmas is about. For
all too many, Christmas is history, a little child in a crib, rather
than mystery, God-with-us.*

*It is a delicate task to move Catholic devotion away from a
child who no longer lies in straw—who is no longer a child. Fortu-
nately for me, the community that worshiped with the Woodstock
College Jesuits in St. Paul's Chapel on the campus of Columbia
University was remarkably open to an effort to probe the mystery.
Not indeed to solve it (even Jesuits have been known to bend low before mystery) but to cast a ray of light upon it from God's own disclosure in the revelation that is Christ.*

*And so, that midnight in 1973, I tried to trace the three stages
of the Christmas epic as the liturgical readings unfolded them—
anxious expectancy (Isa 9:2–7), actual coming (Lk 2:15–20),
what God-with-us means for us (Titus 2:11–14)—not so much as
three chronological stages, rather as three intertwining constants of
human living.*

The Christmas word has been proclaimed to you. As the Church
recaptures it, that word has three stages. There is, first, the anxious
expectancy. It is expressed from the lips of a Hebrew prophet: all
those endless days when a people walked in darkness, when the
land was deeply shadowed, when joy was indeed there but ambiguous and muted, when the experience of God's people stressed a
yoke that weighs, a bar across the shoulders, an oppressing rod.
But He will come.

There is, second, the actual coming. It is expressed in the simplest of narratives: a journey and a delivery, shepherds watching
and angels singing, good news, great joy, to be shared by all. He
has come.

And there is, third, the theological reflection. A pupil of Paul
explains that, in this child so anxiously expected, so simply come,
in him God's grace has been revealed, salvation has been made

possible for all, we are to give up everything that does not lead to God, and we wait in hope. He will come again.

Those three stages, the Christmas epic, are three constants of human living. Not necessarily, not usually, in three chronological stages: he is not yet here, he is here, what does his coming mean? No, in concrete living, in day-to-day existence, the three are constantly intertwining.

I

To begin with—if you are anything like me (which God forbid)—there is the experience of absence, God's absence. That remarkable rabbi Abraham Heschel (who died a year ago yesterday) once summed up the story of his own people in a single sentence: "The inner history of Israel is a history of waiting for God, of waiting for His arrival."[1] Such, I submit, is the story of Everyman.

As I have come to see it, the religious history of every man and woman is "a history of waiting for God." Oh, not passively, not always consciously. But there are days when I walk in darkness, when the land on which I dance is shadowed, when gladness is muted and what I experience is oppression—God does not seem to be there. Have *you* not felt it? The frightening experience of absence . . . the fear that God is not here . . . the doubt that He ever was . . . the feeling that just maybe He simply is not . . . the emptiness? And even if your life is undisturbed, a tranquil awareness of God, you must be ceaselessly in search of Him: how to hear Him, see Him, touch Him whom you confess with your lips. For you must experience the Our Father that is naked syllables and the hour of contemplation that is empty, the Communion that seems only bread and the Church that does not communicate God's presence.

And far from our own comfortable experience of absence, think of the billions who wait in terror or numbness or pain for God to show His face. The billion or so who close their eyes hungry each night; the nine-year-old Vietnamese running toward us, her flesh aflame with napalm; the bitter enemies in the north of Ireland or the Middle East who cannot find God in one another; the unwanted waif who stares at you from eyes that do not understand; the schizophrenic and the Mongoloid.

In some sense, *all* of us wait in anxious expectancy; for none of us is God here as we want Him to be here. He is indeed a hidden God.

II

The second constant of Christian living is the good news, the great joy, to be shared by all. In Christ, God is here, God is with us. Not in a manger—that happened once. Where then? Literally everywhere. For Christ lives in every nook and cranny of His universe. He *has* to, because he is *God*-with-us. Wherever your eye falls, he is there. He *is* everywhere because he is *active* everywhere, because without him the sun could not shine nor the snowflake fall; without him the grass could not grow nor the seas surge; without him the skylark could not sing, the panther prowl, the shad ascend the rivers.

More personally, God is here, among you. Tonight, regrettably, countless Catholics are celebrating the Christmas liturgy with a frightfully unorthodox theology of community prayer. In this vision, a number of individuals (ten or a thousand), unknown to one another, uncaring of one another, come in out of the cold and, in quavering song and stilted prose, petition an absent God to become really present, so that they may receive Him bodily and return each to his or her isolated home convinced that they have been nourished spiritually.

No wonder God is not grasped, because three crucial Christian realities are not grasped. (1) You who come in out of the cold already constitute a community of faith: you come to worship because you believe, because you have been called to faith and conversion, because you have experienced God. (2) Once this believing community comes in out of the cold, your function is not to make God present. He *is* here—and not only tented at the back. He will indeed become sacramentally present: his flesh for food, his blood as drink. But not out of the blue, out of nowhere. He is already here, because you are gathered in his name. He is here in the word proclaimed. He is here in your hearts, because you believe, because you love. (3) Most importantly, your community prayer does not originate within your community, within you. Your prayer is a response. You are able to pray because the God of mystery touches you with His presence. The initiative comes from God—not present coldly, abstractly, distantly, but laying hold of you as a believing community, at the very core of your being. Prayer is you responding to God within you, to God among you.

Indeed God is here, in His Christ. No, unlike his mother, I cannot cuddle him in Bethlehem. Unlike the Samaritan woman, I cannot slake his thirst with water. Unlike the woman with a flow of blood, I cannot touch his garment. Unlike Mary of Bethany, I cannot sit in rapture at his feet. Unlike John, I cannot stand near his crucified flesh. Unlike the disciples, I cannot break bread with him on the beach. And yet it is the same Christ who is here: was here when you entered, spoke to you with his word, links you together with his love, makes possible your prayer, and in a few short moments will touch your flesh in unique fashion with his humanness.

He is here. But, to experience him here, you must cease to be spectators, on the outside looking in. As in all love, you must lose yourself: the ecstasy that means going out of yourself, to celebrate Jesus as he is, as he lives now—beyond us indeed, but God-with-us. If you do not find him here, as he is now, do not look for him in the crib: he is not there.

III

The third constant of Christian living is the ceaseless effort to understand what God-with-us means, and to live it. The reading from Titus suggested four facets of this loving reflection, this reflective loving.

First, in Jesus God's grace has been revealed. More concretely: Jesus is God's love for us in human flesh. "God so loved the world that He gave His only Son . . ." (Jn 3:16).

Second, in Jesus salvation has been made possible for all. More concretely, Jesus is God's love for *all*. The good news, the great joy, St. Luke insists, is to be shared by all. Not a chosen people, not a faithful remnant, not a predestined elite. What he is, each of us is designed to be: Jesus is Everyman. Which is why we weep for every life that is less than human. Mother Teresa caressing the crippled of Calcutta is Mother Mary cradling the crucified flesh of her Christ.

Third, we are to give up everything that does not lead to God. A harsh saying? Not really. It is because of us that not everything leads to God. Because of us the earth is plundered and men are sundered, love turns to lust, and life is made unlivable. Bethlehem is a plea, in God's own flesh, to turn things Godward: yourself and the small world that is your empire, where your loves and your hates make the difference between peace and war.

Fourth, we wait in hope. *There* is the Christmas paradox, the Christian tension: he is here, and still we wait in hope.

Christianity is indeed a historical religion: Christ did come; but we do not survive on nostalgia. Christianity is indeed a present fact: Christ is here, now; but we are not imprisoned in the present. The risk in being a Christian is that you open yourself to a future, and that future is God's future. The first Letter of John is so insightful: "Beloved, we are God's children now; it does not yet appear what we shall be . . ." (1 Jn 3:2). I do not know what tomorrow will bring—only that tomorrow Christ will be there. I do not even know if I will experience his presence—only that my life, like my liturgy, must relive the Jesus who was and celebrate the Jesus who is. Only thus is every risk-laden tomorrow an act of hope in God's future: "Into your hands. . . ." In the moving poetry of W. H. Auden:

> . . . To those who have seen
> The Child, however dimly, however incredulously,
> The Time Being is, in a sense, the most trying time of all.
> For the innocent children who whispered so excitedly
> Outside the locked door where they knew the presents to be
> Grew up when it opened. . . .
> . . . The happy morning is over,
> The night of agony still to come; the time is noon;
> When the Spirit must practice his scales of rejoicing
> Without even a hostile audience, and the Soul endure
> A silence that is neither for nor against her faith
> That God's Will will be done, that, in spite of her prayers,
> God will cheat no one, not even the world of its triumph.[2]

And the day will dawn when that sentence of John will be completed: ". . . it does not yet appear what we shall be, but we know that when He appears we shall be like Him, for we shall see Him as He is."

5
IN GOD WE TRUST
Fifth Sunday of the year with a bewildered Job

The "noon-ten Mass" in Dahlgren Chapel on the campus of Georgetown University is a Sunday happening of profound meaning for many D.C. dwellers. Graduate and undergraduate students, lay faculty, men and women from the surrounding area, others from a distance—these have gradually formed and continue to form a well-knit worshiping community. A week-long preparation by campus ministers, the Liturgical Arts Community, and other interested people usually results in a liturgy that realizes the twin function of liturgy as sacrament: (1) it gives expression to the faith experience of this Christian congregation and (2) it helps mold that experience.

On February 4, 1979, I was privileged for the first time to be the principal celebrant, and therefore the homilist, at Dahlgren's 12:10 Mass. Mulling over the liturgical readings five weeks in advance, I was struck by the apparent one-sidedness of the selection from Job 7. All we are told is that, from Job's bitter experience, life on earth is simply cruel and hopeless. I realized, with uncommon clarity, how misleading a biblical passage can be if it is torn from its context. And so I experimented: I studied Job's total experience, to see where it might lead. To my delight, it cast light on a critical but difficult virtue. Who would have suspected that a community dump could flower trust in God?

If you listened carefully to the first reading (Job 7:1–4, 6–7), you might well be either "turned off" or "way down." To believe Job, your living is slavery; your days are empty; your nights are long and miserable; death comes swiftly and leaves you hopeless.

The problem with any liturgical snippet is that it is not in context. And anything out of context rarely reveals its richness, can even distort. During the Second World War the British Broadcasting Corporation used the opening bar of Beethoven's *Fifth Symphony* as Morse code: 3 dots and a dash = V: V for Victory. This is Beethoven? Or what would you know of *Hamlet* if the only lines left to us were Hamlet's advice to Ophelia: "Get thee to a nunnery. . . . Or, if thou wilt needs marry, marry a fool; for wise men know well enough what monsters you make of them."[1] And so with Job. He does indeed say what the lector read to you; but if you have before you only those six verses, you will not understand Job and so you will not grasp what God is trying to tell you through Job.

39

This being so, I shall do three things: (1) put the Job passage in context; (2) touch this biblical book to a basic religious characteristic; (3) suggest how all this might have meaning for you and your human, Christian existence.

I

First then, Job and the Book of Job. It is a fascinating human story—the experience of a man who has to wrestle with God. He is comparatively young, well off, a good man of high moral standards: the very first verse announces that he "was blameless, upright, feared God, turned away from evil" (1:1).[2] But in a brief space everything he has is destroyed—not only cattle and house and servants, but sons and daughters. He is struck with a disease that gives ceaseless pain, never lets him sleep, makes him ugly to look at. He is barred from human society, lives in a community dump. People spit when they see him; even his wife says: "Curse God, and die" (2:9). It reminds me of a powerful picture in the sixties, *The Pawnbroker*, where Rod Steiger epitomizes despair: "Everything I loved was taken away from me—and I did not die."

Now Job struggles with God. To begin with, he is bewildered, confused. He doesn't understand why this is happening to him; he hasn't done anything to deserve it. He loves God, wants only to please Him, is groping for a more intimate relationship. Then why is God suddenly acting like an enemy, hostile, oppressive? Why does the Almighty torment so unimportant a creature? Is He being sadistic? Was He jealous of Job's happiness? What kind of gift is such a life, such a living death? And so Job curses the day he was born. He begs God to just leave him alone: go away, don't bother me, let me have a little comfort before I die.

Job's friends are no help at all. For them there is no mystery: Job must be suffering for his sins. The logic is impeccable: if Job is not a sinner, then God is unjust. So, dear friend, stop protesting your innocence; your condition is clear proof of your guilt. Repent, and all will be well with you again.

But Job cannot confess what is false; he is not a guilty man. He denies deceit or adultery; he has respected the God-given rights of his slaves and shared his goods with the poor; gold or any creature has never been his god; his door has swung open to every wayfarer; he has never pretended to be what he is not. No, not for sin is he being punished.

In all this wrestling there are two splendid moments. The first is Job's act of faith, of trust. God only seems to have changed; He still cares. If Job's sufferings make no sense, God has His own reasons. Divine abandonment is only for a time; somehow Job will see God.

But if faith dissolves Job's doubts, it does not diminish his desolation. The sharpest torment of all is still there: a dark night of the soul. For all his faith, Job cannot "get through" to God. He used to experience God's presence; now he experiences only God's absence.

The second splendid moment: at last God speaks to Job. He shows Himself to this anguished believer, this rebellious lover, who has raged against his situation, has demanded that God justify His ways. But notice: God says nothing to Job about his guilt or innocence, nothing about suffering and its meaning; He does not explain. And Job does not say: "Ah yes, now I understand. Thank you." The real experience is simply the encounter: God lets Job find Him. And in the encounter Job is happy to disown his speculations, his complaints; he even discards his ultimate support, his cherished integrity, his innocence. "He cannot buy his justification from God; he must accept it as a gift."[3]

II

So much for Job in context. Now let me touch this biblical book to a basic religious characteristic. I mean ... trust—trust in God.

When I trust you, I wed faith and hope. I rely on you to be faithful, to be true to your promises, true to yourself. It is not quite the same as confidence. Trust, Webster's Second Edition Unabridged tells us, "is often more instinctive, less reasoned, than confidence, which is apt to suggest somewhat definite grounds of assurance."[4] I have not tested you out thoroughly, proved to the hilt that you are trustworthy. I have a sense, an instinct, a feeling—not indeed without some basis, but not the end result of a syllogism or a questionnaire. It comes often from some experience of you, an experience not reducible to proof. Sometimes it happens when my eyes meet yours, or when we share something in common. It is most likely to happen if I love you.

Job is a splendid example of trust. He had to face the problem of evil: why do the innocent suffer, the wicked prosper? And in the face of evil, he found human wisdom bankrupt. His anguished questioning ended in a theophany: God appeared to him, not to

defend His wisdom but to stress His mystery. Job trusted God not
because he could prove that God merited his trust, but because he
had experienced God. Ultimately, he trusted God because he loved
Him. Not the other way round: not trust first, then love. He trusted
because he loved.

The Book of Job "does not offer Job's experience as a way to
understand evil, but as a way to live with it. The experience of Job
is that one can support evil only when one experiences a theophany, an insight into the reality of God."[5] Only trust makes evil endurable—trust not because God has offered proof, but because
God has shown His face. The movement in summary: from experience of God . . . to love for God . . . to trust in God.

III

What meaning might all this have for you, for your human,
Christian existence? For many of us, trust does not come easily.
When I was a boy, some shopkeepers had a half-witty sign based
on our American coins: "In God we trust; all others pay cash." But
all too often we prod even God to put His money where His word
is. Nor does it seem unreasonable. Here is a God who insists that
He is ceaselessly faithful, will never let His loved ones down. But is
that true? There are good Jews who will tell you that God died in
Auschwitz. And how do you say "Trust God" to the one billion
who go to bed hungry each night? Can you justify the God of Mongoloid babies? Where was God when Russia raped Hungary, or
when my father and brother died of cancer three weeks apart? The
challenges to trust are legion. Why, even that long-suffering mystic
Teresa of Avila protested to God: "Why do you treat me this way?"
Said God: "I treat all my friends this way." Retorted Teresa: "No
wonder you have so few!"

It will not surprise you that *I* cannot justify God's ways with
man, God's ways with you. Being a theologian does not help: I try
too hard to understand, and so I fashion my God out of my pitiful
human ignorance. It takes me as far as it took Job: I too complain
from the community dump!

No, you will trust God only as much as you love Him. And you
will love Him not because you have studied Him; you will love Him
if you have touched Him—if He has touched you. Even then your
troubles are hardly over. You may still hassle with God. As with
Job, trust will not destroy your desolation, only make it endurable.
Remember that Jesus' own tremendous cry of trust on the cross,
Psalm 22, begins: "My God, my God, why have you forsaken me?"

(Ps 22:1; Mt 27:46). Only if you love will you make that final leap into darkness: "Father, into your hands I commit my spirit" (Lk 23:46).

Recently a remarkable Bahamian priest told me a story that might well end this quest of trust. A two-story house had caught fire. The family—father, mother, several children—were on their way out when the smallest boy became terrified, tore away from his mother, ran back upstairs. Suddenly he appeared at a smoke-filled window crying like crazy. His father, outside, shouted to him: "Jump, son, jump! I'll catch you." The boy cried: "But, daddy, I can't see you." "I know," his father called, "I know. But *I* can see *you.*"

6

FOR YOUR PENANCE, LOOK REDEEMED
Lent with a smiling Christ

Lent is a problem today. As I was growing up, and even much later, words like penance, sacrifice, fasting, and abstinence were part of our Lenten vocabulary. They had been drilled into us—in church, at home, especially in the parochial school. I do not say they have disappeared (witness, for example, the Lenten pastorals), but they no longer dominate our mind-set and speech patterns. This is not the place to argue the reasons: do you indict our culture, or do you blame it all on Vatican II?

Although this movement raises problems for the "old Lenten spirit," I do not find it without value. For one thing, it has compelled me to rethink the meaning of Lent in liturgy and life. The process was brought to a head as I prepared to preach in Georgetown University's Dahlgren Chapel on the first Sunday of Lent 1979.

The fresh (not new, simply rediscovered) approach to Lent in this homily began with a holy card: the "smiling Christ" of Lérins. It concretized questions with which I had been struggling for quite some time. What precisely is the Christian trying to do these forty days? Is there room for Lenten laughter? If there is, what is its relationship to the tears of Lent? Where should our penitential emphasis lie? What ought we to "give up"—besides sin?

I think I learned something about Lent; I know I learned something about myself.

In the famous Abbey of Lérins, on an island off the southeast coast of France, there is an unusual sculpture. It may go back to the twelfth century, and it has for title *Christ souriant*, "the smiling Christ." Jesus is imprisoned on the cross; his head is leaning somewhat to the right; his eyes are closed—in death, I think; but on his lips there is a soft, serene smile.

The smiling Christ—here is my springboard for Lent. And if you prefer Scripture to sculpture, if you need a text to test my orthodoxy, I give you Jesus in Ash Wednesday's Gospel: "When you fast, do not look gloomy, like the hypocrites" (Mt 6:16). I know this raises a problem, and I'm glad it does. As usual, three points. First, a look at Jesus: did he really smile? Second, a look at Lent: is it for laughing or for crying? Third, a look at you: what now till Easter?

44

I

First then, a look at Jesus: did he really smile? Did he actually laugh? One tradition is enshrined in some fourth-century monastic rules of St. Basil the Great: "so far as we know from the story of the Gospel, he never laughed. On the contrary, he even pronounced those unhappy who are given to laughter (Lk 6:25)." Oh yes, he had "joy of spirit," he had "merriment of soul." But as for its "outward expression," as for "hilarity," no. Such a one would not be "master of every passion," would not be "perfectly continent."[1]

True, the Gospels never say that Jesus smiled or laughed, as they twice testify that he wept—over Jerusalem and over Lazarus, over his city and his friend. But I do not understand how one who was like us in everything save sin could have wept from sorrow but not laughed for joy. How could he fail to smile when a child cuddled comfortably in his arms, or when the headwaiter at Cana wondered where the good wine had come from, or when he saw little Zaccheus up a tree, or when Jairus' daughter wakened to life at his touch, or when Peter put his foot in his mouth once again? I refuse to believe that he did not laugh when he saw something funny, or when he experienced in the depths of his manhood the presence of his Father. Too often Christians have been so aware of Jesus' divinity that his humanity became somewhat unreal, artificial. No, he was like us. . . .

I do not say Jesus smiled when his fellow townsmen cast him over a cliff. I do not pretend he laughed in Gethsemane. I do not know if he died with a smile on his lips. There are moments when you cannot smile, when it makes no sense to laugh. But that's not the point. The point is: here is a man whose whole life was a movement to a cross, a man who cried out that he was in anguish until his death should be accomplished—and still he moved through life very much as we do. He attracted not only fishermen and centurions but children, simple folk, women like Mary of Magdala—and he could hardly have done so with thunderbolts, if he had only "spoken with authority," if his face wore ever the stern mask of a judge and did not crease into a smile or break out into merry laughter.

II

Second, a look at Lent: is it for laughing or for crying? Granted that Jesus smiled, is there any place for the smiling Christ these forty days? I say there is. But to understand this, you must grasp a crucial Christian fact: in Lent we are not pretending.

Neither in Lent's liturgy nor in Lent's living dare we make believe that Christ is not yet risen, that we have to wait for Easter to see his resurrection, to live it, to enjoy it. Even in Lent you and I are *risen* Christians. And the twin fact that Jesus is risen and that we have risen with him into a new life must color the way we celebrate Lent, must color our asceticism, our self-denial. Oh yes, during these weeks we re-present the stages of our Lord's pilgrimage to Jerusalem, his way to the cross; but we do it as *risen* Christians. And that means we do right to reproduce in our own Lent, in our own suffering, on our own cross, the smiling Christ of Lérins. The cross is victory, not defeat; and we do not have to wait for that victory, wait for Easter to dawn.

But we cannot pretend the other way either. Simply because we have risen with Christ in baptism, we cannot make believe that Lent does not really exist. Risen we are, but not yet *fully* risen: "We ourselves," St. Paul agonizes, "we who have the first fruits of the Spirit, groan inside ourselves as we wait for . . . the redemption of our bodies" (Rom 8:23). And so we must ceaselessly reproduce the journey of Jesus to Jerusalem, not only symbolically and liturgically but in our flesh and bones and in the wrenching of our spirit. That is why our laughter is not yet full-throated; that is why it is often through tears that we smile; that is why we still have to pray "Father . . . remove this cup from me" (Lk 22:42). We have not been transformed completely into the risen Christ; that transformation will take place only if we go up to Jerusalem with Jesus. The smiling Christ rests on a cross.

Is Lent for laughing or for crying? I say, for both. But I am stressing the laughter of Lent because it is so far removed from our spirituality. It is almost as hard to find a smiling Christian on Good Friday as it is to find a "smiling Christ" in crucifixion art. In my memory, those of us who took Lent seriously, from Ash Wednesday's "dust thou art" to Holy Saturday's empty tomb and tabernacle, only confirmed Nietzsche's cutting critique about Christians: we "do not look redeemed."

III

Finally, a look at you: what now till Easter? I do not reject Jesus' injunction in today's Gospel: "Repent. . ." (Mk 1:15). However turned from sin you are, you stand in need of constant conversion, must keep turning to Christ. And those whose face is turned totally from him, any who need a radical conversion—it is not time for them to smile serenely. Their Lent is limpid: they give up sin. But I assume that you who gather here each Sunday are already on the road to Jerusalem with Jesus. To you I suggest a twin approach to these forty days: what a splendid spiritual writer has called "an asceticism of humor" and "a diaconate of humor."[2]

For yourself personally, individually, an asceticism of humor—a fresh form of self-denial. A young lady once said to me: "Why are you so hard on yourself?" It was the only self-denial I knew: keep that rebellious flesh under control, and be intolerant of imperfection—mine and everyone else's! To you I am suggesting that you give up something sweeter than candy, smokier than Kents, perhaps more destructive than sin. I mean an absorption in yourself—where you take yourself all too seriously, where the days and nights rotate around *you*, your heartache and your hiatal hernia, your successes and failures, your problems and frustrations. For an asceticism of humor, you must distance yourself from yourself, see yourself in perspective, as you really are. I mean a creature wonderfully yet fearfully made, a bundle of paradoxes and contradictions. You believe and doubt, hope and despair, love and hate. You are exciting and boring, enchanted and disillusioned, manic and depressive. You are "cool" on the outside and you hurt within. You feel bad about feeling good,[3] are afraid of your joy, feel guilty if you don't feel guilty. You are trusting and suspicious, selfless and selfish, wide-open and locked in. You know so much and so little. You are honest and you still play games. Aristotle said you are a rational animal; I say you are an angel with an incredible capacity for beer!

If it is the incongruous, what does not fit, that makes for humor, you can indeed smile at yourself. So, let Christ the harlequin, the clown Christ, into your spiritual life: you are not laughing sacrilegiously at him; he is poking gentle fun at you—through tears.[4] St. Ignatius Loyola has a rule for Jesuits: our "whole countenance should reflect cheerfulness rather than sadness...."[5] If *we* don't obey Ignatius, you should!

And your smile will turn to lusty laughter if you only realize how lovable you are—not because of anything you have made of yourself, but because God loves you, because God died for you, because God lives in you . . . now.

But an asceticism of humor dare not remain a private joke. Humor, someone has said, good humor is basically looking at the world, at others, with eyes of love—being in love without restriction. An asceticism of humor must move out into a diaconate of humor: you deacon, you minister, the smiling Christ to others. I do not mean that you paint on a false smile or bellow forever with laughter. Simply that, with your new-found Christian delight in yourself, you go out to your brothers and sisters (even to your husband or wife!)—as you are, where they are.

Where they are. . . . Not far from you is someone who is afraid and needs your courage; or lonely and needs your presence; or hurt and needs your healing. So many feel unloved and need your touching; are old and need to feel that you care. Many are weak in so many ways and need for support your own shared weakness. One of the most helpful words I ever spoke was to confess to a woman that I too had doubts about faith. "You?" she cried. "Oh, thank God!" You will rarely know greater happiness than when through you a smile is born on the face of someone in pain; you will have given birth to a smiling Christ.

Christianity needs men and women who repent of their smallness, fast from their selfishness, abstain from isolation. Lent calls for risen Christians, men and women like the hero of Eugene O'Neill's play *Lazarus Laughed*—the Lazarus who has tasted death and sees it for what it is, whose joy in living is irresistible, whose invitation to the world is his infectious cry:

> Laugh with me!
> Death is dead!
> Fear is no more!
> There is only life!
> There is only laughter![6]

Unreal? In a sense, yes—when you look at the Middle East, Northern Ireland, Southeast Asia; when you touch bellies bloated with hunger or shriveled from cancer. But where does the Christian start—start to overcome fear and death? Here, right where you are; now, not after Easter. By bringing the smiling Christ, the joy of Jesus, to one man, woman, or child reliving his passion. Who knows? It just might be your own healing, your own salvation.

At any rate, if the crucified Christ can look redeeming, the crucified Christian can at least look redeemed! For your Lenten penance, therefore, please . . . look . . . redeemed.

7

ONLY LOVE IS BELIEVABLE
Lent with a loving Christ

> When I preached this homily to the Jesuit community at historic Woodstock College in Maryland on March 12, 1967, the fifth Sunday of Lent was called liturgically the First Sunday of the Passion; previously it had been simply Passion Sunday. That Sunday inaugurated a more intensive concentration on the sufferings of Christ, on his "passion."
>
> During my early years in religious life, we gave liberal attention, in prayer and preaching, to the physical sufferings of Christ, from the bloody sweat in Gethsemane to the last loud cry on Calvary. In large measure this was due, I think, to the insistence of Ignatius Loyola in his Spiritual Exercises that, in meditating on the mysteries of our Lord's life, we do not stand outside as onlookers but set ourselves intimately within the Gospel scene, feel what Jesus felt, experience com-passion. It was good, psychologically and spiritually.
>
> But with the movement of the years, I have moved a fair distance from this stress. Not totally, of course; for the pain of Jesus' passion is not an extravagance indifferent to our redemption or our spirituality. I have simply found it needful, for myself and others, to focus more and more on the motive force without which Calvary would have little human meaning and no salvific effect, without which Christianity and the Christian would be literally unbelievable.

Not long ago I picked up a book. A slender volume. A book in German by a profound Swiss theologian. I never got beyond the title. In a literal translation, *Only Love Is Believable*.[1] It struck me, shiveringly, that these four words sum up Christ, Christianity, and the Christian: the passion of Christ, the impact of Christianity, the power of the individual Christian.

I

Only love is believable. In the first place, only love makes *Christ* believable. Only love makes sense out of the next two weeks, the two weeks of the Passion. For there is a problem, a peril, in the very word "passion" and in the purple that colors it. The passion of Christ: something happened to him; he suffered. The priests plotted against him; Judas kissed him; the crowd laid hands on him; Herod laughed at him; Pilate delivered him to be crucified;

the guards whipped him; the soldiers nailed him to wood; the pass-ers-by jeered at him; a thief cursed him. And Jesus? Why, he died.

Something happened to Jesus. Indeed it did. But what hap-pened to him, what he suffered, makes sense only in the context of what he *did*. And the one thing he did supremely, more than any-thing else, better than anyone else—he loved. St. John highlights this on the first page of his Passion: "when Jesus knew that his hour had come to pass out of this world to the Father, having loved his own who were in the world, he loved them to the end" (Jn 13:1), loved them to the uttermost limit of love, loved them totally, loved them to death.

I do not mean to divorce the two—what happened to Jesus and what he did, the passion of Christ and his love. The two are one: in St. Paul's packed phrase, he "loved me and gave himself for me" (Gal 2:20). The two are one; but it is the love that makes the Passion believable, that makes Christ attractive. Show me a man writhing on a cross, and I will be moved: to pity, to disgust, to hor-ror. Show me a man writhing on a cross in love, surrendering his flesh to crucifixion because he loves me, and I will be drawn: to be-lief, to self-giving, to love.

And precisely this is the challenge of these two weeks: the ef-fort of love to draw love, his love to draw mine. And during these two weeks we can see each day in a specially striking way how his passion and our liturgy interlock: that breathless moment when time turns back and Calvary comes alive in the love-born words "This is my body, which is given up for you; this is my blood, which is poured out for you."

II

Only love is believable. But if love alone makes Christ believ-able, love alone makes *Christianity* believable. It is a tragic fact that the Church of Christ has been least attractive when love has been least evident. I mean whenever Christian sects compete for con-verts on foreign soil; wherever Catholicism retires to a ghetto while human beings love and hate, work and play, bleed and cry and die; when so much emphasis is put on externals that the face of the Church looks cold, forbidding, impersonal. Christianity is not be-lievable when it is comfortable and self-satisfied, well-fed, fat, and sleek.

It is a thrilling fact that the Church of Christ has been most at-tractive when love has been most evident, when the Church presents itself to the world as, like Jesus, a suffering servant. Rarely has the Church come so close to being loved as when Pope John XXIII was servant of the servants of God. Few sentences have come out of the Second Vatican Council that are more attractive than the opening sentence of the Constitution on the Church in the Modern World: "The joys and the hopes, the griefs and the anxieties of the men and women of this age, especially those who are poor or in any way afflicted, these too are the joys and hopes, the griefs and anxieties of the followers of Christ."[2]

The Church is believable when its love is visible. A crucified love. On the streets of Selma and with the grape pickers in Delano; when the Church is shaken by *every* life violated in Vietnam; when it agonizes over hands without work, stomachs without food, human beings without human rights; when it can weep for the tears of a stranger; when nothing that is human is a stranger to it.

III

Only love is believable. But if love alone makes Christianity believable, surely love alone makes the *Christian* believable. For Christianity is not an idea floating freely in outer space; Christianity is people—in a sobering phrase, "God's people." Christ and Christianity will be believable only if my love makes *me* believable.

The paradox is, my love will be believable only if I realize that my love is not believable enough. Only if I am honest enough to confess that Christianity is less attractive than it ought to be because my love is less believable than it ought to be. Only if I admit that Christ alone loved his own "to the end," to the limit of love. Only if I stop thinking that it is the person next to me, or the previous generation, or the bishop, or the institutional Church that is lacking in love. Only if, like Christ, I am not merely a servant, but a suffering servant, sharing the anguish of my age. Only if my share in the passion of Christ comes through to every human being I meet, every man or woman crucified between heaven and earth.

Only love is believable. Here lies the unparalleled importance of these two weeks, the two weeks of the Passion. Love must get through to me, the love of him who is the Suffering Servant beyond compare. It must transform my love, so that the men and women I touch resonate to my touch, because they see on my face the image of Christ, the Christ who loved "to the end," to the very limit of love.

8
LET GO OF YESTERDAY
The puzzle of Passion/Palm Sunday

For anyone with a liturgical memory, the Sunday that opens Holy Week can be confusing. Not too long ago, the two Sundays that precede Easter were called, respectively, Passion Sunday and Palm Sunday. Then they were titled, respectively, the First Sunday of the Passion and the Second Sunday of the Passion. Now the second Sunday before Easter is simply the Fifth Sunday of Lent, and the last Sunday before Easter is Passion/Palm Sunday.

If you must preach on Passion/Palm Sunday, the change and confusion become critical. Is this merely a change in title? After all, the liturgical content is basically unchanged. We recall Jesus' triumphal entry into Jerusalem, then we get down to the grim story of the Passion. We read the two traditional Gospels: hosannas and mockery, triumph and tragedy, life and death. What has changed?

Duller of understanding than usual, it took most of Lent 1979 before I grasped what the new nomenclature is telling us. We dare not divide the paschal mystery into a season of dying (Lent) and a season of rising (Easter). Indeed there was a chronological sequence to the events in Jesus' life. But to stress the history is to miss the mystery. Jesus Christ is risen—and even during Lent we dare not pretend he has not. Lent, therefore, must be an increasingly more intense involvement in the whole paschal mystery, which is the mystery of dying-rising—his and ours. Two sides of a single coin.

How to clarify the liturgical celebration and how to touch it to daily Christian living—such was my task on Passion/Palm Sunday 1979 before the community that worships at noon-ten in Dahlgren Chapel on the campus of Georgetown University.

What we do here today is frightfully important. Important not only for the way we celebrate this liturgy but for the way we celebrate life. Important for the way we worship, important for the way we live.

You see, it's a puzzling Sunday. Today's liturgy is a paradox, if not a contradiction. We have two names for this Sunday: it is Palm Sunday and it is Passion Sunday. In the procession we pray "Today we honor Christ our triumphant King," but in the Mass we pray "You have given the human race Jesus Christ our Savior as a model of humility." In the procession we sing "Hosanna to the King," but in the Responsorial Psalm we sing "My God, my God, why have you abandoned me?" The reading from Paul reminds us that Jesus "emptied himself . . . became obedient unto death," then proclaims that "every tongue should confess that Jesus Christ is Lord" (Phil 2:7–8, 11). The Gospel of the procession cries "Behold, your King comes to you" (Mt 21:5), but the Gospel of the Mass ends "Jesus uttered a loud cry and breathed his last" (Mk 15:37).

You have a tension here. You have palms bending in adoration and reeds that strike a thorn-crowned head. You have a king and a convict. You have hosannas and mockery. You have triumph and tragedy. All in the one liturgy. And so we must ask two questions. First, what are we doing here, right now, in this liturgy? Second, how should what we are doing here affect what we do in the rest of our lives?

I

First then, what are we doing here, right now, in this liturgy?[1] In my past, we did today what we did on all the other Sundays of Lent, what we did all through Lent, what we did in a specially solemn way through Holy Week: we reproduced, we re-presented, we lived again the sufferings of Christ, his dying. Why? So that on Easter we could celebrate his rising. We were looking forward to Easter dawn, when Jesus would rise from the dead and we would rise with him. Today tragedy, tomorrow triumph. Lent, dying; Easter, rising.

I have news for you: this is liturgical nonsense. Lent is no more a preparation for the resurrection of Jesus than Advent was a preparation for the birth of Jesus.[2] This is to emphasize the history at the expense of the mystery. There is indeed a history, a chronology: from desert to cross to resurrection. But Passion Sunday, like all of Lent, gets its liturgical meaning from Easter. And what is Easter? Easter is the paschal mystery, and the paschal mystery is a duality: the dying-and-rising of Jesus. And the fact is, he has already died and risen; we dare not pretend that he has not.[3] Lent is not the dying of Jesus, Easter his rising. The whole of Lent is a progressively more intense initiation into the paschal mystery, into the twin reality of Jesus dead and risen.

If you need proof, go back over each Sunday this Lent. Each Sunday Gospel proclaimed not only dying but rising—in death, life. The first Sunday: Jesus in the desert (Mk 1:12–15). The biblical desert is not only the place of wandering and confusion, of hungering and thirsting, of temptation and searching; it is the place of discovery and covenant, of intimacy and love and new life. It is the Lord who leads into the desert. Remember, in Hosea, how the Lord speaks about Israel? "I will allure her, and bring her into the wilderness, and speak tenderly to her" (Hos 2:14).

The second Sunday: the Transfiguration (Lk 9:29b–36). On the journey of death, Jesus is revealed as the person of life. On the death march, the disciples see his glory. But they fail to grasp the death-life duality. In John Gallen's vivid paraphrase, "Who needs to go up to Jerusalem and die? It is good for us to be *here*. Where? The Sinai Hilton, that's where!"[4]

The third Sunday: destruction of the temple (Jn 2:13–25). In the midst of destruction, resurrection. "Destroy this temple [my body] and in three days I will raise it up" (Jn 2:19). The fourth Sunday: darkness and light (Jn 3:14–21). In the midst of darkness, Jesus is presented as the person of light. Not at the end of the darkness—in its very midst. The fifth Sunday: the grain of wheat (Jn 12:20–33). In dying, the grain of wheat yields a rich harvest. In dying, Jesus lives; in dying, he gives life.

So too for today, Passion/Palm Sunday. We are a historical people; Christianity is rooted in history; and so we do well to recall and reproduce the events that took place when Jesus entered the city of his dying. But if we stop at the history, we miss the mystery. Today we enter with growing intensity into the *whole* paschal mystery. Not palms *or* passion; both. Not triumph *or* tragedy; triumph *in* tragedy. Not a dying *or* a rising Christ; a dying-rising Christ. That is why the paschal mystery will open most intensely not next Sunday but with the evening Mass of the Last Supper; for the paschal mystery is one mystery: life in and through death.

This Lenten Sunday, then, why is triumph wed to tragedy, kingship to degradation, hosannas to curses, joy to sorrow? Because only the Resurrection makes sense out of Passion Sunday. And we are not preparing for the Resurrection; it has already happened! We know how the story turned out, and we should not pretend we do not. Even in Lent, in Holy Week. And not only the history, what factually happened: Jesus died, then he rose to life again. But the mystery as well, God's plan from eternity: life leaped *from* death; death was the springboard for his rising. That is why I find it enlightening and thrilling that when the risen Jesus appeared to his disciples, he showed them the wounds of his dying (cf. Jn 20:26–27). The mystery is one mystery: dying-rising.

II

This leads to my second point: how should what we are doing here affect what we do in the rest of our lives? That it ought to touch our lives is clear. For liturgy, as sacrament of Christian belief, does two things: it gives expression to the faith experience of a people, and it molds that experience, shapes it, fashions it.[5]

But how? What does Passion Sunday say to Christian experience, to the shape of my life? Underlying the answer is a truth I left out of my first point, a truth essential to the paschal mystery: Jesus Christ died and rose *for us*. Not only did he himself journey to Jerusalem; he commanded us to follow him on that journey. It is a journey that goes to life through death; and death gives life not only when we breathe our last, but all through our Christian existence. Because the journey is structured that way, we cannot avoid talking about death, about our dying, our daily, ceaseless dying.

In our journeying to life, we die in two ways; for death comes to us from two sources. Death comes to us, first, from sin—from the sins of our own fashioning and from "the sin of the world," all the weight and burden of human transgression from Adam to Antichrist. And "the wages of sin is death" (Rom 6:23). Not the soul leaving the body; not some abstract absence of God. The results of radical sin, of "mortal" sin, are within me. It unmakes me, undoes me, unravels me, misshapes me. In sin, in radical sin, I am a different person; for Life has left me.

To the death that is sin we have been dying since our baptism. And the dying is never ended. For dying to sin is not something negative; dying to sin is turning to Christ, and turning to Christ is a constant conversion. If sin is rejection, dying to sin is openness: openness to God's presence poured out on us through every flower that opens its chaliced petals to us, every breeze that caresses our skin, every man or woman whose eyes meet ours, the awesome presence of the Holy One Himself tabernacled within us. In dying to sin, we live to God.

Death comes to us in a second way: from the very shape of the journey—even apart from sin. For the human journey to go forward, to move ahead, you have to let go of where you've been, let go of the level of life where you are now, so as to live more fully. It's never far from you. Whether it's turning 21, 40, or 65; whether it's losing your health or your hair, your looks or your lustiness, your money or your memory, a person you love or a possession you prize; whether it's yesterday's applause or today's rapture;

whether it's as fleeting as Fort Lauderdale or as abiding as grace—you have to move on. Essential to the human pilgrimage, to the Christian journey, is a self-emptying more or less like Christ's own emptying: time and again, from womb to tomb, you have to let go. And to let go is to die a little. It's painful, it can be bloody; and so we hang on, we clutch our yesterdays like Linus' blanket, we refuse to grow.

But no, it will not do—especially for a Christian. You are commanded to let go. Not invited—commanded: "Follow me!" It is a sticky, risky thing, this letting go of yesterday, if only because you cannot be certain where it will lead, except that the journey is in the tracks of one who laid aside his divine glory to clothe himself in our flesh, let go of Nazareth and his mother, the hill of Transfiguration *and* the garden of Gethsemane, the sinners he had touched with his forgiveness and that unpredictable band of mixed-up apostles—let go of the very miracle of being alive.

The comforting thing, the thrilling thing, is that you let go for a purpose; kenosis, emptying, dying is not its own end. You let go of yesterday because only by letting go, only by reaching out into a shadowed future, can you *grow* into Christ, come to be increasingly conformed to his dying-rising. Only by letting go can you *grow* in loving communion with God, with the crucified and risen images of God, with the breath-taking beauty of His creation all about you.

Only by dying, not only to sin but to yourself, can you come fully to life. You don't *forget* your yesterdays; they are part of who you are today. You simply refuse to live in them, to wallow in them, to pretend that there, in some near or distant yesterday, there life reached its peak or died its death.

Many years ago I was intensely moved by a movie. It was titled *Come Back, Little Sheba*. The male lead, Burt Lancaster, is a reformed alcoholic. His wife, Shirley Booth, is a devoted woman with a big heart; but she bores him endlessly by ceaselessly recalling the good old days. Remember when . . . ? Time and again she walks out on the porch calling for Little Sheba, the dog that has disappeared, the dog that is a symbol of those bygone days, a symbol of dashed hopes. And for twenty years these two good people live what Thoreau called "lives of quiet desperation."

No, my brothers and sisters, stop calling for Little Sheba. Passion Sunday is a different call: the paschal mystery, your involvement in the dying-rising of Christ, is *now*. Die a little, to live more richly. Let your yesterdays be yesterdays, the joys and the sorrows, so that *today* you may listen to the Lord's voice (cf. Ps 95:7), receive his flesh and blood for *today's* food and drink, go out to a little acre of God's world where crucified men and women need so badly a Christian who has died to sin and self, who lives to God and for others . . . today.

9
THE EUCHARIST IS OUR EXODUS
Liturgy of the Last Supper

Each year the Catholic University of America schedules a so-called University Mass for Holy Thursday. Classes are still in session that day, but one hour is withdrawn from academic time so that students, faculty, and administrators may be free to share a special community worship.

For the 1977 liturgy, celebrated in the crypt of the Shrine of the Immaculate Conception, I found one homiletic approach especially alluring. I had, in the past, preached on the Last Supper as Jesus' response to a threefold challenge to his love, a response concretized in the Real Presence, the Mass, and Communion; and I had preached on the Eucharist as sacrament of oneness, the oneness of all in Christ Jesus (see my All Lost in Wonder *[Westminster, Md.: Newman, 1960] 87–97). But in '77 the liturgical readings took me in a different direction. Exodus 12:1–8, 11–14 recalled the Jewish Passover, memorial of the escape from Egypt. 1 Corinthians 11:23–26 reminded us of the Last Supper, the springboard of Jesus' own "going out" from us. John 13:1–15 is the famous foot-washing, with its two different interpretations in Johannine circles.*

In this context it seemed good to center my homily on the word "exodus," on the experience of exodus. For each of the three readings focused on a historical moment, and each of those moments is an exodus, a departure, a going out.

If any single word could sum up today's liturgy, I suggest it might be "exodus." Today's three readings focus on three historical moments: the thirteenth century before Christ, the year 28 or 30 of the Common Era, and our own 1977. Each of those moments is an exodus, a departure, a going out. There is, first, the exodus of the Israelites from the land of Egypt. There is, second, the Last Supper, the point of departure of the new exodus, Jesus' own passage from this world to the Father. And there is, third, your exodus and mine, our departure today from all that is sin and self. A word on each reading, to put it into perspective; then a word on ourselves.

I

First, the original Exodus. In Jewish history the escape from Egypt is the marvel of marvels. Without it there would be no Jewish history. This passage over the Red Sea is a prototype of libera-

58

tion—deliverance from slavery to serve the Lord God in freedom. That is why, in the Seder today, each Jewish family faithful to traditional faith commemorates the Exodus, raises its cups to proclaim:

> Therefore it is our duty to thank, praise, laud, glorify, uplift, extol, bless, exalt, and adore Him who did all of these miracles for our fathers and for ourselves. He has brought us forth from slavery to freedom, from sorrow to joy, from mourning to festive day, from darkness to a great light, and from subjection to redemption.

The Seder re-enacts a historical deliverance. But with this re-presentation of the past, each Passover fuses an expectation, the expectation of future liberation, a freedom to come. Each Passover "is a feast of hope which deepens messianic expectation; in the course of a paschal night, the Messiah will come!"[1]

Second, the tradition St. Paul hands on, the saving word he "received from the Lord." It reminds us that, in the Christian vision, the lamb the Lord ordered the Israelites to eat prefigures "the Lamb of God who takes away the sins of the world." It reminds us that, as Paul put it, "Christ, our paschal lamb, has been sacrificed" (1 Cor 5:7). It reminds us that this supper, this passover, which Jesus yearned with all his heart to eat with his disciples before he suffered (cf. Lk 22:15), is not bread and wine but his own flesh and blood, given for us, given to us. It reminds us that the Last Supper is the springboard of Jesus' own exodus: with this meal of love he begins to "go out" from us—a passage to the Father that will be marked with blood—thorns on his brow, spittle on his face, lashes on his back, nails in his hands and feet. It reminds us that to eat this bread and drink this cup is to "proclaim the death of the Lord until he comes." With *this* re-presentation of the past, *our* passover fuses an expectation, the expectation of future liberation, the perfect freedom of the children of God. Each Eucharist "is a feast of hope which deepens messianic expectation": the Messiah will come—again.

Third, the Gospel reading. On the face of it, it seems so simple. Jesus washes the feet of his disciples, gives an example of humble service. But the Gospel text reveals something more complex. In Johannine circles two different interpretations of the foot-washing arose, and both find place in our Gospel reading.

The first interpretation we may call Christological. When Jesus lowered himself to wash the feet of his followers, his action was

prophetic and symbolic. It was prophetic: he was acting out beforehand his humiliation in death—somewhat as Mary, in anointing his
feet (Jn 12:3), acted out beforehand the anointing of his body for
burial. It was symbolic: it signified the service he would render in
laying down his life for others. That is why his response to a protesting Peter was almost harsh: "If I do not wash you, you will have
no heritage with me" (Jn 13:8). That is why he can say his washing
makes his disciples clean (v. 10). The foot-washing symbolizes Jesus' death in humiliation for the salvation of others. That is why,
when Jesus explains his action, explains that he must die to bring
men their heritage with him and cleanse them of sin, Peter submits.

The second interpretation that grew up is somewhat different:
Jesus has acted out for his disciples a moral example, an example
of humility, which they must be ready to imitate. "The rabbi has
done for the disciples an act of service that occasionally generous
disciples might do for a rabbi; the disciples must be willing to do
similar acts of service for one another."[2] "What I just did was to
give you an example: as I have done, so you must do" (Jn 13:15).

II

You can sense, can't you, that these readings are wonderfully
woven of mystery—the mystery that is salvation, redemption, liberation. But granted this, granted the readings are theologically profound, what, if anything, do they say to us here and now, on this
campus in 1977? Much more than a short homily could ever ex-
haust. For your reflection I propose a single facet. The Last Supper
that inaugurated Jesus' exodus from this world to the Father, the
Eucharist that brings to breath-taking fulfilment the paschal lamb
of the Israelites, should spark our own exodus. I mean our departure from so much that is sin, so much that is self.

First, within Christianity the Bread of Life is not primarily an
individualistic thing, a solitary supper, my private party. Its function is to form a community. St. Paul phrased it beautifully: "Because the Bread is one, we, though many, are one body; for we all
partake of the one Bread" (1 Cor 10:17). The Lord who locks himself in the tabernacle of my body is none other than the Lord who
nourishes the man or woman beside me, my next-door neighbor,
the same Christ who feeds the Lebanese, the Japanese, and the
Thai, the African, the German, and the Czech. Christ is not divided, Christ is not multiplied. There is one and the same body, one
and the same Christ, for all. In his flesh we are one.

A peril within Catholicism today is that the Eucharist which should make us one threatens to divide us. Catholic communities are unchristianly rent by warring loves: Shall we offer the Mass of Pius V or Paul VI? Shall we stand or kneel, pray in an ageless Latin or an ephemeral English, receive Life in our hands or on our tongues, wish peace with a touch or a word, blare forth Bach from an organ or strum a Christian love song? For all too many, these are not academic debates or Christian options; they are life-and-death struggles—so much so that some Catholics will not worship with other Catholics save on their own terms, even suicidally refuse the Bread that gives life. Is it for this that the Word-made-flesh offered that flesh the night before he died: "This is my body, which is given for you"?

Even more crucially, there is the world outside our altars. Outside these walls is a hungry world. Hungry for bread: 460 million are starving, and each day 10,000 of the hungry die. Hungry for justice: in South Africa 18 percent of the population dominate the rest, and the world's women are still an oppressed class. Hungry for peace: blood reddens the barriers of Belfast, an uneasy truce heats the sands of Sinai. Hungry for understanding: so many human hearts, close by you, are waiting hopelessly for a word of love or the touch of your hand. In that context—millions of men, women, and children struggling desperately to live human lives, struggling even to live—talk about the Bread of Life can sound awfully empty, suspiciously hollow. And it will be empty, will be hollow, unless there is a Christian exodus, unless we go out of our small selves, unless we who feed on the Eucharistic Christ are ourselves eucharists for the life of the world.

This is not insubstantial poetry. The Eucharist is central to Christians for a complex of reasons. It is a presence, a real if hidden presence, a presence without peer, a presence of Christ's whole person, a presence which leaps from love and leads to life, a presence which is a promise, a promise of good things which our eyes have not yet seen, our ears not yet heard, blessings it has not entered our minds to imagine. If I am to be a eucharist for the life of the world, my feeding on the flesh of Christ must take me from church to world, to wash the feet of my brothers and sisters. I must begin to be present to others, present where they are, present in ways that respond to their needs, to their hungers—for food or freedom, for justice or understanding, for peace or God. I must be really present—I, not merely my money or my mind—somewhat hidden at times but always totally committed, because as a Christian my life is love and only love can bring life, can light dulled eyes with hope, can promise somebody somewhere that tomorrow will be more human, will be worth living.

A Eucharistic prayer from the second century speaks of "this broken bread" which "was scattered over the. hills," then was "gathered [and] became one mass,"[3] one Bread. We must reverse that process. The one Bread we eat must be given back, must be transformed into a bread we break for the millions, must be scattered again over the hills, into the valleys, through the deserts until each brother of mine, each sister, from Appalachia to West Africa, can smile each night and murmur: "I am full."

That is what I mean by an exodus spirituality. The Christ of Holy Thursday not only feeds me. He does with me today what he did that night with the bread: he takes me, and he blesses me, and he breaks me, and he gives me. The broken bread—then as now, Christ or I—the broken bread is a force for healing, for freeing. But then as now, Christ or I, the bread must be broken. Otherwise it cannot be given—especially to those who are themselves broken. And once we are given to others, we shall find that it is they who give to us. Given to the oppressed, the enslaved, we shall be lifted from our own oppression, our slavish centering on ourselves. In the broken we shall find our own healing. In such an exodus the Messiah will really come—to them and to us.

10
JESUS CHRIST IS LORD
Feast of Christ the King

In preparing a homily for the liturgical feast of Christ the King in 1976—a homily to be delivered first at the Catholic University of America and later that day at Holy Trinity Church in the Georgetown area of Washington, D.C.—I came to the conclusion that the feast faces us with two problems, one apparent, the other real.

The apparent problem stems in large measure from an American reaction to kings. We don't like kings: they conjure up the tyrant and the despot—too much power in one man's hands. And yet Jesus did claim to be a king, did claim absolute authority. Not too much trouble solving that problem, at least in principle. Jesus' kingship is neither political nor despotic; he is not interested in replacing Caesar; he is a "king of hearts." And the liturgical reading from John 18:33–37 can be helpful. It shows how Jesus, confronting Pilate, moved away from the rhetoric of kingship to describe his role in terms of truth—truth in the biblical sense, founded on experience of God.

The real problem, as I saw it, does not lie with Jesus or with Pilate. The real problem is ourselves: how do we relate to him who is Truth? Is he our Lord? Another way of phrasing it, are we men and women "of the truth" in the biblical sense? The feast of Christ the King challenges not so much our intellectual perception as our Christian fidelity.

Today's feast is a unique feast. The Church titles it "Christ the King." But the very Gospel the Church chooses suggests that "king" is a title Jesus Christ would rather not have. Where does this leave our liturgy? Do you have to choose between Rome and Jerusalem, between a tiara and a crown of thorns? Suppose we try to see—which, of course, means three points: (1) the apparent problem; (2) the solution; (3) the real problem.

I

First then, the apparent problem. It stems from three sources: from us, from Jesus, from Rome.

The problem stems in part from us. For most Catholics, Christ as king is not our thing. "King" sends out bad vibrations. It connotes power, force, violence; it suggests dominion, domination, despotism. King conjures up bloody kings like Herod or mad kings like Ludwig—Herod who killed all those children, Ludwig who built all those castles. And kings paint pictures of pomp and circumstance: ermine robes, crowns of gold, the wolfish appetite of Henry VIII. Kings sit on thrones; courtiers fawn on them; jesters clown for them; the common folk grovel at their feet. No, a king is not our thing.

The problem stems in part from Jesus. King is not a title Jesus liked very much; today's Gospel suggests strongly that he would rather dispense with it. But the fact is, at the most critical moment of his life he does not *deny* he is a king. His response to Pilate, "*You* say I am a king," is not a categorical denial; it is not the unequivocal "no" Pilate would have liked, some Catholics would prefer. And whether you call him king or not, he did claim absolute authority. Before ascending to his Father, he sent his disciples on their mission with a solemn preface: "All authority [absolute power] in heaven and on earth has been given to me" (Mt 28:18). And Paul told the Christians of Corinth that at the end of time Christ will "deliver the kingdom to God the Father. . . . For he must reign until he has put all his enemies under his feet. . . . For God has put all things in subjection under his feet" (1 Cor 15:24–27).

The problem stems in part from Rome. So much of today's liturgy speaks a language that can turn us off: "He received dominion, glory, kingship; nations and peoples of every language serve him" (Dn 7:14). "The Lord is king; he is robed in majesty" (Ps 93:1). "Jesus Christ is . . . ruler of the kings of earth" (Rev 1:5); he is "the king of all creation."

So then, an apparent problem: the Church proclaims Christ king; he does not deny he is a king; but kings and kingdoms alienate us—they smell too foully of force, of despotic power, of threats to freedom and human living.

II

Now this problem, the apparent problem, finds its solution in today's Gospel. First a negative solution. Jesus reassures Pilate: my kingship presents no threat to the sheerly political interests of Rome. My kingdom does not belong to this world; like me, my kingdom comes from above. I do not have subjects, I have followers. I do not compel, I attract. The only force I use is the compelling power of love. My kingdom is *within* you, else I have no power over you at all. I did not take flesh to sit on Caesar's throne.

But Jesus is not concerned to keep Pilate happy. His response shifts to the positive; he moves from the rhetoric of kingship to describe his role in terms dear to the Evangelist John: "The reason why I have been born, the reason I have come into the world, is to testify to the truth. Everyone who belongs to the truth listens to my voice" (Jn 18:37). And with that it is now Pilate who is on trial, not Christ.

To grasp the significance of that shift, to thrill to those few bald words about truth, you have to plunge into the atmosphere out of which they burst. Truth here is not Greek truth, the truth of Augustine and Aquinas, the truth of the Neo-Scholastics. It is not reality somewhere out there, something that exists whether I am thinking of it or not; it is not linking my *mind* to what *is*. It is a different approach to truth, a notion of truth founded on religious experience, on encounter with God. It is the biblical notion of truth.[1]

Old Testament truth is remarkably rich. Basically, it has to do with being stable, proven, reliable, dependable, trustworthy. That is why in the Old Testament truth properly belongs to God. God is a "God of truth" (Ps 31:5; Jer 10:10). But not in an intellectualist sense. The God of truth comes to consummate clarity in the context of the covenant and His promises. Moses puts it splendidly to Israel: "Know that Yahweh your God is God, the God worthy of trust who keeps His covenant of love forever with those who love Him" (Deut 7:9). When the Psalmist sings to God "The sum of thy word is truth" (Ps 119:160), he tells us that God will never go back on His word, He will always perform for His people His wonderful works of salvation.

But this God of truth demanded "men [and women] of truth" (Exod 18:21; Neh 7:2). But not in some rationalist sense. Men and women of truth were not intellects in conformity with objective reality, but persons unswervingly conformed to God's will. Oh yes, they had to *know* God's will; but this was not enough—they had to *do* God's will. Men and women of truth were the people of God who were faithful to His covenant, His law—yes, men and women who were faithful to one another (Gen 47:29; Josh 2:14; Zech 7:9).

In impressive fashion the New Testament reflects the Old. St. Paul's formula "God's truthfulness" (Rom 3:7) is God's faithfulness, His fidelity to His promises; and for men and women, a life of truth is a life of righteousness, the kind of life Paul expects to find among Christians (Col 1:6; 2 Cor 13:8). But something new has come into being: "the truth of the gospel" (Gal 2:5, 14). For Paul, truth is the word he preaches, God's mystery revealed, to be ac-

cepted by faith, to be lived in love—not an abstract set of propositions but the person of Christ (2 Cor 4:5): "truth is in Jesus" (Eph
4:21).

But for all the richness of Paul, it is in John that we discover a
theology of truth. Truth is the word Christ heard from the Father,
the word he came to proclaim, the word that should lead us to believe in him (cf. Jn 8). This, John insists, is a fresh truth, a new revelation: "grace and truth have come through Jesus Christ" (1:17).
In fact, the thrilling newness of Christianity is that Christ is himself
the truth (14:6): he has in himself the fulness of revelation, he
makes the Father known. It is summed up remarkably in that glorious sentence, "I am the way and the truth and the life" (14:6). The
three nouns are intimately linked. Jesus is the *way* to the Father because, as *truth* in flesh, he conveys to us the revelation of the Father
in what he says and what he is, and in this way communicates to us
the *life* of God.

In consequence, a Christian's task, in John's eyes, is to "belong to the truth" (18:37). But this is possible only if the Christian
who has been born of the Spirit in the surrender of faith abides in
the word of Jesus, allows all his actions to be guided by the truth of
the gospel, works with and loves his brothers and sisters by the
power of the truth within him, adores the Father with a worship inspired by the Spirit of truth and by the truth of Jesus (cf. 4:23–24).
This is the truth that makes for Christian freedom (8:32)—freedom
not from necessity but from sin. Truth is not so much, therefore, a
complex of statements or ideas, not really speculation about the
world or salvation. It is an address of God to man in concrete encounter, and man's response to that address—an address and a response inseparable from the person of Jesus, who is himself the
truth and the way to the truth. "Everyone who belongs to the truth
listens to my voice."

III

If *this* is the truth Jesus came to proclaim, Pilate's question
"Truth? And what is that?" was more profound than he could have
suspected. The truth stood before him in person—and he could
not see. Which leads to my third point: the real problem.

You see, the real problem in today's liturgy is not Pilate and it
is not Jesus; it is you and I. Pilate is no longer on trial; but you and
I are. The problem is not whether Jesus has some title that connotes despotic rule; the problem is, how do you and I relate to him

who is truth and the way to truth, who is life and the way to life? Kings may be anathema to us, but our Christian tongue must confess with St. Paul that "Jesus Christ is *Lord*" (Phil 2:11). The question is . . . *is* he? I mean, is he *your* Lord and *my* Lord?

How can you tell? One question is basic: Who or what commands your love, rules your heart? Can you say, with full integrity, that no one, no thing, takes precedence over Jesus in your life, in your day-to-day living? What motivates you, moves you, possesses and thrills you from dawn to dusk? Is it some other human person? Is it lust . . . for power, for recognition, for honors, for glory, for a man or woman, for comfort, for personal satisfaction? What makes you go, makes you tick? Who or what rules your heart? Something does—or someone does. Or—dreadful thought—perhaps nothing does.

Another way of looking at it: How do you relate to truth? Not to philosophical truth: Does what is in your mind correspond to what is out there? That will pass an exam on campus; it is not enough for God. Rather, biblical truth: Are you a man or woman "of the truth"? How faithful are you? How full of faith, how reliable?

Each of you has a covenant—with God and His images—perhaps several covenants: promises that stem from baptism, from religious profession, from ordination, from marriage. They are hard promises. That you will love the Lord with your whole heart, the person next to you as you love yourself. That you will share the poverty of the poor, the virginity of Mary, the blood-soaked obedience of Christ. That you will be a man or woman of the Church, critical perhaps but always from love. That you will be faithful, not only not unfaithful, to one man or woman—not only in flesh but utterly reliable: the other can trust that you will never go back on your word.

And don't forget the subcovenants that are yours: the scholar, the teacher, the student, the administrator—whatever the work you do. These are not just contracts with an impersonal institution (contracts that may seem to call for a bit of occult compensation); they touch your relationship to a living God and living people. How faithful are you? *Full* of faith and *utterly* reliable?

In sum, my brothers and sisters, Christ the King is a problem not so much for Christ as for you, a challenge not so much to research and exegesis as to reflection and conscience. Jesus Christ is indeed Lord; but is he *your* Lord? God is indeed a God of truth, utterly faithful to His promises; but what He expects of *you* as He addresses you in concrete encounter, in the daily events of your Christian existence, is that you be a man or woman of truth: not merely an intellect in harmony with reality outside of you, but a whole person in tune with the God within you, the good and faithful servant of the brothers and sisters who are one flesh with you.

SACRAMENTS AND
SACRED COMMITMENT

11
A STRANGE GOD, A STRANGE PEOPLE
Baptismal homily for an unsuspecting child

> *We feared for this child—feared that God might take her soon after her coming to birth, as He had taken her sister one short day into this life. And so we prayed—her father and her mother, those who worshiped each Sunday with the Woodstock Jesuits in St. Paul's Chapel on the campus of Columbia University, friends far and near—we prayed for Sonia Maria with trust and trembling. In His goodness, God gave her back to us (and since then her smile has delighted the landscape of New Brunswick in Canada, Berkeley in California, and New Orleans). And so, when we gathered for the Sunday liturgy at St. Paul's on May 12, 1973, the blessed water we poured on her was laced with thanksgiving beyond forgetting.*
>
> *What to say at a baptism encircled with such memories, within a living Christian community? How keep the homily from being just another routine remembrance of baptismal grace, to which only Sonia Maria might respond with a cry from the heart? The answer came suddenly, unexpectedly, excitingly, as I lounged on the roof of a Jesuit residence on Riverside Drive, gazing pensively over the Hudson River to the Jersey shore beyond. Why not talk directly to Sonia Maria, address my baptismal reflections to the child about to be baptized? Why not tell her about this awe-full, dread-full, danger-filled thing we were about to do to her: initiate her willy-nilly into our community?*
>
> *Not surprisingly, the grownups listened.*

You and I are about to exercise an extraordinary act of love. We are about to welcome a child, an infant, into a community, into the Christian community. It is an awesome, fearsome, perilous thing that we do; for in effect we are saying to this child:

Sonia Maria, like it or not, you are being initiated into our community. You will become part of a people, God's people. This God is a strange God, and His people is a strange people.

I

This God of yours is a strange God, a God of contradictions. For your God is now the God of Moses and Abraham, the God of Ezekiel and Isaiah, the God of Jesus and Mary, the God of John and Judas. This God thunders His commands from a mountain, beckons to you from a burning bush, whispers love from a cross. He

71

permits a Pharaoh to enslave you, and divides a sea to save you. He
leads you into a wilderness to face hunger and death, then feeds
you with bread from heaven. He promises you a progeny without
end, but commands you to sacrifice your only son. He will be endlessly faithful to you, and yet let you, like Israel, "play the harlot
with many lovers." He loves you even when you forsake Him, and
proves it by crucifying His Son. He will let you rest on His breast
like John, and kiss Him like Judas.

He loves mothers (there is even a mother of *God*), yet He ex-
iles them to Egypt, lets their little ones be bloodied in countless
Bethlehems, colors some black and leaves them to white mercies.

His kingdom within you is joy to the full, joy which "no man
can take from you," yet you can enter this kingdom, share it, only
through tears—and the tears are not wiped away till the new Jerusalem descends from heaven. You have already experienced His
heavy hand; for He took your sister after one short day, and even
for *you* we were afraid and we wept.

If you decide really to serve Him, He will shake you and shiver
you and shatter you, yet at the darkest moment you will say with
the Psalmist: "Though He should slay me, yet will I love Him."
And one day He will in a sense "slay" you, the day you say "Lord
Jesus, come"—but only that you may be a new creation, that the
life you begin today, His life, may be intensified and eternalized
within you, beyond the power of sin and death to destroy.

II

A strange God. A stranger people; a people of contradictions.
For we are proud, are glad, to call ourselves a community of faith, a
community of hope, a community of love. And yet, as you grow up,
Sonia Maria, you will often be scandalized; for you will discover
that we are all in some measure faithless, hopeless, loveless.

Week after week we cry with our lips: "I believe in one God
the Father . . . in one Christ Jesus, who died for us . . . in the Holy
Spirit . . . in one church, in the communion of saints, the forgiveness of sins, life everlasting." We do indeed believe it. But you will
find our faith long on propositions, short on self-giving. We forget
that without a yes to Jesus a yes to propositions is sterile, useless to
save. As St. James put it, even the devils believe: believe that God is
one and three, that God became man and died for our sins, that
God punishes and rewards; and still they are severed from God
forever. Side by side with suffering servants you will spy lip ser-

vants, serving many masters: power, greed, knowledge, comfort, whatever our "thing" is—those thousand and one masters that are not Jesus.

"Our hope is in the Lord." You will hear us chant this endlessly, from the diaphragm. And you will be disenchanted to discover how often our hope is not in the Lord but in man—in what we can see and what man can do. Your hope, I hope, will reflect St. Paul's four incisive sentences to the Christians in Rome: "Our salvation is founded upon the hope of something. But hope would not be hope at all if its object were seen. And if we are hoping for something still unseen, then we need endurance to wait for it. Only, the Spirit comes to aid us in our weakness" (Rom 8:24–26). Please God, Sonia Maria, you will always hope *for* God *from* God.

On the basis of Christ's own command, we call ourselves a community of love: "A new commandment I give to you, that you love one another. By this all men will know that you are my disciples, if you have love for one another" (Jn 13:34–35). Here too, Sonia Maria, you will grow up in a community of contradiction. This is what we should be, but so often are not. Who looks at the barbed wire in Belfast, the scorched earth of Cambodia, the decaying schoolhouses in Appalachia, the slums of our own city, and thinks of us as a community of love? You will not find us less color-conscious than our unbelieving neighbors. You will wonder why, in this breathless mystery of the Mass, in this re-presentation of God's total self-giving, millions of Catholics just want to be left alone, millions of Catholics find it repulsive to turn to another human person for whom Christ died and say "Hello." You will find it mind-blowing, perhaps faith-shattering, that within this community of love we tear and rend one another, while the unbeliever shakes his head in unbelief: "See how these Christians hate one another."

And still, Sonia Maria, despite our inner contradictions, the community to which we welcome you is not just another sin-ridden establishment. There is a Presence here that is not of this world, a Presence that pervades and invades us, a Presence that breaks through our smallness and our sinfulness, makes us better than we are—a Presence that is awfully real because it is a Person, a living, pulsing, risen Person. Here, Sonia Maria, you will find Jesus.

You will find him all the more easily because it is not we, your fellow Christians, who put him here. He *is* here. Oh yes, we can make him sacramentally present ("This is my body"), but he is already here: in the proclaimed Word; because two or three are gathered here in his name; because his Spirit, the Holy Spirit, is our lifeblood. Please God, you will also find him in us: in the smiles that crease our faces, in the joy that makes us *look* redeemed, in the love that lights our waking moments.

III

Sonia Maria, before we welcome you through symbol and ritual into this paradoxical people, this community of contradictions, let me make an uncommonly honest confession. In the course of a half century (and more), I have seen more Catholic corruption than most Catholics read of. I have tasted it. I have been reasonably corrupt myself. And yet I joy in this Church, this living, throbbing, sinning people of God; I love it with a crucifying passion. Why? For all the Catholic hate, I experience here a community of *love*. For all the institutional idiocy, I find here a tradition of *reason*. For all the individual repressions, I breathe here an air of *freedom*. For all the fear of sex, I discover here the redemption of my *body*. In an age so inhuman, I touch here tears of *compassion*. In a world so grim and humorless, I share here rich *joy* and earthy *laughter*. In the midst of death, I hear here an incomparable stress on *life*. For all the apparent absence of God, I sense here the presence of *Christ*. . . . I pray, Sonia Maria, that your life within this community, your experience of a strange God and a still stranger people, will rival mine.

Come now, Sonia Maria, and take your first steps into a kingdom you can only enter through hardship and tribulation, into a community that will not wipe away your every tear but does promise that we will touch each tear with our love.

12
NOT YET IN CHRIST
Baptism as first conversion

*When a preacher has a homily that has struck fire, he is tempt-
ed to use it again . . . and again . . . and again. So much encouraging reaction had filtered back to me after my baptismal homily "A
Strange God, a Strange People" that I repeated it, with the necessary modifications of course, when baptizing the boy child of two
dear friends in Philadelphia several years later. But then the boy
child got himself a little sister, her parents sought out the same homilist, and the homilist was caught with a very small baptismal
bag.*

*Still, a promising possibility began to sprout from seminars I
had conducted over the years at Woodstock College and Catholic
University on the development of the doctrine of original sin. Exis-
tential and personalistic philosophies, a newly-awakened Christo-
centric view of reality, evolution, modern biblical scholarship, fresh
interpretation of the Council of Trent—all these have compelled re-
consideration of the doctrine, with some exciting results. Naturally,
such developments do not turn into a homily, but they did have the
effect of focusing my remarks less on Adam and more on Christ.*

*It was a graced day for me too, that gracing event on Novem-
ber 5, 1978, in historic St. Joseph's Church, Willings Alley, Philadelphia. Then it was I saw, with incomparable clarity, Christ our
Lord taking a child's hand on the first small steps of a lifelong
Christian journey not to end this side of eternity.*

My brothers and sisters in Christ: Most of you don't know it, but
we theologians are doing our best to make the sacrament of baptism difficult for you. You recall, of course, what baptism does to a
child: he or she is cleansed of original sin and made a member of
Christ's Body. But theologians can no longer agree on what this
original sin is of which the child is cleansed.

When *I* was baptized, it seemed simple enough. I was a fallen
god. In a distant Paradise there had been a prehistoric catastrophe.
The first man, at the peak of human powers, rebelled in cold blood
against his Creator. In punishment, he lost God, self-mastery, endless life—not only for himself and wife Eve, but for all who would
be seeded from him. And so I came whimpering into the world de-
prived of God's presence, guilty because I shared mysteriously in
Adam's no, unable to recapture a Paradise lost, enslaved to passion, destined for a life in which, like St. Paul, "I can will what is
right, but I cannot do it" (Rom 7:18).

Not quite, say recent researchers into sin. The Adam myth must be reinterpreted; the perspective has to be not a fall from perfection but a movement forward; the center has to be Christ. My status at birth was not a solidarity in sin with a historic Adam; it was the human condition: I was not-yet-in-Christ. And I was not-yet-in-Christ because I was situated in a sinful world, in a world constituted by the whole history of sinful deeds from the first to the latest. Within each child born, before any personal choice, there is a deep-seated bias, "a kind of will not to love God . . . a bias stemming from the very fact that the individual has been born into the human family. . . ."[1]

I've taken this little excursion into theology not to show you how smart I am, but to bring out a central facet of Christian living. As so often, a fresh confusion in theology, new disagreements, have made clearer than ever an aspect of baptism we have been prone to forget. In baptism the central figure is not Adam but Christ. In the past as I remember it, the stress was on original sin. We had to rid the child of it, and quickly, lest he or she languish in Limbo forever, near God but yet so far from Him.

I am not downgrading sin, especially the "sin of the world" that affects each child conceived. Whatever it is, however you define it, it is awfully real, all-pervasive, at the root of our being. But there is a danger here: we have tended to see in the unbaptized child a little monster from outer space, pockmarked or blackened by Adam's sin, not yet loved by God. A core of truth, indeed, but it can be strangled by the imagination.

The emphasis on Christ rights the balance. Elizabeth Ashley is not-yet-in-Christ. Her Savior has not yet taken possession of her; he will in a few short moments. When I pour water on her head in the name of the Trinity, that action will not only initiate entrance into our believing community. It will be the first stage in a process, a journey, of conversion. The grace of Christ will begin to remove the bias toward evil, the deepseated desire to be held captive, the unconscious connivance with sin that lies at the root of all newborn being. It is unimportant that she will *feel* only cold water and not warm grace; God will be at work in the depths of her person. Christ her Lord will be preparing the way for a free, personal, total turning to him when she is fully aware of his liberating presence. The Christ who already loves her, who loved her from her first human moment, will be incredibly active in her. He will take her hand on the first small steps of a lifelong Christian journey, the conversion, the turning to him, that can never be final this side of eternity.

Conversion can never be final. This sober thought turns us from Elizabeth Ashley to ourselves. Christian living is a constant conversion to Christ, a turning to him afresh as our Lord. It does not end at baptism; it begins there. The encouraging, glorious, salvific fact is that in all conversion God takes the initiative, God starts the process. That religious truth is strikingly evidenced in Elizabeth Ashley's baptism today: she does not know that God is taking her hand. In like fashion, He works on and in us in countless ways, most of them beyond our recognizing—in the events of every day and the people who cross our path, through the sacraments of the Church and the sacrament that is this moment. Of us He asks a response, a response He will one day ask of Elizabeth Ashley: that we turn more totally to Him in loving awareness.

Today we shall bring a variety of gifts to Elizabeth Ashley. One gift none of us should forget to bring: our own conversion, our own fresh turning to Christ in love. He is there, you know—wherever you are.

13
PRIESTHOOD AND RECONCILIATION
The ordained priest and Christ's passion

In preaching the word—God's and my own—I have long felt partial to priests. Not primarily because I belong to "the club." Rather because I am convinced that the continuing education of priests ranks among our most urgent Catholic needs. Besides, I am aware, at times uncomfortably, that I myself have been gifted with a continuing education for almost half a century. The least I can do is to give liberally what I have liberally received.

For some years the Diocese of Bridgeport in Connecticut heard more from me, for better or worse, than any other diocese in the country. In 1975 I was asked to introduce Holy Week to the Bridgeport priests with a type of meditation homily that would link priesthood and the sacred days to come.

From several rich possibilities I chose the rubric of reconciliation. It is an important, if not frequent, Pauline word (see 2 Cor 5:17-20); it is an "in" word today even in some secular discourse; and—a powerful moving force—I had given six radio talks on the subject in January and February 1974 which were published that year in a booklet Towards Reconciliation *by the United States Catholic Conference. Those talks, however, had not addressed the role of the ordained priest in reconciliation, nor the relation of that role to the death and resurrection of Christ. In eighteen minutes the subject is hardly exhausted, but perhaps a beginning has been made.*

My fellow priests in Christ: Holy Week is your week. It is the week of priesthood and reconciliation. The terms are complementary. Priesthood has for purpose reconciliation, and reconciliation is a priestly task. That was true of Christ, and it is true of you—true of the Eternal High Priest, and true of us who share his priesthood. Let me speak first of Christ, and then let me speak of you; for this is your week.

I

However you interpret the Fall, however you understand original sin, a catastrophic rupture rent humanity. On four levels. We were severed from God; we were divided within ourselves; we were ripped from our brothers and sisters; we were alienated from nature, from the nonhuman. An incredible disharmony: God, myself, others, things.

78

Such rupture cried for reconciliation, the destruction of disharmony. But in God's plan no mere man, no sheerly human person, could redeem: not Abraham or Isaiah, not John the Baptist or Mary of Nazareth. It would take a God-man—someone who could plead for man because he himself is man, plead successfully because he is God.

A priest did this—the High Priest of the new covenant. On the four levels. (1) To all who welcomed him he gave power to become children of God, all who believe in his name. (2) Our schizophrenia, our inner division, the struggle of which St. Paul complained "I do not do what I want but the very thing I hate," this "body of death," who delivered us from it? In St. Paul's triumphant cry, "Jesus Christ our Lord" (Rom 7:15, 24–25). (3) The hate that reddened the earth with the blood of Abel, a brother's blood, that hatred God-in-flesh conquered with a new commandment: "Love one another as I have loved you" (Jn 13:34). Not only did he *command* love; he gave us *power* to love. (4) He made it possible for us to live at peace not only with the animal but even with the atom— not so much to subdue the earth as to bring it to redemption with us.

How did Christ the Priest do this? The most remarkable week in salvation history. Four moments: he changed bread and wine into his body and blood; he delivered that body to death on a bloodspattered cross; he rose from the dead; and he gave to his apostles the power to forgive sin in his name. The two prime sacraments of reconciliation: Eucharist and penance; sacrificial death and triumphant resurrection, the first fruits of redeemed humanity.

For your meditation on Christ this week, therefore, I urge on you four incomparable biblical "words": (1) "This is my body, which is given for you; this is my blood, which will be poured out for [you]" (Lk 22:20; Mt 26:28). (2) "My God, my God, why hast thou forsaken me?" (Mt 27:46). (3) "Why do you seek the living among the dead? He is risen; he is not here" (Lk 24:5; Mk 16:6). (4) "Peace be to you. Receive the Holy Spirit: whose sins you forgive, they are forgiven them" (Jn 20:22–23). A word on each.

(1) "This is my body." Anguished by his love for the disciples ("Eagerly have I desired to eat this passover with you before I suffer" [Lk 22:15]), agonized by awareness that he must leave us, yearning to remain with us, he invents a solution that stuns our mind, staggers our imagination: he will leave us *and* he will remain with us; he will go *and* he will stay. He will take from us the Christ who walked the dusty ways of Galilee, whose face creased into a

smile, whose eyes blinked away tears—*that* no one will ever see again; in that sense he will go. But he will leave with us the reality of that presence: he *is* there, and his presence is *real*. The same Christ of Palestine will be with us at the beck and call of a priest.

(2) "My God, my God. . . ." The Last Supper was not a lovely interlude before the storm. "This is my body" Christ murmured on Thursday with an eye to Friday. Not just "This is my body," but "This is my body given for you." Thursday and Friday are one day; it is all one sacrifice. His body is given indeed—given to death. Death for us—for every man and woman from Adam to Antichrist. In his body indeed we are reconciled to God; but it is a blood-stained body, a body that twisted and turned and was racked on two beams of wood, while a whole little world cried to him in mockery: "If you are the Son of God, *come down!*" (Mt 27:40). We are reconciled not simply in the sacramental Christ; we are reconciled in the crucified Christ. Sacrifice is consummated not reclining around a table but hanging by nails on wood. *So* are we reconciled to God and to one another.

(3) But that is not quite true. Sacrifice is consummated not in death but in resurrection. Easter is joy unconfined because the resurrection of Christ ("This Jesus God raised up" [Acts 2:32]) is for us the visible proof that the Father was pleased, that God and humanity were no longer in a situation of hostility, that we were one once again with God, that the Eternal Priest had offered an *acceptable* sacrifice, accepted by the Father for "the sin of the world" (Jn 1:29) and for the sins of the world. In the triumphal cry snatched from the Psalms by the Church at Easter and touched to the tongue of Christ, "I have risen and am still with you."

(4) That same night the risen Christ, the risen Priest, appeared to his own priests with the visible marks of his passion—beyond passion indeed, but eternally "passioned." That night he revealed to them the power of his priestly passion, the way to reconciliation: "Whose sins you shall forgive, they are forgiven them." The reconciliation realized by *the* Priest in his blood is channeled to the world through human persons graced to share in his priesthood.

II

And what of *you*? This week should strengthen you and shake you. Without any merit on your part, simply because God has chosen you, you are His minister of reconciliation. But your ministry is neither magic nor naked nature. You will minister reconciliation only if your priestly existence re-presents the Holy Week of Christ—not only this week but every week.

(1) The sacrament of reconciliation par excellence is the Eucharist. Here, more perfectly than anywhere else, man's redemption is daily accomplished. Here must be the center of priesthood. Even if the individual priest be called to serve the Church in classroom or chancery, in a Bridgeport slum or on the campus of Catholic University, priesthood—in fact, the Church itself—revolves around Eucharist. Here the body of Christ fashions one Body of Christ, sacramental body builds Mystical Body, sinners (all of us) become one with God One and Three, one with one another. If priestly ministry, reconciliation, is not realized around the Eucharistic sacrifice and sacrament, it will not be realized anywhere else. A pertinent (perhaps impertinent) question: In *your* vision of priesthood, is Eucharist central? And how do you celebrate it? Perfunctorily? Routinely? Out of obligation? Or is your Eucharist a visible sign that Christ is really present—because every word, every gesture, your very face is instinct with meaning, with conviction that here is Christ, here is forgiveness?

(2) Is *your* Thursday oriented to Friday? Do you mean it when you say, in the person of Christ, "This is my body, *which is given for you*"? If your priestly existence is not sorrow-laden, if you do not anguish in reconciling, if you do not share in some way the crucifixion that forces from your people a ceaseless "My God, my God, why have you forsaken me?" then your Eucharist will be largely unreal—consoling to you, perhaps a needed reassurance that you are a priest, but only half Eucharist: sacrament but not sacrifice. You will reconcile automatically, *ex opere operato*, but not as a whole person, as the Christ who gave his *own* body for the sins and sorrows of the world.

(3) To be an effective agent of reconciliation, to be Christ in the midst of your sinful people, you must be "raised with Christ" (Col 3:1). In the concrete, this demands, first, that the risen Christ be central to your spiritual life. He *is* your life. "If any man loves me, my Father will love him, and we will come to him and make our home with him" (Jn 14:23). Are you afire with this risen Christ, not somewhere out there, but deep within you? It demands, second, that your words, your gestures, your face, your life mirror the risen Christ within you—that in the teeth of sin and war, of disease and death, you can joy in living, because in the midst of death you have discovered life. For you, as for St. Paul, "life is Christ" (Phil

1:21)—Christ now and Christ forever. You are alive, and your life is the risen Christ. How else can you link human persons with the *risen* Christ? The German philosopher Nietzsche had a profound complaint against Christians: we do not *look* redeemed! The least your people can expect of those who mediate redemption to them is that you look redeemed—look risen.

(4) One of the most touching, most effective words of reconciliation you speak as priests is "I absolve you." In effect: "By the power of God and in the name of Christ, I say to you: 'Your sins are forgiven you. Go in peace.' " These words are sacramental. I mean, they are not your ordinary sign, simply pointing to an absent reality: "50 miles to New York City." No, these words are an efficacious sign: they effect what they signify; they express a *present* reality. With your words, through your words, the sinner's sins *are* forgiven; he or she *is* reconciled to God and to the Christian community.

The danger is precisely there: the sign, the rite of reconciliation, is efficacious; as long as I say the words, the sinner is reconciled. And so you have our long, sad history of humdrum, routine confessions—humdrum and routine not only because penitent after penitent repeats the age-old litany of human weakness, but even more tragically because *we* get used to saying "I absolve you." As priests, we are dealing with persons; we are touching human hearts. We are not sacramental computers: feed into us any mass of sinful data and out comes a penance. Each penitent is a unique person in need not of some impersonal "thing" called reconciliation, in need rather of the reconciling Christ—in need of you. The new structure of penance looks to this, at least allows for it—a personal encounter. Penitent meets Christ—and the Christ he or she sees (God help us) is you and I.

My brothers in Christ the Priest: This is your week. A week of many colors, many shades. A week that symbolizes, foreshadows *your* life, your priestly existence, your role as reconciler. Think on it in fear and trembling; but think on it, too, with joy and delight.

14

WHAT YOUR LOVE MEANS TO US
For two young people saying yes for ever

Inasmuch as I have not been a parish priest, save for a single month decades ago, weddings are events at which I officiate only rarely (twice annually on an average) and for close friends. And yet experience taught me quite early that a nuptial homily has its own special problems. It dare not be long, especially within a Mass; it addresses a man and a woman at a uniquely intimate moment in their lives; it is delivered by a priest who ordinarily has not experienced the relationship that links this couple; and it should include a message to the congregation.

Out of many efforts, the homily I reproduce here has proven the most effective, and it is the one I like best. It moves out from an admission: no one, certainly no priest, can tell a couple entering marriage what their love means to them. What we dare express with a measure of confidence is what their love means to us. Here the possibilities are legion, and much depends on the concrete context. But I am quite happy with the three ideas that are no more than suggested in the homily to come; for they encapsulate personal reactions of mine that over the years have made the nuptial liturgy a flesh-tingling spiritual experience for me.

I have given this homily a number of times in substantially the same language, and so I have thought it prudent not to insert the names of any couple actually addressed. Let two traditionally popular Catholic names, John and Mary, serve as an appropriate disguise.

Mary and John: No one can tell you what this hour means to *you*; for no one can tell you what your love means to you. Only you know the depths of your love, its varying currents, yes its agonizing perils. For us to enter into this—what your love means to *you*— would be somewhat sacrilegious; for we would enter a sanctuary where none of us belongs—not even a Jesuit!

What we can tell you—ever so briefly—is what your love means to *us*—to us who know you more than a little and love you more than much.

First, there is a splendid *freshness* that comes through to us. As we grow older, it is increasingly easy to be bored and to bore, to be blasé and worldly-wise and sophisticated and all those adjectives that really mean we have lost the power to wonder, to be surprised and delighted and amazed. We no longer run our fingers through grass and water, no longer shout at the stars, no longer make faces at the moon. But the way you two look out *at the world* together in love makes us aware once more of what the poet Gerard Manley Hopkins called "the dearest freshness" that "lives deep down things."[1] Your love helps us to come alive again.

Second, there is a splendid *humanness* that comes through to us. What strikes us on all sides today is the horrifying inhumanity, the appalling hate, that stalks the earth—from Northern Ireland to Southeast Asia, from Rhodesia to the streets of America. What does not come through enough is that human beings are genuinely human only to the extent that they are freed for love. But the way you two look *at each other* in love is a striking symbol to us of what it means to be a person: to be "for another," to be "for others." Your love is humanity in miniature. You symbolize what *our* lives should be like, but often are not.

Third, there is a splendid *hope* that comes through to us. The generation that conceived and bore you is sometimes puzzled by you (as you are by it)—puzzled because you think so differently, talk so differently, sing the songs that you do, and dream the dreams that you do. Today's wedding will not change all that, will not quite bridge the gap. But the way you look *at us* in love should make us think more profoundly, make us see more vividly what richer hopes rest with the young and the new, with the creative and the dreamer, with the passionate and the committed, with the smashers of idols.

A Swiss theologian has written a book with a fascinating title: in translation, *Only Love Is Believable*.[2] The glorious thing today is, *your* love is believable. And because it is believable, it gives us fresh hope, and it promises deeper love on our part—for you and for every human person whose life we shall from this moment touch. Here indeed, in your love, here are man and woman; and because man and woman are here, here is God—not as a cold word, but as a warm reality—a God in whose likeness you have been fashioned.

Come then, Mary and John—come and, in this sacrament, give to each other the two who are most dear to you. Give to each other . . . yourselves, and give to each other . . . God.

15

TAKE, O LORD, MY LIBERTY
Final vows of a Jesuit

The final, solemn religious profession of a Jesuit is not a simple subject for preaching. To begin with, the three "vows of religion" raise problems, perhaps more so in our time than in several centuries. Besides, in pronouncing his "final" vows, a Jesuit is not moving from the temporary to the perpetual, from vows for a time to vows for ever: the vows he uttered many years ago, at the end of his noviceship, were confessedly permanent. Then, too, a homily is not a lecture: you cannot write a treatise on the vows analogous to St. Jerome's defense of monasticism and the veneration of saints against Vigilantius in 406.

This specific profession late in 1978 had a further complication: it was December 8. It would hardly do, in a liturgical celebration on that date, to simply pass over "Mary conceived without sin." Accustomed by now to barging in where a prudent angel might fear to tread, I decided to tackle the complication head on: what connection can we uncover between Mary immaculately conceived and a Jesuit vowing poverty, chastity, and obedience?

The event was uncommonly touching for me. It was a quarter century since Gerald P. Fogarty and I had first met, quite accidentally, one Sunday afternoon at Woodstock College in Maryland— he a Loyola High School student, I a fairly young theology professor at Woodstock. Now he was teaching in the Department of Religious Studies at the University of Virginia. The several hundred friends, associates, and students who crowded the Church of St. Thomas Aquinas in Charlottesville were a tangible testimony to professional competence and warm priestliness. But they also provided a challenge: how do you put meaning into this consecration on this *festival?*

This evening three issues should concern us, three problems should challenge us. There is, first, today's feast, the Immaculate Conception of our Lady. There is, second, today's happening, the final vows of a Jesuit priest we know and admire. There is, third, the connection between today's feast and today's happening.

I

First, today's feast. Today the Catholic world puzzles the non-Catholic with yet another Marian mystery. That mystery is enshrined in a solemn declaration by Pope Pius IX in 1854: "the

Blessed Virgin Mary, in the very first instant of her conception, by an extraordinary grace and privilege of almighty God, in view of the merits of Christ Jesus Savior of the human race, was preserved free from all stain of original sin. . . ."[1] Now this joyous day is not made for debating the doctrine; not ours to argue whether any creature has the competence to proclaim infallibly what God has revealed. Let me try rather to cast some light on today's feast by casting it in the context of some exciting Catholic theology.

Protestants have long been concerned that the privileges Catholics concede to Mary lift her above our common humanity, raise her to the level of the saving Christ, elevate her to divinity. Quite the contrary, we say. We have rediscovered an early Christian vision of Mary: she is type or figure of the Church. She does not exist in icy isolation. Quite the contrary. Mary's meaning for us lies in this, that in the mother of Christ God has realized first and perfectly what He has designed for every Christian. In her life and person she expresses to perfection what it means to believe, to love and be loved, to be graced, to be saved. What Mary is, that we are destined to be.[2]

The most vivid expression of this idea is the Incarnation. Mary's answer to an angel is symbol of each Christian's response to Christ, each human response to God. "Be it done unto me according to thy word" (Lk 1:38) is the perfection of faith. "Greatly troubled" (Lk 1:29), able to say no, not knowing all that God's call implied, a Jewish teen-ager spoke a total yes to whatever God wanted. With that yes she gave birth to God within her, would give Him to a waiting world.

And such is the task of the believing Church, the faithful Christian. We are to continue through space and time Mary's murmured yes, co-operate in redemption by loving faith, and so bring God to birth within ourselves, share Him with others.

Even the first moment of Mary's humanity—what Catholics call the Immaculate Conception—speaks not merely of Mary but of man. Her first human moment declares dramatically that love begins above; oneness with God starts with God; God takes the initiative in all salvation. Before she could say yes or no, God linked Himself to her in love, enveloped her with His amazing grace. It is a striking reminder that redemption stems from God's mercy and not our own deserving—not even Mary's. God gives the very beginning; God loves before we do.

Oh yes, God's initiative is incomplete; it looks forward—to a response. As with Mary, so with us, God's embracing grace, "the

Lord is with you" (Lk 1:28), will come full circle only when we murmur "Be it done." But "Be it done" is a response, and even that response, for all its freedom, is itself God's gracious giving.

II

Second, today's happening. To some, it is as much a mystery as the Immaculate Conception. This evening a man of flesh and blood confirms solemnly what he first vowed seventeen years ago. As he closes early adulthood, the summer of life—what recent research claims "may be the most dramatic" season of a man's existence[3]—at the height of his human powers, he makes an astounding decision. He reaffirms in mid-life maturity what he promised in the first flush of manhood: he vows poverty, chastity, and obedience in the Society of Jesus till the end of his earthly days.

In this vowing Father Fogarty takes a radical risk: he risks not becoming a man. By these three vows he is in danger of declining what a profound Jesuit theologian called "the encounter with three elemental forces ... encounter with the earth, with woman, and with [his] own spirit."[4] By the vow of poverty, he risks declining responsibility for his livelihood, risks "an inert, parasitic life—living off the collectivity," risks remaining irresponsible.[5] Vowed poverty can impoverish. By the vow of chastity, he risks refusing to enter the world of Eve, risks a premature senility (sex is dead), thinking himself whole when he is not. He risks remaining the proverbial bachelor, "crotchety, emotionally unstable, petulant, and self-enclosed."[6] By the vow of obedience, he risks declining "the most bruising encounter of all,"[7] the encounter with his own spirit and its power of choice. He risks being other-directed, with his choices made for him, refusing ultimate responsibility for them. He risks "an end both to aspiration and conflict"; he can spare himself "the lonely agony of the desert struggle."[8]

He knows this. He may not have known it seventeen years ago, when "the world [was his] oyster"[9]—and just about as small. This evening ignorance is no excuse; his glasses are no longer rose-tinted; the three vows are not the three Graces of Greek mythology, Brilliance, Joy, and Bloom. He knows that, like the prerogatives of Mary, the vows of a Jesuit do not set him above the common herd; they fling him brutally into the human situation. This he knows not as abstract principle but as soul-shivering experience. And still he chooses it. Coolly, serenely, dispassionately, he will say "Take, O Lord, take all my liberty."

III

But do these vows make sense? Some insight may dawn if we can connect today's happening with today's feast. I suggest two parallels.

In the first place, in both there is the mystery of God's initiative. It is God who calls. I do not mean that anything and everything anyone does in God's name is a response to God; the recent Guyana suicides destroy that thesis. I do mean that we must take care not to confine the whisperings of God's Spirit to what makes rational sense to us. Under that condition, Mary would have told the Angel Gabriel to "get lost," and the Lord Jesus would never have consented to be crucified. God is constantly calling us to go beyond ourselves; the gospel summons us to what is foolishness in the eyes of the world.[10]

I am simply suggesting that you leave room for the possibility that forms of self-giving which are not in obvious contradiction to the gospel may well be an inspired challenge to worldly values. I am implying that vowed poverty, chastity, and obedience, distasteful as they might be to human sensibilities, may be God's way of speaking to a culture that prizes "making it big" and "scoring" sexually and "doing your thing." God does take the initiative. His grace envelops us in ways beyond our foretelling. And His call, to a girl in Nazareth or to a Jesuit in Charlottesville, does not make final sense in a syllogism or a computer.

This leads into my second parallel. How *do* you know it is God who has taken the initiative? Very concretely: by results. Yesterday's yes, Mary's "Be it done," brought God to birth and earth, gave you and me a flesh-and-blood Savior, the compassionate Christ. Today's test you yourselves can grade. Does Father Fogarty's threefold surrender to the divine make him more human? Since you have known him, has the yes to God he first uttered seventeen years ago become a yes to the world and to life, to spirit and sexuality, to pulsing persons? Has it become a yes to *his* world, *his* life, *his* spirit, *his* sexuality, a yes to you?

Put another way, have the vows he solemnizes today freed him or enslaved him? Has the vow of poverty actually liberated him from a slavish attachment to things, to possessions, to what is "his" to clutch and to keep? Has the vow of chastity released him for warm human relations that draw you not only to him but to Christ, freed him from a confining absorption in any one person *and* from a "play the field" mentality? Has the vow of obedience delivered him from a damnable preoccupation with his own wants, his own good pleasure, his own satisfaction, rather than the will of God and the agonizing needs of God's people?

If, as I believe, the answer to those questions is a thumping, resounding yes, then it is a good thing Father Fogarty does this evening. Then we can say with the Psalmist:

> This is the *Lord's* doing;
>   it is marvelous in our eyes.
> This is the day which the *Lord* has made;
>   let us rejoice and be glad in it.
>   (Ps 118:23–24)

Yes, let us rejoice in a good man's inspired self-giving to God and to you. At the same time let us remember that the struggle his vows trigger will never end this side of eternity; for religious vowing, like all Christian commitment, is a ceaseless struggle to transcend, to go beyond yourself, beyond where you are now; you leap with fearful faith into God's unknown. His strength stems from this, that the God who took the initiative will always be there—a God whose faithfulness makes our fidelity possible, a God who remains faithful through all our infidelities, whose yes to us is never revoked by our no to Him.

It will strengthen him beyond measuring to know that you too will be there. With your friendship, of course; but even more with the fidelity to God and man to which each of you has been summoned. For his yes today, his yes to God and to you, will have its full effect only if you echo it in your own lives, only if you too can say, with Mary and with him, "Be it done unto *me* according to thy word."

ANNIVERSARIES AND ANNUAL EVENTS

16
THE RISK AND THE JOY
After a quarter century of teaching

[*Francis X. Winters, S.J., dean of Woodstock College in New York City, wrote the following paragraphs as a Foreword to a private printing of the following homily, delivered November 21, 1971.*]

Father Walter J. Burghardt, S.J., has often been called upon during the last twenty-five years to deliver an "occasional" sermon, a religious statement appropriate to a significant event, such as an inauguration, an anniversary, or the death of a prominent person. In his sermons on such occasions, Father Burghardt has repeatedly demonstrated his unique capacities as a theologian and an artist.

The sermon presented here is such an occasional sermon. The occasion was a very special one, the preacher's twenty-fifth anniversary as a faculty member of Woodstock College, now located in New York City. Those who were present in St. Paul's Chapel, Columbia University, understood that, for the preacher, these years have not simply turned in a repetitive cycle. Twenty-five years of teaching historical theology have a history and, indeed, a theology of their own. For those who were present, "the risk and the joy" were not merely the words of a title; they were an interpretation of that bit of religious history that we have been privileged to share and to shape.

The audience, too, was a very special one: the faculty he has loved and led, his students and former students, friends from many parts of the United States, and the Christian community which worships weekly with the Jesuits of Woodstock. Their reaction to the sermon was a moment of silence, followed by several minutes of warm applause. They were responding to more than the words printed here. They were applauding the Christian life which has found such graceful expression in his sermons over the years.

After twenty-five years, those who know me would be scandalized if my silver homily were not plated with three points. Several divisions have been suggested by "friends": the child, the Jesuit, the man; before Woodstock, at Woodstock, after Woodstock; even, before celibacy, during celibacy, after celibacy.

I shall indeed have three points. But the three points have to do with three facets of this quarter century that have shaped me. I mean priesthood, theology, and Woodstock. I am a priest; my "thing" has been theology; and my home has been Woodstock. Largely because of these I am the man I am.

These realities I select not simply because they spell "me";

more importantly because they involve you. For if any single word sums up my words to come, it is "change." And if any one reality rends the people of God today, it is your reaction to change.

I

First, then, I am a priest. I have always sensed that there is something stable about priesthood, aspects that abide, that are not likely to change. As Father Raymond Brown has brought out so beautifully, the New Testament furnishes four facets of Christian ministry which the Church sees as basic in her priests.[1] Not all were present from the beginning in one and the same person; but the Church has gradually brought them together to fashion her notion of what a priest is.

To be a priest is to be a *disciple*. To be a disciple means to be "called," as Peter and James and John were called, to follow one only master: Jesus. And the response to his "follow me" must be total, not part time, and not just for today. I am not a disciple of Jesus if Jesus is not my whole life. And this master whom I follow is a bloodstained master who came not to be served but to serve, who warned his disciples against honors and first places, who turned savagely on Peter when he rebelled against the passion of his Lord.

To be a priest is to be an *apostle*. To be an apostle is to be "sent," as the original apostles were sent, to serve others. The keynote is service—St. Paul's "I will most gladly spend and be spent for you" (2 Cor 12:15). And what the priest carries to others is always Jesus—not only his message but his presence. "We preach," St. Paul declared, "not ourselves but Jesus Christ as Lord, with ourselves as your servants for Jesus' sake" (2 Cor 4:5).

To be a priest is to be what the New Testament calls a *presbyter*, responsible for the pastoral care of the churches. With St. Paul, I must "hold firm to the sure word" I "was taught" (Titus 1:9), with an authority that does not dominate, that is softened by being wonderfully warm and human.

The point is, I represent an institution. No matter how charismatic, how prophetic, even if called to protest the sins and corruption of institutions, of the Church herself, I must represent more than my personal insights. Like it or not, I am a churchman. I cannot, as a priest, stand outside my institution; I am an official part of it, even when most critical of it. For this institution is the setting where faith is born and grows; this institution is the locus and focus of worship; this institution is the community of love. This is what I represent.

To be a priest is to *preside at the Eucharist*. For here I do what St. Paul insisted must be done: "proclaim the Lord's death until he comes" (1 Cor 11:26). Whatever else I do—in library or lecture hall, in city slum or county jail—at some point I must gather a people around an altar, about a table, to share with them a thanksgiving where the work of redemption is accomplished and in unparalleled fashion man is made one with man and God.

Called to follow Jesus and sent to serve others, man of the Church and minister of the Eucharist—this is the priest in his stability, almost his timelessness. But today the stable is shot through with the unstable, the predictable with the unpredictable. Today's priest must be far more open than yesterday's: open to new ideas (like Protestant churches being communities of salvation), open to fresh ways of doing things (like letting the laity into parish administration), open to a wider world (like the Jew next door and the unbeliever turned off by religion).

Today's priest must be uncommonly courageous; for he must face up to and live with his deep doubts, or his sense of inadequacy, or his loss of nerve, or his feeling that he is not free, or his low standing in society. John Courtney Murray used to say: "Courage! It's far more important than intelligence."

Today's priest responds more eagerly to the need for unusual or unexpected witness: in a California vineyard or a Connecticut jail, in a Harlem tenement or a Milwaukee ghetto.

Today's priest will experiment with priesthood: live in low-cost housing, work in a factory, rap all night in a coffeehouse, picket against privilege. He makes more decisions on his own, and suffers the anguish that afflicts every sensitive human who finds himself in conflict with legitimate authority, with parent or president, with pastor or pope. He does not always know whether he is preaching Jesus or himself. He is more liable to err, because he takes more chances, convinced that today the name of the game is risk, that to be a priest may well call for heroism.

Today's priest may even wear a tie, let his hair grow, and find that his people, like the Pharisees of old, are concerned to clean only the outside of the cup, refuse to look within, where good and evil really lie.

II

My second point: my "thing" has been theology. After twenty-five years, I am convinced that in reaching for the real, few subjects rival theology. What I started as an academic discipline has changed for me to a searing search. For theology is unreal unless it is a search for God and man, through systematic reflection on experience.

In theology, I have been searching for God. Not for a God who dwells only in light inaccessible, outside time and space. Rather for a God who has a history—a history shaped by every star and every stone, by each blade of grass, each buck and doe, each human heart. For a God who graces His universe, not only the product of His power, but the breath of His love. For a God whose pulsing image is every man. For a God who *became* man.

And in theology, God-talk though it is, I have been searching for man. For, in St. Irenaeus' felicitous phrase, "God's glory is man alive!" Searching, therefore, for what it means to be man, what it means to live—and what it means to die.

And where have I sought Him? In the stuff of theology's search, in experience. *My* experience indeed, for it is I who am searching. But not in some narrow sense. My experience must include the community experience that spans ages and continents. And so I have felt the Hebrew experience of Sinai and the desert; the New Testament experience of God's break-through in the flesh of His Son; the conciliar experience from Nicaea I to Vatican II; the experience of theologians like Augustine and Aquinas, mystics like Tauler and Teresa.

I have shared the experience of non-Roman communities, their pens and their pews and their pulpits; and there I have found Christ, have heard the whispering of his Spirit. My theology been leavened by the arts—from Peanuts' reflections on another Woodstock, through Samuel Beckett's mind-blowing "Two times anything equals zero," to *Godspell's* glorious "God is dead; long live God!" I have come to agonize over the experience of living man, as he cries to me that he cannot discover God in my abstractions, as he stands mute before an immutable Lord who does not weep when man bleeds, as he insists that, if he is to find God at all, he must somehow find him in man.

In all this is the stuff of theology, the experience that calls for agonizing reflection.

To do theology in this way is often to be lonely; for despite the dialogue and the collaboration, the honorary degree and the kudos in *Time*, your most searing search is centered in solitude.

To do theology in this way is often to wonder whether it's all worth doing; for you are exegeting John while the world is burning, arguing abstract love while real men are locked in hate, recapturing Chalcedon while Christ is crucified again in his little black images.

To do theology in this way is often to feel frustration; for to hard questions there are no easy answers; pop theology is an illusion; and at times you joy that you know not the solution but the problem.

And still, as long as the search is real, you feel not only the agony but some of the ecstasy. The ecstasy that is a "going out" of your lone self, into the fire and cloud that is God, into the clay and spirit that is man. It is splendidly summarized in a thrilling paragraph from Aquinas:

> There are two ways of desiring knowledge. One way of desiring knowledge is to desire it as a perfection of one's self; and that is the way philosophers desire it. The other way of desiring knowledge is to desire it not [simply] as a perfection of one's self, but because through this knowledge the one we love becomes present to us; and that is the way saints desire it.

Yes, through theology the God I love and the human persons I love have become present to me: man in God, and God in man.

III

My third point: Woodstock. There this priest played the theologian. No matter what the travels and where—Oxford or Rome, Geneva or Jerusalem—Woodstock in Maryland has been more home to me than any other place in my life. Seven years of study, twenty-four of teaching. All the openness of 650 acres, all the privacy of a goldfish bowl. And profoundly home.

What I had to learn is that Woodstock is not primarily a place. It takes much learning. For there is something that grabs you in blades of grass that sing in the breeze, and earth that gives beneath your feet day upon day; in a small room that smells of your sweat and imprisons your deepest thoughts; in a chapel underground, carved by a friend for you and your Sacrifice out of that eternal granite; in library shelves that you have learned to read eyes closed; in a recreation room that echoes the cultured tones of a Murray and the wit of a Weigel; in a cemetery that looks back on a century of love and forward to endless life; even a homemade golf green with your one consistent par.

But Woodstock, like purgatory, can never be a place. I learned that the hard way—by being torn from it. For to make Woodstock a place is to make it a *then*. And Woodstock, for all its peerless past, is a *now* or it is nothing. Somewhat as tradition, in its most thrilling theological sense, is all the Church's yesterdays gathered into a mighty now for a future in hope, so Woodstock is yesterday's century-in-Maryland (all its life and love, all its agony and ecstasy, every footfall and heartbeat, every insight and prayer) gathered into New York's today to fashion a fresh tomorrow—somewhere. This alone is Christian living, for institution as well as individual. We live *on* the past, yes; we dare not live *in* it.

What I am saying, I suppose, in all three points, is this: to live really is to risk everything, to smash through the boundaries that imprison us, to die stretching and reaching. It is Nikos Kazantzakis in his old age standing before the abyss tranquilly, fearlessly: "There are three kinds of souls, three kinds of prayers. One: I am a bow in your hands, Lord. Draw me lest I rot. Two: Do not overdraw me, Lord. I shall break. Three: Overdraw me, and who cares if I break! Choose!"[2]

Only in this way, I now believe, can a human being become real—by risking all for God and for man. And it is indeed a process of *becoming*—ceaseless, endless becoming. Do you remember that delightful little book by Margery Williams, *The Velveteen Rabbit or How Toys Become Real*? The toy rabbit and the toy horse are engaged in dialogue that is deceptively simple:

> "What is REAL?" asked the Rabbit one day.... "Does it mean having things that buzz inside you and a stick-out handle?"
> "Real isn't how you are made," said the Skin Horse. "It's a thing that happens to you. When a child loves you for a long, long time, not just to play with, but REALLY loves you, then you become Real."
> "Does it hurt?" asked the Rabbit.
> "Sometimes," said the Skin Horse, for he was always truthful. "When you are Real you don't mind being hurt."
> "Does it happen all at once, like being wound up," he asked, "or bit by bit?"
> "It doesn't happen all at once," said the Skin Horse. "You become. It takes a long time. That's why it doesn't often happen to people who break easily, or have sharp edges, or who have to be carefully kept. Generally, by the time you are Real, most of your hair has been loved off, and your eyes drop out and you get loose in the joints and very shabby. But these things don't matter at all, because once you are Real you can't be ugly, except to people who don't understand."[3]

Two glorious ideas: (1) You *become* real. (2) Once real, you can't be ugly, except to people who don't understand. Here is my risk and my joy. Risk because I dare not be static, am rarely at rest even in research, am always in movement to another moment, another dimension of the real. Joy because in the eyes of you who understand me I can't be ugly.

For both these facets, the risk and the joy, I am singularly grateful to all of you who have crossed my path. For you have helped me become real: hostile or loving or indifferent, you have kept me alive, aware that to live is to evolve, at times to retract my yesterday, always open to tomorrow. That is why my feeling for you, and my prayer for you, is best expressed in St. Paul's letter to the Christians at Philippi (Phil 1:3–11):

> I give thanks to my God each time I remember you. Always, in every prayer of mine for all of you, I make my prayer with joy, so full a part have you taken in the work of the gospel from the day it first reached you till now.
>
> Of this I am certain, that He who began the good work in you will bring it to completion, ready for the day when Christ Jesus comes.
>
> It is only fitting that I should feel this way about all of you: you are close to my heart, and I know that you share the same grace I do in defending and asserting the gospel.
>
> God is my witness, how I yearn for you all with the tenderness of Christ Jesus.
>
> And this is my prayer for you: May your love abound more and more, in the fulness of its knowledge and the depth of its perception, so that you may learn to prize what is of real value. May nothing cloud your conscience or hinder your progress till the day Christ comes. May you reap through Jesus Christ the full harvest of your justification to God's glory and praise.

17
THE MAN WHO LIVES WITH WISDOM
To a half century of uncommon priesting

*On February 27, 1976, the Catholic University of America
celebrated liturgically the fiftieth anniversary of the ordination of
one of its most distinguished professors. Expert in patristics, Christian archeology, and the history of early liturgy, Johannes Quasten
had come to C.U. in the fall of '38, largely because his teaching
faculties at Münster had been withdrawn two years before by the
Nazi government. More effectively perhaps than any other expert in
early Christianity since World War II, Quasten communicated to
the American Catholic community (and others) an awareness of
cultural contexts, a realization that Christianity is inescapably in-
volved in the ebb and flow of time, that the ancient Church cannot
be understood without a thorough knowledge of classical culture.
Music and monuments, men and movements, texts and transla-
tions—with these Quasten has left us an imperishable heritage.*

*I was fashioned by Quasten the teacher; I have collaborated
with Quasten the scholar; but, most touchingly, he has been for half
my life my friend. I have felt the heart that hides beneath the shy
academic exterior; I have touched the loneliness that shadows so
much of a scholar's existence; I have sipped the cognac that puts a
fitting finale to "an evening with Quasten."*

*My homily (moving out from Wis 6:12–17, Eph 1:2–12,
and Lk 2:41–52) was an effort to capture—for the hundreds who
packed the crypt of the Shrine of the Immaculate Conception—a
multifaceted man who weds so entrancingly the past and the present, the old world and the new, the scholar and the priest.*

A persistent note in today's liturgical readings is . . . wisdom. That
insistent theme lured this playboy in patristics to invade the sanctuary of Scripture. I wanted to discover who the wise man is, and
what he does that is so wise, and how he comes to be wise. The
spoils of that invasion have proved delightfully rich for today's festivity. As sentence follows sentence in this scriptural summary, I
would ask you to keep in mind our principal concelebrant.

I

First then, who is the wise man? In the Old Testament, wisdom is an art: it is the art of living well. The wise man is the expert
in the art of good living. Passion does not sear him; he is self-pos-
sessed. Wrath does not wrack him; he is patient. A fiery spirit is not

his; he is cool. He is a knowledgeable man, has mastered a field, may even have academic knowledge; but, more importantly, he is at home with his knowledge, it rests lightly yet securely upon him. In him, technical competence is compatible with an artistic sense. He is a reflective man, reflects on existence, existence human and nonhuman—but not like a metaphysician. Rather, he has a sixth sense of where he sits in human existence, never ceases to scrutinize his destiny. Insightful in matters religious, he is pious in its profound sense. Aware that God rules the world, he has a salutary fear of the Lord.

Second, what does the wise man do that is so wise? He does indeed do something; for the wise man of the Old Testament is not just an observer of the human scene, ensconced on a *sedes sapientiae,* a "seat of wisdom." Old Testament wisdom is practical wisdom; it is a technique whereby the wise man can make his way through the perils of life to the goal he has in view. He maps out rules for human living; he distinguishes the good from the evil. He is intimately interested in others—interested not only in "the people" but primarily in persons. He knows the human heart, its joys and its sorrows. He senses man's grandeur and his wretchedness, his solitude, his anguish in the face of suffering and death, his sense of life's nothingness, his uneasiness before God. With all and each he wants to share his wisdom. Marvel of marvels, the wise man knows how to enjoy life. He knows the defects of the world that surrounds him, the sinfulness and selfishness of man, the hostility of created nature; he does not approve them, but neither do they shatter him. Through all of this he walks with sympathy and serenity; he enjoys being alive.

Third, where does the wise man of Scripture get his wisdom? From three sources. (1) There is the tradition of the Fathers—the accumulated wisdom of the past. (2) There is his own personal experience: from openness to all that is real, he has grown in wisdom, never ceases to grow. (3) It is, at bottom, a gift of God. Ultimately, the master of wisdom is Jesus: he is the Wisdom of God, in whom the sapiential texts find their definitive meaning; he it is who, as Wisdom incarnate, communicates wisdom not to the wise of the world but to his little ones.[1]

II

My brothers and sisters in Christ: We have been privileged to know Scripture's man of wisdom. Three and thirty years ago I came callow to Catholic U., to learn from a master how to . . . learn. It was a thrilling experience. Sworn enemy of the fast degree, he was a demanding teacher. Under him you learned, like him, to be intolerant only of superficiality and to eschew the glittering generality. Not dynamic in the usual sense, quite undramatic, his pedagogical charism was his ability to fire the few with a fresh vision of the past. At high moments you shared his vision. You began to believe and to live his quotation from Harnack: "You will achieve as much as you are willing to sacrifice for." Under such a master I lived to learn.

A whole generation has passed. During those years the master and the apprentice have grown into friends, and an even more thrilling experience has been mine. Under the master I lived to learn; with the friend I have learned to live. For to me he is in the flesh the wise man of God's word: he knows how to live. And that capacity stems, I take it, from Scripture's three sources of wisdom.

First, the tradition of the Fathers. From the experience of early Christianity overleaping the bounds of Palestine, this man from Münster first learned what he would have to live—learned what it means to leave home and hearth, to come to terms, as the early Church did, with an alien culture, to become part of it without ceasing to be himself, to profit from its wisdom and baptize it with his own. Those who watch his planes take off and return know that he bestrides two worlds, the old and the new. And many who sit under him in class or with him at table sense that this movement symbolizes his Christian existence and the existence of Christianity: the tension between continuity and change. Like the Church he loves, he can live comfortably in the present because his roots are ruggedly in the past. Like his Church, he is cosmopolitan and . . . catholic.

Second, personal experience. Like the wise man of Scripture, this wise man of Washington has learned how to live by . . . living. He is splendidly open, not only to a new manuscript but to new ideas, fresh faces, different ways of doing things. The shortwave broadcast from Germany and the Washington *Post*, a foible from C.U.'s past or some ecclesial mischief in Rome, an exhibit in a museum or an exhibition in the Tidal Basin[2]—all these and a thousand more are grist to his daily mill. But, above all, he learns living by loving: he enjoys people. Whether baptizing the child of a former colleague in Germany or cheering local hearts with wine in his book-lined study, he simply loves people. And, I am happy to say, for him people are not unisex. He lives the second and better half of St. Jerome's pithy advice to a priest in 394: "Omnes puellas . . . aut aequaliter ignora aut aequaliter dilige": as for women, "either skip them all or love them all."[3]

I envy him above all because he has come to terms with reality, with human living. The daily small happenings that ulcerate the rest of us, these he takes in stride. In some form or other, he has seen them all. Not that he is jaded or does not care; he simply does not lose his biblical cool. He may well be Brookland's last unflappable man. To see him stride the campus tall and confident is to grow in hope: God must be in His heaven, and the world cannot be all that bad.

I am persuaded that this "cool" quality stems from the third source of biblical wisdom: it is God's gracious giving. Here is no Stoic walled off from passion by an iron will, no secular humanist bemused by beauty. His wisdom he would edit in capital letters: it is the Christ who lives in him and walks with him, the Christ who talks between the lines of his *Patrology*, the Christ he will shortly summon to this altar with priestly lips. Here, ultimately, is the Wisdom who makes him the wise man he is, the Wisdom to whom he has consecrated whatever wisdom is his.

I have said so little about his priesthood—and so much. For this man of wisdom, priesthood is not a life within his life, a half hour of Sacrifice each day. He is not a schizoid, torn between the sacred and the secular, the altar and his desk. No moment of these fifty years has not been priesthood. For the priestly task committed to him by the Church has been simply and profoundly this: through the wisdom that is his from the tradition of the Fathers, from his own experience, and from the grace of God, to shape men and women of wisdom, in the image of Wisdom incarnate. And for this God loves him; for, in the words of Solomon's Wisdom, "God loves nothing so much as the man who lives with wisdom" (Wis 7:28).

Father Quasten, you have given us at Catholic University exactly half of your years; but you have given us the whole of your heart. We are the wiser for your wisdom: more human, more Christian, more priestly. From the depths of our hearts . . . thank you!

18

FOR THEM I CONSECRATE MYSELF
Silver jubilee in a changing priesthood

On November 19, 1978, the Jesuits of Georgetown University and hundreds of friends celebrated, liturgically and socially, the twenty-fifth anniversary of the ordinations of four members of the University community: John E. Bennett, main campus chaplain; Timothy S. Healy, president; Richard A. McCormick, professor of Christian ethics at the Kennedy Institute for Ethics; and Leo P. Monahan, counselor at the University's medical and dental schools.

Anniversary homilies threaten to be either maudlin recollections or premature canonizations. How cling reasonably close to reality, to the priestly existence of these four men over a quarter century, and have it speak to us meaningfully today? I concluded that a potentially fruitful approach would be to engage the undeniable fact of change: look back on the year of their ordination (1953), contrast with it this year of celebration (1978), and see what reflections such a comparison might inspire.

It was a delicate task. A homily is not the place for swift historical judgments. And in this instance I could all too easily open old wounds, aggravate deep-seated sensitivities. But my fears proved unfounded—perhaps because I stressed not the specific changes (though these were not passed over) but the underlying principle that seems beyond challenge: new needs, fresh responses. If the priest of '78 is not the priest of '53, it is because the world of '78 is not the world of '53.

Those of you with a passion for liturgical detail may have noticed that the Word of the Lord and the Gospel of the Lord just proclaimed to you are not the Word and the Gospel for the Thirty-third Sunday of the Year. The Sunday readings seemed less than appropriate for today's celebration. The reading from Proverbs asked: "A perfect wife—who can find her?" (Prv 31:10). Paul told the Thessalonians: "We should not go on sleeping, as everyone else does" (1 Thess 5:6). And Matthew described the servant who took "the one talent" his master had given him and in fear buried it (Mt 25:18, 25).

Not in those directions does our celebration run: wife, sleep, fear. Our thoughts focus on the words of the Lord to Jeremiah: "to all to whom I send you you shall go. . . . Be not afraid. . . . I have put my words in your mouth" (Jer 1:7–9). We are looking upon men who have been "called by God, just as Aaron was, to offer gifts and sacrifices for sins" (Heb 5:4,1). Our concentration is on Christ, who in his priestly prayer tells the Father that he has "consecrated" himself for his disciples, has offered himself as a sacrificial victim, that they too may offer themselves for those whom God has given them (Jn 17:19).[1]

But to celebrate one hundred years of priestly existence, the task of a homilist is neither to bury these men nor to praise them. I want to do something still more difficult. I shall, first, go back twenty-five years to their ordination, to see where a priest was then. I shall, second, return to today, to see where a priest is now. I shall, third, reflect on that movement from then to now, to see what it says to us about a priest . . . what it says about four priests.

I

When these four priests offered their first Mass, the ritual was highly stylized, quite solemn; their backs were to the people, for the Eucharistic emphasis was exclusively on the high priest Christ. When they preached in '53, the sermon was a stepchild; the stress was so much on the sacrifice that you could miss the Word and not miss Mass. Ceaselessly the four raised tired arms in absolution, for a sense of sin was pervasive. Believers besought them for solutions; and the solutions were given—clearly, objectively, with authority. Priesthood, like medicine and law, had status: some Catholics still tipped their hats as priests walked by, and thousands of young men felt called to priestly service. The prayer of priests was regular, regulated: breviary and meditation, thanksgiving after Mass and examination of conscience.

In '53 the clergy were clean-shaven; hair dared not defile our ears. We wore the cassock—to the altar, to table, almost to bed; only on the golf course did we don the world's trousers. Rome expected us to be "out of this world," separated not only from evil but from much that is good; and in large measure we were. Friendships with women were discouraged; woman was indeed a soul to be saved, but a dangerous species. Jesuits rose from sleep at 5:30 (our enemies said, 5:30 twice a day), and we were supposed to be home at a civilized hour.

In '53 the priesthood may not have been paradise, but it was studded with stability and security; it was fenced about with fidelity. You could commit yourself with confidence to a celibate existence for life, be respected for it, and expect to die in the warm arms of the Society of Jesus. We knew who we were, and it was good.

II

Twenty-five years have passed, and the passage has been soul-searing. A new world has been born, a new America, and in it a new man and a new woman. We have all been changed: by Vatican II and Vietnam, by the bloody emergence of a Third World, by the abortive rebellion in Hungary and the Soviet invasion of Czechoslovakia, by black power and woman's revolt, by the assassination of the Kennedys and Martin Luther King, by the campus riots of the sixties and the waves of Watergate, by the anxieties of aging and the cry for freedom that rings round the world.

Change has cut the Church to its marrow. We are torn within—from the kiss of peace through contraception to one true Church. Seminaries and convents have closed their doors; those that remain open seem to some all too open. In ten years ('67 to '76) ten thousand American priests left the priesthood; not nearly as many replace them.

One result of change? A new look to priesthood, new demands, fresh expectations, unfamiliar confusions. Mass now brings me face to face with you; I may not lay the whole burden on Christ; the buck stops here; I must come through to you as a person. The homily is "in": when I speak, you want my mind to be filled with God's word, my heart raptured by the Spirit, my tongue touched with fire. Less often do you come to me for God's forgiveness. Counseling is a two-way street, where you and I meet on the same level, where I too am frightfully vulnerable, I too am "beset with weakness" (Heb 5:2). Priesthood means little; what matters is this priest. I cannot appeal to a profession, to my collar; I can only offer my priestly witness. And ever so many priests are not sure what priestly witness is.

You want us to be one with God *and* one with you. You expect us to be awfully close to you, warmly human, and still chaste and celibate. You challenge our pretensions to poverty. Our obedience leaves you cold when it does not free us for service—to the poor and oppressed, to the aging and the lonely. You demand that we feed your faith *and* search for justice.

Now we even share your insecurities: how to find and keep a

job at Georgetown, how to retire without bitterness, how to survive in old age, how to die believing, hoping, loving.

III

What does this movement from then to now say to us about a priest? About these four priests? One point I shall *not* make: which is better, '53 or '78? A homily is not a debate. But this I do say: against all the odds, these twenty-five years give us reason to rejoice, to celebrate. Not for the obvious reason: a hundred years of priesthood. That is a sheer statistic. More importantly, today reminds us that priesthood is not a frozen entity, a changeless state; it never was. The Church's ministry, from first-century Jerusalem to twentieth-century Washington, is a story of change: different models, varying emphases, new ways of serving.

We have experienced the jurisdictional model, where the priest holds the plenitude of authority in a perfect society, where to teach is to impose authoritative doctrine as a matter of obedience. The cultic model, where the priest is primarily the performer of sacred mysteries. The monastic model, where the priest is the holy man, the guru, withdrawn from the world and its vanities. The prophetic model, where the minister is predominantly proclaimer of God's word, calls to conversion.[2] The pastoral model, where the priest is community leader, brings his people together, activates their charisms for the benefit of all.

Oh yes, core functions are constant: to preach the word, to build the community, to serve mankind, to preside at worship. But the way this is done, where the stress falls, this changes; it can never be frozen. Why? Because the Church's ministry is in function of the Church's mission. And the Church's mission is not to an abstract humanity, but to a concrete world, to these pulsing people, to these loves and these hates, these sins and these needs, this frustration and this emptiness. If the priest of '78 is not the priest of '53, it is because the world of '78 is not the world of '53. Exhibit A: Georgetown.

We celebrate these four priests today because they were ordained in '53 and they are living in '78. Not just living . . . alive! President of a university and moral theologian, counselor and chaplain, each has moved into a new age with enthusiasm and joy, because here is their ministry as the Church sees it *now*; here is where they must respond, in new ways, to the needs of a whole little world with more colors and smells, more problems and pressures, more anxiety and despair than the Lord Jesus himself experienced. It is good that they have been "called by God, as Aaron was." It is good that they have gone, as Jeremiah went, where God sent them. But best of all, they have "consecrated" themselves: like Jesus, each has offered his life and his love, even unto crucifixion, for those whom God has given him. They live for you . . . in '78. For this, above all, we celebrate them; better still, for this we celebrate . . . God.

19
LOOK, LOVE, LAUGH
Homily for a college graduation

On a number of occasions I have been asked to deliver bacca-laureate homilies or commencement addresses: for example, at Catholic University and Georgetown in the District of Columbia, Loyola in Baltimore, St. Joseph's in Philadelphia, Wheeling College in West Virginia, Spring Hill in Mobile, St. Bonaventure and Canisius in Western New York. At no small risk, I have even given graduation talks at high schools: Fordham Prep, D.C.'s Gonzaga, St. Peter's Prep in Jersey City.

In many of these situations I have developed, with somewhat varying emphases and modifications dictated by world events and intramural realities, the same basic theme. Background for the theme is my conviction that most graduates are in process of decid-ing what it means to be alive, to live, to be human, to be a man or woman. In this context I have found it most effective to share with a graduating class what, after more decades than I care to count, I feel it means to be human, alive—especially, to be alive in the Spir-it. My basic theme has three facets: to be alive is to look, to love, to laugh.

Here I present this address in the form it took most recently: a baccalaureate homily at Saint Mary's College, Notre Dame, Indi-ana, on May 19, 1978. The outdoor liturgy was inspiriting: 422 women graduates (largest of that impressive institution's 131 com-mencements) and thousands of relatives and friends; Bishop Wil-liam E. McManus presiding with customary grace and wit; a fine sense of the sacred whispering in the spring breezes.

The minutes to come could be painful minutes. You don't know me, and I don't know you. You know nothing about me. Except that I obviously stem from an earlier, more wrinkled stage of hu-manity's evolution. And I know nothing about you. Except that you must be wondering what I will say that could possibly be of interest to you—and how long it will take.

More than that: you and I are very different people. You do not look at the world the way I do, do not use words the way I do, do not quite think the way I do, do not dream my dreams or sing my songs. Even your experience of God may be different from mine. And so I feel very much in tune with Rod McKuen when he sings:

> I make words for people I've not met,
> those who will not turn to follow after me.
> It is for me a kind of loving.
> A kind of loving, for me.[1]

The words to come are "a kind of loving." For I want to share with you not abstract aphorisms ("the pen is mightier than the sword"), not eloquent exhortations ("do unto others as you would have them do unto you"), not sentimental slush ("love is never having to say you're sorry"). I want to share ... myself. At this critical moment, when you are in process of deciding what it means for you to be alive, to live, to be human, to be a woman, I want to tell you what, after a half century and more, *I* feel it means to be human, to be alive—especially, to be alive in the Spirit. What *I* feel. Not *a* priest, but this priest. Not *a* theologian, but this theologian. Not talking to just anybody, but talking to you. And I shall develop three ideas sketchily. I shall say that to be alive has three facets: to be alive is to look, to love, to laugh.

I

First, to be alive is to *look*. You see, I am not genuinely alive simply because there is life in me. Simply because I watch a time clock from nine to five, or a Late Show from eleven to one. Simply because my standard of living is high, my cholesterol low. Simply because I offer the Sacrifice of the Mass each day, or am perpetually poor, chaste, and obedient. Simply because I sit at a desk or dig a ditch, wash diapers or trump aces. Simply because I eat and drink, weep and laugh, rock and roll. Simply because I am going through the motions of living—all the routines that enable a man or woman to get through life without living it.

The point is, I am not genuinely alive simply because I am not medically dead. I am alive to the extent that I am looking. With my mind, to begin with. For with this mind I look into a microscope and am filled with the wonder of life the naked eye cannot see. With this mind I speed over oceans more swiftly than the jet and touch human persons from Siberia to Somalia, from Egypt to East Germany. With this mind I flee back into the past and rediscover a universe perhaps five billion years old, rediscover an America five centuries young. With this mind I pluck meaning from the strings of a harp and the whisper of the wind, from a sonnet or a sonata, from Michelangelo's *Pietà* and the Mona Lisa, from Beethoven's *Pastoral Symphony* and Tchaikovsky's *Swan Lake Ballet* and Verdi's *Aïda*—yes, from Linda Ronstadt and the Aztec Two Step. With this mind I look into the minds of philosophers from ancient Greece to modern Britain, from Plato's world of ideas to Whitehead's experience and process, to share their tortured search for what is real, for what is true. With this mind I look into the mind of God as He reveals Himself in creation, on a cross, and in the lines of His own book.

Indeed I look with my mind. And only if I look, only if my mind is open, do I come face to face with what makes life come alive, makes life not endurable but entrancing and enrapturing, bewildering and challenging, mind-blowing and soul-searing. I mean the experience of mystery. I mean the realization that reality, the real, is incredibly complex and perplexing, profound and open-ended. Whether it's the inner you or outer space, whether it's a blade of grass or the ocean floor, whether it's God in His heaven or the person next to you, the real is a fascinating, frustrating wedding of what I can grasp and what is still beyond my grasp.

That is what a remarkable rabbi, Abraham Joshua Heschel, saw so clearly and lived so completely. Interviewed on NBC shortly before his death, he was asked: What is the essence of being? What does it mean to live a human life? He replied:

> Actually, the greatness of man is that he faces problems. I would judge a person by how many deep problems he's concerned with. A person who has no problems is an idiot. Because a man has problems. And the more complicated . . . he is, the deeper are his problems. I'm not against pleasure, but the greatness of life is the experience of facing a challenge.
>
> In a very deep sense, religion is two things. It's an answer to the ultimate problems of human existence, and it is a challenge to all answers. This is a deep ingredient of existence—problems. And the tragedy of our education today is that we are giving easy solutions: be complacent, have peace of mind, everything is fine. No! Wrestling is the issue. Facing the challenge is the issue.

To be alive is to look. But not merely with my mind—I am not naked intellect. If I am really to respond to the real, my whole being must be alive, vibrating to every throb of the real. Not only mind but eyes; not only eyes but smell and taste, hearing and touching. For reality is not reducible to some far-off, abstract, intangible God-in-the-sky. Reality is pulsing people; reality is fire and water; reality is a rainbow after a summer storm, a gentle doe streaking through a forest; reality is a foaming mug of Michelob, Beethoven's Mass in D, a child lapping a chocolate ice-cream cone; reality is a striding woman with wind-blown hair; reality is Christ Jesus.

And your looking will be most real when you no longer analyze what you experience or argue it, no longer describe what you see or define it, but are *one* with it; when you no longer move around the real but enter into it; when you simply "see" and what you see you love.

II

Which brings me to my second point. To be alive, to be human, it is not enough to *know* the real; I must *love* it: God's people, God's things, God Himself. Thomas Aquinas summed it up splendidly:

> There are two ways of desiring knowledge. One way is to desire it as a perfection of myself; and that is the way philosophers desire it. The other way of desiring knowledge is to desire it not [merely] as a perfection of myself, but because through this knowledge the one I love becomes present to me; and that is the way saints desire it.

The point is, I am most human when I go out of my small self, when I share not what I have but who I am, when I am "for others." My life is genuinely divine, therefore utterly human, to the extent that it reflects the very Being of God, where to be Father is to be turned totally to His Son, and to be Son is to be turned totally to His Father. To be human as a Christian should be human, my existence should be Godward and manward: turned totally to God, totally to God's images on earth. This is what it means to be a person, to be a Christian; this is what it means to love.

But precisely here I am profoundly discouraged. Why? Because the gut issues of '78 are so hate-full and we are so loveless.

At this moment, four billion persons walk or lie on this earth. At least one billion go to bed hungry each night, at least one out of every four. Each day ten thousand of the hungry die; but for each one who dies, another takes his place—and soon two may take his place. At this moment, 200,000 of the hungry "live" in the streets of Calcutta, build little fires to cook scraps of food, defecate against the curbstones, curl up against a wall to sleep—perhaps to die. Tonight ten million Americans will fall asleep hungry; twenty-five million more are undernourished; sixty million are poor: two out of every seven.

At this moment, human rights are being violated, human persons raped by injustice: the nonwhite eighty-two percent in South Africa, the political prisoners in the Philippines, twelve million Russians in any given year imprisoned or tortured or killed in the Gulag Archipelago, the world's women still largely second-class humans.

At this moment, human blood is reddening the earth, from South Africa to the north of Ireland to the streets of your home city.

If those facts and figures sound abstract to you, here is how many years you could expect to live if you grew up in certain other countries: Cambodia, 44; Kenya, 43; Burma, 42; Sudan, 40; Ghana, 39; Madagascar, 38; Libya, 37; Cameroon, 36; South Vietnam, 35; Togo, 34; Chad, 32; Nepal, 25 to 40. And beneath these naked figures smolder volcanos of envy and resentment, of fury and frustration and hate.

War and race, poverty and politics—these issues are hate-full in large measure because we are loveless. Oh, not everyone. But so many of us, the community called Christian, we do not come across as a community of love. Who looks at the barbed wire in Derry or the hot sands of Sinai, the stinking streets of Calcutta or the decaying schoolhouses in Appalachia, and thinks of Christians as a community "for others"? Who sees us as turned totally to God, totally to man?

Today's world tells me forcefully that no definition of love, no protestations of love, will touch the gut issues of '78. Only persons in love can do that. And you are not in love if your horizons are narrow, if your arms do not reach out beyond your own country, your own color, your own creed, your own college, your own private cell. You are not in love if you are unwilling to risk, if you clutch defensively all you have gained, if you build a fence around your home and your possessions, your dear ones and your love. You are not in love if you imprison the Spirit of love.

For you graduates, the gut issue of '78 is not Belfast or Beirut, not Appalachia or Calcutta. The gut issue is . . . you. Can you honestly define yourself, can you answer the question "Who are you?"

with "I am 'for others' "? If you can, who are these "others"? Only those who look like you, who love you? Or are you turned toward *every* other—not only the white *or* the black, but the white *and* the black *and* the red *and* the brown *and* the yellow? Not only the clean and the love-laden and the respectable, but the dirty and the hate-choked and the repulsive? The gut issue is: whose hand can you touch in love? Answer that question and you will know how profoundly the Holy Spirit has laid hold of you. Whose hand can you touch in love?

III

My third point may sound strange to you: to be alive, to be human, is to *laugh*. And yet it follows inescapably from points 1 and 2. For if you look and love, if you respond to the real with every fiber of your being and are turned totally to others, you will laugh. For laughter is not hysteria; laughter is not primarily a belly explosion over a vulgar joke; laughter is . . . *joy in living*. And therefore laughter is splendidly human, utterly Christian. And conversely, sadly, half the human race is less than human because it cannot joy in its living, and it cannot joy in its living because that living is less than human.

Eugene O'Neill once wrote a play—a muddled play in many ways, but a play with a splendid insight. It dealt with the life of Lazarus after the Son of God summoned him from the grave. O'Neill called his play *Lazarus Laughed*. It is the story of a lover of Christ who has tasted death and sees it for what it is—the story of a man whose one invitation to men is his constant refrain:

> Laugh with me!
> Death is dead!
> Fear is no more!
> There is only life!
> There is only laughter![1]

And O'Neill tells us: Lazarus "begins to laugh, softly at first," then full-throated—"a laugh so full of a complete acceptance of life, a profound assertion of joy in living, so devoid of all fear, that it is infectious with love," so infectious that, despite themselves, his listeners are caught by it and carried away.

This, I submit, is intelligent Christianity. It is not that you blind yourself to sin and war and disease and death. These will touch you as cruelly as they touch the man or woman who does not believe, who cannot hope, who refuses to love. And still you can laugh, can joy in living. Why? Because in the midst of death you are constantly discovering life: in a glance or a touch or a song, in a field of corn or a friend who cares, in the moon or an amoeba, in a lifeless loaf transformed into the body of Christ. But you will discover life only if you look and love, only if you open your whole self to a whole world of experience, open your whole self to others. Otherwise you will see only death; and when you see nothing but death you are . . . dead.

Graduates of '78: I have said nothing about individual courses and basketball hoops, even about Mass and sacraments. Not that these are unimportant, unrelated to scholastic existence. But the fact remains: St. Mary's is not a factory for facts; it is not a sauna for overweight Christians; it is not even a chapel, where faith is fortified against infidelity. Please God, you have amassed facts, lost fat, kept faith. Please God, you *will* leave here learned slender believers.

But more to the point, you will leave here "educated" to the extent that a college guided by the Spirit has opened you to looking and loving. You will leave here "educated" in the measure that St. Mary's has revealed a world that excites you with its mystery and its promise and has disclosed the "other" without whom you are not quite a person, not quite human, not quite alive. Looking and loving, you can leave here . . . laughing.

20
IN NO OTHER NAME
Baccalaureate for a dying institution

On May 13, 1973, Dunbarton College, a liberal-arts college for women founded in 1935 by the Sisters of the Holy Cross from Notre Dame, Indiana, held its final commencement. Located in our nation's capital, Dunbarton had attracted students not only from a majority of the states and the District of Columbia but also from Puerto Rico and a number of foreign countries. Its alumnae were uncommonly devoted to Dunbarton—a tribute to a small but competent and concerned faculty, an openness to educational experimentation, and a friendly atmosphere that helped to fashion a genuine community.

But pressures of the late sixties and early seventies (too complex to be detailed here) dictated that Dunbarton close. The decision was a difficult one for the administrators who had to make it, and a terrible blow to thousands who had lived and studied there. I myself was deeply stirred, for I had come to know and love the college from a number of retreats to the students and an occasional lecture, had made some close friendships that remain even today.

The invitation to preach at the final baccalaureate Mass was an honor I appreciated but could hardly rejoice in. Moreover, my anguish was the more acute because not long before this it had been decided that my own institution, Woodstock College, would soon have to close its own doors. The two events came together in my homily.

Each of today's three readings[1] contains a remarkably pertinent sentence—remarkably pertinent because each touches intimately not only your general Christian existence but your Dunbarton bonds as well. First Peter, then John, then Jesus—each has something to say to you this morning.

I

First, St. Peter: "In no other name is there salvation save in the name of Jesus" (Acts 4:12). Here is basic Christianity. Oneness with God, grace, divine life, redemption, salvation—call it what you wish—all this comes to you, to me, to each age, to the world, only through Jesus. Others may help, should help—Church and churches, pope and priests, Scripture and sermons, faith and works, husband and wife, nuns and novenas—but, to use one of those annoying fundamentalist graffiti, "Jesus saves." Your Christian existence must focus on the words of Christ the night before he died: "*This* is eternal life: to know the one true God, and Jesus Christ, whom He has sent" (Jn 17:3). More graphically in that haunting song from *Godspell:* "To know you more clearly, to love you more dearly, to follow you more nearly." For he *is* life; all others *share* in his life, or they are not really alive.

This basic Christian affirmation (Jesus saves) says something about Dunbarton. *Jesus* saves—Dunbarton does not. I do not say this coldly, coming to you from outside, from a secure Jesuit existence. I share your sadness in a unique way. In January it was decided that Woodstock College—the oldest American Jesuit seminary (104 years), the most prestigious Catholic seminary in the U.S., the only Catholic seminary that has consistently held the admiration of non-Catholic America for its academic excellence—Woodstock would phase out and close. Woodstock has been my adult life: 7 years study, 28 teaching. For Woodstock to close, as for Dunbarton to close, is tragic; it could even be a mistake. I shall not argue either case here. But the *Christian* meaning of our closing—yours and mine—is agonizingly clear: only Jesus is indispensable, irreplaceable. Dunbarton and Woodstock are *moments* in the story of salvation. Important moments, indeed—perhaps they should be longer moments—but they are still moments. Like the famous Christian School of Alexandria in the third century, so for us: a Christian institution is born, it peaks, it dies. It plays its part in God's mysterious scenario for salvation—and it disappears. Only Jesus goes on—because only Jesus saves.

II

Second, St. John. Remarkable words for every Christian: "It does not yet appear what we shall be, but we know that when he appears we shall be like him, for we shall see him as he is" (1 Jn 3:2). The whole thrust of Christian living is to become increasingly like Christ. Oh, not in physical appearance—that is so much a matter of race and sex and culture, of unimportant resemblances—strong nose, dark beard, flowing robe. To be like Christ is to live with his life. It is St. Paul's anguished prayer: "My little children, with whom I am in travail, in labor, *until Christ be formed in you*" (Gal 4:19). I mean the Christ who wept over Jerusalem and over Lazarus, over his city and his friend. I mean the Christ who loved every human person—the world with its hundred hues, its thousand tongues, its countless shapes and agonies—loved them all even unto crucifixion. I mean the Christ whose touch was a healing, whose look was a loving, whose words were woven of compassion, whose smile was strength for the sinful, hope for the hopeless, light for the darkened, life for the lifeless. I mean the Christ who was so utterly human that, as St. Athanasius put it in the fourth century, he even "borrowed death from us."

"It does not yet appear what we shall be." All that matters, however, is that when he comes again "we shall be like him." Only then will all our human striving—the agony and the ecstasy, the pride and the passion, the wrestling and the dancing, every cry of delight and sob of sorrow—find its fulfilment, its meaning, its joy: when we are so utterly like him that we can cry with St. Paul "I live—no, it is not I that live—Christ lives in me" (Gal 2:20).

And so with Dunbarton, so with Woodstock. In one sense we know what we shall be. The Dunbarton you know—like the Woodstock I know—will be no more. It will no longer be a place you can come back to. It will cease to be a place.

But that is relatively unimportant. Dunbarton is not primarily a place. It is, in a way, something like the Church, like tradition. Tradition is all the Church's yesterdays, gathered up into today, for a future somewhere tomorrow. So, too, for Dunbarton. Dunbarton is all of your yesterdays—gathered up into your today—for a tomorrow somewhere. In a word, Dunbarton is you. It has a future: you.

And therein lies the risk and the joy. *Risk*, because tomorrow is clouded with uncertainty: "it does not yet appear what [you] shall be." Dead tomorrow, or alive in 2025? Total self-giving, or incessant self-getting? Love without possession, or possession without love? Aware of Christ within you, or anguished by the feeling of God's absence? Imprisoned within four walls, or open to a whole world of experience? Still comfortably in the Church, or somewhere on the edge, or utterly outside? Tomorrow is not yours to know—and therein lies the risk in human living: "it does not yet appear what [you] shall be."

But therein lies the *joy* as well. Your whole life can be, should be, a ceaseless struggle to become a person, to become real. Where, despite sin and war, disease and death, each dawn is a new dawn, a first dawn; where each day is mind-blowing because you are alive and in love; where age is not an enemy but time to grow; where pain is not to be avoided and deadened, but you love and live the wounds that open you to others' pain; where even death is not resignation to a grim reaper, but an "I do," your yes to a loving Lord. This is the joy of human living. Live like this—the risk and the joy—and Dunbarton will stay alive in you. Dunbarton need not close today. The closer you come to the Christ within you, the more you resemble him who is so wonderfully human, the more Dunbarton stays alive. This is not pious pap, insubstantial poetry. This is the Real. Dunbarton is not a place; Dunbarton is persons—women—women in love: in love with Christ, in love with men, in love with life.

III

Third, Jesus: "I lay down my life in order that I may take it up again. No one takes it from me, but I lay it down of my own accord" (Jn 10:17–18). Two crucial affirmations for any Christian: (1) *I* lay down my life. (2) If I do, death will give birth to *new life.* This was the mystery of Christ's own existence—the paschal mystery. "If the grain of wheat does not fall into the ground and die, it remains alone; but if it does die, it produces much fruit" (Jn 12:24). "Was it not *necessary*," he asked the two discouraged disciples on the road to Emmaus after his rising, "was it not *necessary* that the Christ suffer these things *and so* enter into his glory?" (Lk 24:26). Because he died, you and I are alive. To me, the most thrilling words in the Gospel are the short words our Lord spoke to his friends the night before he died: "I have life, and you will have life" (Jn 14:19).

A recurrent theme, a paradox, in John's Gospel is that those who share Jesus' life never really die. Oh yes, there is an obvious superficial dying: the widow's only son at Naim, Lazarus in the tomb three days, Christ himself carried within the rock. But this, for all its agony and tragedy, is a surface dying. Those whom the Spirit of Christ, the Holy Spirit, invades and transforms, they never really die. That is why Jesus was dissatisfied with Martha's faith-filled affirmation: "I know that my brother will rise again in the resurrection on the last day." No, he declared to her, "those who believe in me will *never* die" (Jn 11:24, 26). For, as long as the life of Jesus, the Spirit of Christ, has hold of you, you are genuinely alive; and this Spirit of Christ need never leave you, even in physical death—*will* never leave you, as long as you lay down life of your own accord—as long as death is an "I do"—as long as your life's constant prayer is the life-filled prayer of the dying Christ: "Father, into your hands I commit my spirit" (Lk 23:46). Into your hands. . . .

Several years ago, in a Phoenix hospital, a sixteen-year-old girl lay dying. She knew it. One day, perhaps a day or two before her death, a Carmelite friend, Father William McNamara, came to her hospital room. He looked harried, worried, for he loved her dearly. Janet, hours from death, looked into his eyes, then said simply: "Father, don't be afraid."

So, too, for Dunbarton. Only if at this moment in *God's* history you lay down Dunbarton's *obvious* existence *of your own accord* will new life spring from the dead. For that, you don't have to believe that the Holy Spirit perched on the limbs of superiors, spoke infallibly through them—that human decision equals God's decision equals death. No, you simply start with a fact: surface death—real yes (that is why it hurts), but quite superficial. Then a trust-filled "Into *your* hands." And with that the Christian confidence that somehow, in so many places, life will spring from this death of yours. For the Spirit of life, the Spirit that Jesus sends, is not tied to 2935 Upton Street Northwest (not even 1600 Pennsylvania Ave.). The Holy Spirit inhabits not so much places as persons, not so much a chapel as a human heart. In you—in the life you live, the children you create, the world you fashion, in the ideas you spark and the love you unleash—in a thousand ways seen and unseen, life will leap from the ashes, from apparent death.

Dear friends of Dunbarton: This year you and I die a little. In Dunbarton's dying and Woodstock's, you and I die a little. And if you're anything like me (God preserve you from that), you hurt—and you *will* hurt. And with the Christ of Gethsemane you will pray in anguish: "Father, if at all possible, take this bitter cup away—don't ask me to drink of it." Peace will come (it hasn't come to *me* yet) when you can see more faithfully that only Jesus is irreplaceable, when you can trust more hopefully in God's uncertain future, when you can say more lovingly "I do. . . . Into your hands."

Till that day dawns, I have for you only the Christian wisdom of a sixteen-year-old girl whom the Spirit of Jesus never left: "Don't be afraid. . . . Don't . . . be . . . afraid."

21
AS GOD HAS DONE UNTO YOU
For a Red Mass

The Red Mass, a votive Mass in honor of the Holy Spirit, is celebrated in many Catholic dioceses at the opening of the judicial year. It has a venerable history that traces back to thirteenth-century France, England, and Italy. On the origin of the name, scholars are not at peace. In one theory, the priest-celebrant was vested in red, and so the judges of the High Court in Edward I's reign (1272–1307), all of them doctors of the law, conformed to ecclesiastical tradition and also wore red robes. Others hold for an origin with more profound content: the liturgical red signifies a willingness to defend the truth inspired by the Holy Spirit, even to the shedding of one's blood.

On April 5, 1979, a distinguished congregation gathered at the Co-Cathedral of St. Thomas More in Tallahassee. Besides the six Catholic bishops of Florida, this Red Mass was graced by Governor Bob Graham, members of his Cabinet, three justices of the State Supreme Court, the president of the Senate, members of the legislature, and some judges and lawyers. A highly ecumenical turnout—a dramatic demonstration of the remarkable changes that have transformed the religious temper of Tallahassee.

The purpose of the Red Mass is clear enough: it invokes God's guidance and strength during the court term to come. But the homilist has a problem: he cannot content himself with invocations. Research, reflection, and prayer finally focused my approach on the single word "justice"—the concept of justice as chiseled by the wise on earth, but more importantly the exciting insights unveiled in God's word.

For those of you who have been captive to a Red Mass homilist all too often, a word of comfort. I shall not lecture you on your legal and judicial duties; my ignorance would dismay you. I shall not expound the natural law; this is divine worship, not a classroom. I shall not castigate the Supreme Court on abortion; constitutional lawyers have raised enough learned eyebrows. I shall not laud St. Thomas More; his spirit surrounds you in this cathedral, perhaps in your lives.

What, then, is left? Why, to raise your sights. Every professional needs that every so often. As a theologian, I must remind myself that my floundering efforts to grasp God intellectually make little sense unless I believe in God and love Him. At times Joseph Califano must lift his eyes from his 184-billion-dollar budget and focus on a hungry child in Appalachia, on the people his purse strings should serve. Even the Pope, as he plays the politician with Poland or flays the rape of the poor at Puebla, must raise his heart to heaven. And those whose frightening task is to mete out human justice—to give other men and women what is due to them—must ask what is the justice God demands of you, not on a bench but in your fuller lives, in your broader living. For it would be ironic if, while dealing out justice by the standards of men, you were yourselves unjust stewards by the standards of God.

I shall, then, do two things. I shall probe God's own word, to see what justice means in the Old Testament and the New. Then I shall return to you, to see if anything in all this might speak to your total living.

I

First, God's own word on justice. It is fascinating to flit through the Old Testament and hear the God of Israel as He impeaches His people. Through Isaiah and Hosea, through Amos and Micah and Jeremiah, He ceaselessly tells Israel that He rejects just those things they think will make Him happy. He is weary of burnt offerings, does not delight in the blood of bulls or lambs. Incense is an abomination to Him. Their appointed feasts His soul hates. Their prayers and the melody of their harps He will not listen to. He does not want rivers of oil, thousands of rams, even their first-born. Then what is left? What can God possibly want? Two things: their steadfast love and that they execute justice.[1]

That God should want Israel's love is understandable. But that the second great commandment should be "execute justice" is not what we would expect. Is there not a higher commandment, such as the Lord's demand in Leviticus: "you shall love your neighbor as yourself" (Lev 19:18)?

The point is, the justice God asked of Israel was not an ethical construct. It did not merely mean: give to each what is due to each, what each person has a strict right to demand, because he or she is a human being, has rights that can be proven by philosophy or have been written into law. No, justice was a whole web of relationships that stemmed from Israel's covenant with God. The Israelites were to father the fatherless and feed the sojourner, the stranger, not because the orphan and the outsider deserved it, but because this was the way *God* had acted with *them*. A text in Deuteronomy is telling: "Love the sojourner, therefore; for you were sojourners in the land of Egypt" (Deut 10:19). In freeing the oppressed, they were mirroring the loving God who had delivered *them* from oppression, had freed them from Pharaoh. In loving the loveless, the unloved, the unlovable, they were imaging the God who wooed Israel back despite her infidelities, betrothed her to Himself forever (cf. Hos 2:14–23).

Justice, for the Jew, was not a question simply of human deserving, of human law. The Jews were to give to others what they had been given by God, were to act toward one another as God had acted toward them—and precisely because God had acted this way. Their justice was to image not the justice of man but the justice of God. For Israel, the practice of justice was an expression of steadfast love, a demand of steadfast love—God's love and their own love. Not to execute justice was not to worship God.

This is the tradition that sparked the ministry of Jesus: "I will put my Spirit upon him, and he shall proclaim justice to the Gentiles. . . . He will not break a bruised reed or quench a smoldering wick, till he brings justice to victory" (Mt 12:18–20). In harmony with Hosea, he wants not sacrifice but compassion, mercy (cf. Mt 12:7; 23:23). And the just man or the just woman is not primarily someone who gives to another what that other *deserves*. The just man, the just woman has covenanted with God; this covenant demands that we treat other human persons as *God* wants them treated in His covenant plan, treat friend and enemy as He treats them. And how does He treat them? He "makes His sun rise on the evil and on the good, sends rain on the just and on the unjust" (Mt 5:45).

The early Christians seem to have grasped that. If *anyone* is hungry or athirst, naked or a stranger, sick or in prison, it is always Christ who clamors for bread or water, Christ who cries to be clothed or welcomed, Christ whom you visit on a bed of pain or behind bars (cf. Mt 25:31–46). And the first Letter of John is terribly uncompromising: "If anyone has the world's goods and sees his brother in need, yet closes his heart against him, how does God's love abide in him?" (1 Jn 3:17).

II

All well and good—a superb scenario of scriptural justice. But what does it have to say to you—to you whose burden is precisely to give others what is their due, you who should not be swayed from justice by love or sentiment, should not be swayed by anything less than the law on your books or the need to correct injustice—you whose goddess is the Roman *Justitia*, the lady with scales and a sword, her eyes blindfolded or closed in token of impartiality?

Ladies and gentlemen, you are an incredibly powerful group. For this nation is founded on law, and so in large measure it is founded on you. True, our legal hands are not lily-white. We look back with shame on a Dred Scott decision that declared slaves to be property. We blush that in this "land of the free" women have been second-class citizens. We weep because justice is so slow, weep when human beings rot in jail for months before they can be tried. We cannot applaud when programs for the poor and underprivileged are cut back for inadequate reasons. We get cynical when the powerful can delay or gerrymander justice. And you must surely cry for those colleagues of yours for whom the law is a game whose name is victory and wealth, where the prize goes to the brilliant and the prestigious, to the crafty and the manipulator.

And still the law is a proud profession. "Equal before the law" is still an ideal, but you are moving relentlessly toward it. With maddening slowness you are fashioning a society where the laws are just, where the just are free, where the accused can hope for justice. Without you this would be a nation in anarchy, a nation singularly unfree. And so I do not hear the Lord God saying to you: "I am weary of your governors and your legislatures. I no longer delight in your Cabinets and your courts. I will not listen to your endless arguments and your charges to the jury. Your appeals to a higher tribunal my soul hates, and your 4-to-3 decisions are an abomination to me."

No, I do not hear the Lord God saying that; but something else I do hear Him saying. You see, for all your understandable absorption in matters legal, despite the high importance of the law you serve, you dare not limit your life to living by the law. No more than I can rest satisfied with an intellectual appreciation of God's mighty acts in history, an objective presentation of the same to students, some competent books and a hundred articles under my name. It is good, but not good enough. My life has to transcend theology, and your life has to leap beyond the law.

For me, the knowledge of God that stems from study should lead to the only knowledge of God that saves, where to know God is to be like Him, to get to be in His image, to share in His holiness—that knowledge which is essentially union, oneness in love with a loving God.[2] For you, the quest for justice as defined by the wise among mortals should be the springboard for a fuller life; the love of law should lead to the law of love.

Why? Because, for your personal life, human law is not enough to save you, to make you one with God; only "steadfast love" of God can do that. And for the nation, although human law may preserve us from anarchy, it is not enough to bind up the country's wounds. You can give blacks and women equality, and you should; but unless whites and males give themselves in the process, we shall have only an armistice, not genuine peace. The law of the land is no substitute for the Sermon on the Mount. Courts of law are effective equalizers, but they cannot mandate love.

What, then, does this demand of you? A return to the biblical vision of justice. The justice you *live* must be a whole web of relationships that stem from your covenant with God. Your presence here implies that you have such a covenant. Perhaps not in a religious community, but still a genuine commitment to the God of Abraham, Isaac, and Jacob, to the Father of Jesus Christ. In that commitment it is not enough to give to others what they "deserve," what they have earned by their efforts. You are to act toward others as God has acted toward you—and precisely because God has acted this way. Your commitment commits you to a style of godlike living where no man or woman is a stranger to you, because no man or woman is a stranger to God.

What this means for you in the concrete, no outsider can tell you—especially a visitor from Washington! But this much I dare say: Florida is not a tight little island cut off from the mainland of human suffering. Here too you have the hungers of the human family. Here too children cry for food and grown men despair of work. Here too the old are anxious how they will live, and find so few who will love. Here too race makes for hate, the young are restless, migrant workers are a problem, alcohol and drugs destroy bodies and souls. Here too the powerless lift pitiful hands to heaven, and the middle class tremble to an uncertain future.

Here too, then, your commitment to *God's* justice makes demands on you. It is not enough to be incorrupt, to go to your people with clean hands; those hands must be outstretched. It is not enough to be learned jurists and skilled practitioners; your people need understanding and love.

By all means, confront your constituents with your competence, inspire them with your integrity. Give them what any man or woman can claim from the law. But give them more. For your salvation and theirs, give them yourselves. Act toward them as God has acted toward you. A fresh, exciting, incredible ideal. No longer "Do unto others as you would have them do unto you," but "Do unto others as God has done unto you." Who knows? You just might transform the tear-streaked face of Florida. You just might make this the "Sunshine State."

HUMAN AND
CHRISTIAN LIVING

22
LIFE, GOOD LIFE, ETERNAL LIFE
To those who yearn to be alive

Guideline is a network (NBC) radio presentation produced at the present time by the United States Catholic Conference's Office of Communication for Film and Broadcasting. Its origins go back almost four decades, and it has played a significant role in spreading the word of God to the far reaches of our country. Many of the series presented on Guideline have dealt with major social issues, and the audience has proven to be gratifyingly ecumenical.

I have been invariably happy to accept invitations to speak on Guideline. Carried at different times in different places, it reaches hundreds of thousands each week: in homes, institutions of various kinds, even beach traffic. In fact, I suspect that in my four series (1972, 1973, 1974, 1976) I have reached more people than in the thousands of more personal homilies and addresses I have given in almost forty years as a priest. My booklets Towards Reconciliation *(Washington, D.C.: United States Catholic Conference, 1974) and* Seven Hungers of the Human Family *(Washington, D.C.: United States Catholic Conference, 1976) reproduce two of my series on Guideline.*

The address which follows is reproduced here because I think it will serve as an appropriate introduction to this section on human and Christian living. It stems from my October 1972 series and it tries to summarize what it means for a human being, for a Christian, to be alive. It might be interesting to compare this with Homily 19 above, which deals with the same problem in quite a different way.

From the second century there has come down to us one of the most remarkable short sentences in Christian literature. Penned by our first theologian, Bishop Irenaeus of Lyons, the sentence runs: "God's glory is man alive."[1] It is theologically courageous, perhaps brash, to make God's glory depend on anything that is not God; and the affirmation echoes with special irony today, when life is such a precarious possession, when it is death that dances everywhere, death that lurks on the streets of Belfast, in the rice paddies of Vietnam, on the sidewalks of New York.

The problem, of course, is, what does it mean to say "God's glory is man alive"? I shall sketch an answer in three stages. For "man alive" has three facets—what another early theologian, Clement of Alexandria, saw so perceptively when he spied our imaging of God in (1) life, (2) the good life, (3) eternal life.

I

First then, sheer life. For a human being to be alive, to breathe, for a human being simply to be, is itself a glorious thing. Not because it is somehow better to be than not to be. Rather because to be alive at all is only possible because life is a gift. Not merely from mother and father; life is a gift "from above," from the God who gives "all that is good, everything that is perfect" (Jas 1:17). But not as *we* give gifts, where some *thing* passes from hand to hand. The gift of life is a sharing in Him who *is* Life, in the God whose Godness is summed up in the pithy phrase "He who is." You live because He lives.

More than that: human life is a glorious gift because it is a gift of love. God has not just fashioned you to be. Your gift of life is a gift of love because it is a special kind of existence. You share "being" with so much else on earth: with stone and star, with sea and sand. You share a form of life with winter wheat and quivering aspen leaf. With the birds of the air and the beasts of the field and the fish of the sea you can see and hear and touch and taste and smell. But what makes you human is a twin power you alone of earth's creatures share with God. You are human because, whatever your blood or skin or accent, male or female, you come into this world sharing two of God's precious perfections: you have the power to know, and you have the freedom to love. You are someone; you are a person; you are like God.

That is why human life is so sacred. Oh yes, in a genuine sense all that exists bears the mark of the sacred, because all that is bears the imprint of Him who is. And so all God's creation cries out to me "Handle with reverence!" But for all my awareness of man's inhumanity to the nonhuman, I will not abide the ecologist for whom God's air and God's mountain ash and God's Pomeranian bitch are on the same level of sacredness as God's man or woman. Human life mirrors divine life as no other life can.

That is why the intelligent Catholic is so sensitive to life at its dawning and life in its twilight, to the rights of the unborn and the dignity of the age-worn. Granted we find it difficult to demonstrate that a fertilized egg is instantly human; we agonize over what drugs to withhold from a cancer-ridden, coma-fogged lump of clay on a hospital bed; and we are torn between what God says to us on fetal life and what may be written into law for all. But these are details, inescapable human problems that call for ceaseless probing, problems where here-and-now values clash with always-and-everywhere principles, problems on which men and women of good will inevitably disagree. Where no disagreement should exist, no conflict sever us, is in the recognition that life is sacred, all life, particularly human life; the conviction that, if life is to be taken at all, in Hanoi or a city hospital, it must be taken with reluctance, with a stifled cry of pain, with a horrifying realization that not another cipher but someone unrepeatable is being destroyed, that with his or her death I myself am somehow diminished—and God is not glorified.

II

God's glory is man alive—sheer human life mirrors Him who *is* Life. A second facet: the good life. I do not mean "wine, women, and song," though I do not exclude them. In the Christian scheme of things, you are not genuinely alive simply because you are not medically dead. In fact, you are not humanly alive just because you have mind and will, have understanding and heart. Every dictator from Herod to Hitler has had purpose and passion, has been amazingly alive, whether he has focused on newborn babies in Bethlehem or on aged folk in Dachau. Sinners can be astonishingly alive, especially in their sin: Saul "breathing slaughter" (Acts 9:1) on the road to Damascus; Augustine "in love with love"[2] in semi-pagan Carthage; every fictional daredevil with the morals of James Bond. Knowledge and freedom indeed image Him who *is* Mind and Love. But knowledge and freedom are only the potential for what is crucial in human mirroring of the divine; the potential must be dynamized. Not any sort of knowledge will do; not every expression of freedom reflects divinity.

What then does? Rarely has the answer been given so pithily as by Aquinas. You can desire knowledge in two ways. One way is as a perfection of yourself; that is the way philosophers desire knowledge. The other way is not merely as a perfection of yourself, but because through this knowledge the one you love becomes present to you; that is the way saints desire it.

The human spirit will never call a halt to knowing; it is incurably curious, will never cease to wonder. And so the geneticist will continue to probe the properties of sickle-cell hemoglobin, and the physicist will blast a rocket to Venus; a Toynbee will reconstruct the past, and a Teilhard will project man's ceaseless surge to an Omega Point; behavioral psychologists will search out the frontiers of freedom, and a child will run his fingers lazily through grass and water; the young will reach for reality through music, and all ages will seek in film the meaning of man. For this is the life of embodied spirit, a constant quest for the real.

But this quest can look to myself alone, or it can bring living persons together in love. Knowledge can destroy, and knowledge can unite. Knowledge can kill, and knowledge can create. Knowledge can cause compassion, and knowledge can breed envy, hatred, war. Knowledge can incinerate Southeast Asia, and knowledge can make love to flame.

Our knowledge, our awareness, mirrors the mind of God when its energies are directed to compassion and creativity, to peace and oneness, to love. For the God I would mirror with my spirit is the God in whom understanding and love are one, the God whose self-revelation is a gift of love. Be it an atom I know or a person, the way in which my knowing is genuinely human is if it leaps from love and leads to love. Here is authentic human life, because it images God's own life, total self-giving.

I mean the Trinity, where there is indeed "I and thou"—Father, Son, and Spirit—but no "mine and thine." I mean creation, which is God sharing His life and His goodness, God's love bursting to give what is His, imprisoning His perfection in something imperfect but "very good" (Gen 1:31), in rainbow or rivulet, in petal or panther or newborn babe. I mean redemption, which is God delivering Himself to death so that man can come alive again. This is what human life images when Mother Teresa caresses the crippled of Calcutta, when Dag Hammarskjöld gives his life to unite the nations, when Martin Luther King bleeds and dies so that black and white can touch without hate.

III

This "good life," where knowing leads to loving, suggests the third facet of man's divine imaging: eternal life. It is not easy, not always possible, to say where the good life becomes eternal life. You see, "eternal life," as Jesus put it, "is to know the only true God and Jesus Christ whom He has sent" (Jn 17:3), to love God and His Christ, to love every human person with a love born of God and His grace. Eternal life, therefore, does not begin with death. It has its roots in the past: in the new life that sprang from Christ's death. It looks to the future: ceaseless life with Him who *is* Life. And still it is a here-and-now reality; eternal life has its beginning now. "If any man love me," Jesus proclaimed, "my Father will love him, and we will come to him and make our home with him"

(Jn 14:23). Eternal life is a specially intimate presence, an indwelling of Trinity, where God-within-me is the source of my activity, transforms my thinking, transfuses my freedom—in a genuine sense, is my life.

This is the mystery of grace. Not some thing, but persons fused in love. On God's side, grace is God offering Himself to me, communicating His life to me, demanding from me love and fidelity. On man's side, grace is I offering myself to God, I transformed, shaped to Christ. Grace is God present to man in a new way, man responding to God in a new way. Grace is what the Greek Fathers never wearied of repeating: "God became man to make men gods." Grace is a share in God's secret life. I can love the Father with the Son, like the Son, because of the Son and by the Son, all by the power of the Holy Spirit.

This life in Christ is not easy to grasp. It may well be that you can understand it only by living it. It may well be that Augustine was profoundly right when he wrote:

> Give me someone who loves, and he will understand what I am trying to say. Give me someone whose heart yearns, who is hungry, who feels the nostalgia of loneliness in this exile, who is athirst and sighs for a fatherland eternal; give me such a one, and he will understand what I am trying to say. But if I must explain myself to ice-cold indifference, he will not understand.[3]

Sheer life, good life, eternal life: Are you surprised that the committed Catholic sees life, touches life, lives life with awe and wonder, in fear and trembling? If *God's* glory is you, you alive, dare *you* glory in less than life, in loss of life, in death?

23
A CHANGING CHURCH?
To the baffled and the hurt

While teaching at Woodstock College in its transplanted New York City setting, I was asked to preach on April 8, 1973 at a parish church in Greenwich, Connecticut. The request stressed a problem hardly confined to Connecticut in the early seventies: would I address myself to a divisive parish issue—change in the Church?

I have said yes to such invitations when they call for a lecture. But a sermon? In a liturgical context? In fifteen minutes? To a captive congregation, unknown to me and unable to respond? The challenge proved irresistible, and so I disregarded the sage counsel implicit in John Courtney Murray's honest admission: "I'm a brave man but not a hero." A hero I would be—perhaps a martyr.

The decision was easier to make than to implement. A preacher is presumably presenting the word of God. But that divine word has to be interpreted by a human mind, expressed in halting speech. Especially in controverted areas, the perennial peril is that the word of man may betray the word of God. And if Christian passions have been inflamed, one whose task is to reconcile must walk as if on fragile eggshells—or broken glass.

I do not know what effect my sermon had in Greenwich. I take some consolation from a reaction to substantially the same talk given at a benefit luncheon in New York City the next year for a Jesuit missionary in Japan. A lady wrote: the address "has given me life, even joy. Not since I was young have I been a joyful Catholic. It is like finding my way out of darkness into light."

I come before you an uncommonly fortunate man. For much of my life I took intense delight in a Church that was solid rock; for the past fifteen years I have reveled in a Church that rocks and rolls, a Church that changes. I enjoy being a priest, would not exchange it for the world; and still I envy those to whom married love has brought fulfilment. I am convinced that in Catholicism Christ's dream for his Church is more perfectly realized than in any other community; but nine years of ecumenical dialogue with Lutherans have given me a new vision of *other* churches where the grace of God is working salvation. I am at once a theologian and a historian; and so my faith is fed at once by profound reflection and by the facts of the Church's past. I am the only theologian in captivity who is banned in Owensboro and quite acceptable in Rome. I am indeed a fortunate man.

But today I want to talk about *you*. About you and this new age of the Church, these changes that can be so confusing, this renewal that looks like retreat, this reform that reads like Reformation. Is anything left of the old Church? Is everything up for grabs? Must you resign yourself to uncertainty, to the latest Religion column in *Time*?

I shall make three brief points: (1) There is something very sure and secure in the Church, very *certain*, because it depends ultimately on God. (2) There is something constantly insecure, *uncertain*, changing in the Church, because it depends ultimately on man. (3) You should be gloriously *joyful* within this Church, because this wedding of God and man, of certainty and uncertainty, of security and insecurity, is what gives life to your Catholicism.

I

First, there is something very sure and secure in the Church, very *certain*, because it depends ultimately on God. I mean your faith. I do not mean simply the Act of Faith so many of you remember from the catechisms and prayer books:

> O my God, I firmly believe that thou art one God in three divine Persons, Father, Son, and Holy Ghost. I believe that thy divine Son became man and died for our sins. I believe these and all the truths which the holy Catholic Church teaches, because thou hast revealed them, who can neither deceive nor be deceived.

This is indeed important to your faith. You are saying yes with your mind, your intellect, yes to truths that were disclosed by God through Christ nineteen centuries ago. This is important because within a faith that is Catholic, doctrine is precious. Doctrine is part of "the faith."

But faith is not *primarily* a matter of propositions. My act of faith is, in the first instance, a yes not to a set of truths, but to our Lord Himself. It is my *total* response to God communicating Himself interiorly to me in grace, offering Himself to me in friendship. It is primarily not an assent of my intellect, but a total self-giving: "I myself, entirely myself, yield myself to you."

Without this total self-giving, your yes to propositions ("I believe in one God") is sterile, utterly useless to save you. As St. James put it, "even the devils believe" (Jas 2:19): believe that God is one and three, that God became man and died for us, that God punishes and rewards. . . . And still they are severed from God forever.

The heart of your faith is: "I give myself entirely to you." And this is possible because it is God who makes it possible: God within you, offering Himself to you, God faithful to His promises, God always there, alive and loving. Here is the Catholic certainty: God making Himself *your* God, God within you. The only thing *uncertain* about it is you. At any given moment, do you really want Him? Or is there something you want more than Him?

He is faithful, utterly faithful. He lives within you. He asks for your love, and all the while He makes it possible for you to love, to say yes. Here is the joy which, our Lord promised, no human being can take from you—no human being save yourself. Here is the Catholic certainty, the one reality that is changeless: Christ, the same Christ, yesterday and today and always, the same Christ loving you and demanding your love. Lose him, and you have only yourself to blame—not your husband or wife, not your pastor or neighbor, not some theologian from Sin City.

Here is your certainty and mine: Christ our Lord.

II

My second main point: there is something constantly insecure, *uncertain*, changing in the Church, because it depends ultimately on man—on men and women. Here three areas are crucial: the way we think (theology), the way we live (morality), the way we pray (worship).

(1) *The way we think.* Theology, unlike faith, is an effort to understand. A ceaseless effort. To understand what? To understand him who is God's revelation—Jesus Christ. And because he is divine mystery, and I (for all my obvious brilliance!) am human mind, my efforts will always be failures. Small rays of insight, and much inadequacy, fumbling, error. We shall never fully grasp here below what it *means* to say God is one and three, what it *means* to say I inherit sin, what it *means* to say God died, what it *means* to say I receive Christ in Communion "body and blood, soul and divinity," what it *means* to say Christ lives in me, what it *means* to say I shall see God face to face.

The Church *grows* in understanding—the whole Church—even the pope. But growth is a painful process. Understanding is not something that comes out of a computer in Rome. Understanding is a collaborative effort: many minds, inner anguish, discussion and debate, name-calling and even excommunication.

(2) *The way we live.* Morality is not spelled out in ten commandments. Christian life is not reducible to perpetual purity. The relation between authority and conscience, between an abstract principle and its application to me here and now—this is not automatic, not easy. Oh yes, the Church can come down clear and hard; but, when all is said and done, *I* must still make the final decision. Please God, it will be what official Catholic doctrine affirms; but if it is not, do not make things harder for me, by using a power not given to you: the power to excommunicate me. Theologians are arguing seriously and profoundly on what it means to be "in the Church." Don't add your ignorance to our massive stockpile.

My point here is: Catholicism is a whole way of life. And we grow in our understanding of what that way of life demands. Today we ask, with an urgency hardly rivaled in the past, what do I do with power, when so many are powerless? What dare I do with my money, when one billion human beings on this earth go to bed hungry? What am I doing with my freedom to free the enslaved? To a man whose whole life is spent lifting a fender to a Ford, I cannot simply say "You are imitating Joseph the Carpenter," and let Christian living stand at that.

(3) *The way we worship.* In the past ten years, our liturgy has been transformed. Sometimes almost beyond recognition. The stately Latin has been replaced by a vulgar English; Christ is off somewhere to the side; the organ is silent (save in St. Patrick's) and someone strums away about loving all God's children; it is impossible to pray quietly; you must shake hands; and you even have to see the priest's face!

What has happened? From the first Mass at the Last Supper to the last Mass at the Second Coming, the Church is engaged in a ceaseless effort to make this central act of worship a symbol of what the Church is all about; the liturgy is the Church in miniature. Ten years ago we were stressing one aspect of that mystery: *my* personal relationship to the sacramental, hidden Christ. Now we are trying to right the balance: more emphasis on the Church as *community*, as praying together, as a single family, as a family where the members know and love one another. And so the Church experiments: the altar a little closer, the people a little closer, priest and people a little closer. None of it is infallible; none of it is instant cure; none of it is calculated to make everybody happy. The individual change is unimportant; what is important is the purpose: to create *oneness*. How can this mystery of love be celebrated in such a way that you *care* for the stranger next to you, that strangers cease to be strangers? What worries me mightily, what saddens me profoundly, is that, in this breathless mystery of God's total self-giving, millions of Catholics just want to be left alone, millions of Catholics find it repulsive to turn to another human person for whom Christ died and say "Hello." Here is where your children are more Catholic than their parents.

III

My third main point: you should be gloriously *joyful* within this Church. A provocative French novelist once put on the lips of one of his characters a stinging challenge: "You say you are a Christian. Then where the devil is your joy?" There, for many a pagan, is the real Christian scandal. He does not demand that we be heroes, simply because we are Christians. He may not even expect us to be good. But he does expect us to be happy. And so many of us are not. Where is that joy which Christ said "no man shall take from you" (Jn 16:22)? Where is our response to St. Paul's "Rejoice always! I say to you, rejoice!" (Phil 4:4)? I am afraid we have impressed unbelievers with one half of one Beatitude: "Blessed are they that mourn" (Mt 5:5); blessed are the melancholy. Little wonder that the German philosopher Nietzsche complained about us, about Christians: we do not look redeemed!

And yet you *should* look redeemed. You should radiate a joy no human person can take from you. You have a deathless faith—I mean your total response of love to a God who offers Himself to you in love. And you live this faith within a community, a Church, which is alive. Alive not because it has a hatful of answers. Rather because, for all its human imperfections, this Church brings to you a *message* that saves, a *way of life* that makes each day a new creation, a *worship* that can unite not only God and you, but all of you with one another—if you will only open yourselves to God and to one another in risk-laden love.

Let me make an uncommonly honest confession. In the course of a half century, I have seen more Catholic corruption than you have read of. I have tasted it. I have been reasonably corrupt myself. And yet I joy in this Church—this living, pulsing, sinning people of God, love it with a crucifying passion. Why? For all the Catholic hate, I experience here a community of *love*. For all the institutional idiocy, I find here a tradition of *reason*. For all the individual repressions, I breathe here an air of *freedom*. For all the fear of sex, I discover here the redemption of my *body*. In an age so inhuman, I touch here tears of *compassion*. In a world so grim and humorless, I share here rich *joy* and earthy *laughter*. In the midst of death I hear here an incomparable stress on *life*. For all the apparent absence of God, I sense here the real presence of *Christ*.

My dear friend, the late Father John Courtney Murray, was one of the theological experts at the Second Vatican Council. In fact, he more than anyone else was responsible for the Declaration on Religious Freedom. At the end of the Council, he made a prophetic remark:

> As was the experience of Vatican II, so must be the postconciliar experience: the contemporary Catholic, like the bishops at the Council, must begin with a good deal of confusion and uncertainty, will therefore pass through a period of anxiety and tension, but can expect to end with a certain measure of light and of joy.

So be it.

24
LIFT UP YOUR HEARTS
To the frustrated

*"Lift Up Your Hearts" is not a homily. I include it here be-
cause it could be a homily. It was an address at the Waldorf-As-
toria in New York City on November 14, 1975, on the occasion of
the annual Jesuit Mission Dinner, which pays honor to Jesuit missionaries and the people at home who support them spiritually and
materially. One dynamic man honored then with the Xavier Award
was Msgr. James W. Asip, who through almost three decades in the
Brooklyn Diocese's mission office had channeled to the missions
more than sixty million dollars.*

*I found it imperative not only to confront a concrete Christian
issue, but to suggest its resolution on the basis of mission—to link
what is happening "back here" to what is happening "out there."
Before me were about a thousand Catholics, many of whom had
grown up, and some grown old, in a style of thinking, living, and
worshiping often called "pre-Vatican II" (I am not using the term
disparagingly). So much had changed so quickly that many were
understandably confused: this was not the Church they knew. More
agonizingly, many felt frustrated in the face of movements beyond
their control.*

*My effort at resolution—helping these loving and lovable peo-
ple to understand—focused on the fact that the Church, the whole
Church, is on mission, is mission; and a Church on mission is inescapably a Church in change, but equally a Church in hope. But to
see that, we have to raise our gaze, have to lift up our hearts.*

More than four centuries ago, the pioneer of Jesuit missionaries,
Francis Xavier, wrote a stinging letter from India to King John of
Portugal. The context of that letter was Francis' profound frustration. On fire for Christ and the human images of Christ, he had
been sent by King and Pope to Portugal's new empire in India. He
had set sail, dreaming of countries white for the harvest, of princes
and peoples hungry for the religion of the beloved Portuguese. He
landed at Goa, and before his eyes stretched the slave market.
Here human beings were paraded like beasts, sold for silver, beat-
en with whips while their Catholic masters counted the blows on
their rosary beads. Living in open sin, with gold for their god, they
would help Xavier, of course—if it did not interfere with their precious traffic. And so Christ was sold for cloves and pepper. In this
context Francis wrote to Portugal's King:

It is a sort of martyrdom to have patience and watch being destroyed what one has built up with so much labor. . . . Experience has taught me that Your Highness has no power in India to spread the faith of Christ, while you have power to take away and enjoy the country's temporal riches. . . . It will be a novel thing . . . to see yourself at the hour of death dispossessed of your kingdoms and seignories, and entering into others where you may have the new experience . . . of being ordered out of paradise.[1]

Dear friends in Christ: This evening I want to pick up one sentence from Francis' cry of frustration: "It is a sort of martyrdom to have patience and watch being destroyed what one has built up with so much labor." I want to pick up on that because it expresses the agonizing cry of so many hearts today: from barbed wire in Belfast to buses in Boston, from rice paddies in Vietnam to ruined missions in China, from English Masses to parochial schools, from food stamps for the elderly to the disappearance of old neighborhoods, from marrying priests to miniskirted sisters, from emptying churches in America to no visas for India, from the death of the liberal arts in our colleges to the life of co-ed housing. It is a new world, apparently a new Church, and so many Catholics moan with Xavier in despair: "It is a martyrdom to watch being destroyed what one has built up with so much labor."

It is my thesis tonight that this attitude is understandable but that it is less than Catholic. To grasp that thesis, you must understand three realities, three Christian imperatives: (1) The Church is on mission, the Church *is* mission. (2) This mission is a mission of the whole Church, not only of priests and foreign missionaries. (3) This mission demands a confidence in God's Spirit which is the Christian response to frustration, the only acceptable missionary spirit.

I

First then, the Church is on mission. Until recently it was common to say "the Church *has* missions." The Church has a missionary thrust: the Jesuits have a mission in Japan, the White Fathers have a mission in Africa, the Maryknollers have missions in Latin America, the Medical Sisters in India. Today theologians are more nuanced. They prefer to say "the Church *is* mission." The point is, in the totality of its being, the Church is an outreach; it is the

Church's essence to be God's living outreach to the world. The Church is a corporate apostle; and an apostle is by definition one who is "sent."

In Catholic theology, mission has a high-level, exciting history; for in Catholic theology, mission is the story of God and man. Mission (remember your Latin verb *mittere*?) is a sending, and the root New Testament revelation has to do with a sending. For the root Gospel revelation is the thrilling affirmation that God *sent* His only Son. Sent Him when? The day an angel brought the glad tidings to Mary? Sent Him where? Into this world, to every human person sin-scarred and tear-stained. Sent Him why? That the world, we, might not die but have life—rich and full and overflowing. The first Trinitarian mission was God's unique outreach to sinful man: in Christ, God Himself was sent.

Consequent on this radical mission of God's only Son is another mission equally incredible: the Father and the Son sent the Holy Spirit. Sent Him when? On the first Pentecost. Sent Him where? To the Church. Sent Him why? Vatican II put it well: "The Holy Spirit was sent on the day of Pentecost, in order that He might forever sanctify the Church."[2]

Intimately wed to this sending of Son and Spirit is the mission of the Church: the Church is sent—sent by the Son in the Spirit. This mission was foreshadowed before the Church was born, when the Lord "called the Twelve to him, and began sending them out, two by two. . . . So they went out and preached, bidding men repent; they cast out many devils, and many who were sick . . . they healed" (Mk 6:7–13). But the definitive sending came only after Christ's resurrection. It started in fear, behind locked doors, when the risen Lord showed the disciples his hands and his side, and spoke that exciting sentence: "As the Father sent me, I also send you." And with that he breathed on them: "Receive the Holy Spirit" (Jn 20:21–22). That sending took on added meaning on the mountain in Galilee where the Master issued his missionary mandate: "Go, make disciples of all nations" (Mt 28:19). That mandate was dynamized in a house within the City, where "gathered together in unity of purpose . . . they were all filled with the Holy Spirit," and forth they went, a fellowship of faith and hope and love, so that "every soul was struck with awe, so many were the wonders and signs performed by the apostles in Jerusalem" (Acts 2:2, 4, 43).

The Church, then, is mission, is sent, is apostle—all three mean the same thing. And if you know your New Testament, the implications are electric. For if to be a disciple meant to follow, to follow one only Master, to follow Jesus, to be an apostle meant to serve, to serve not oneself but others, to serve men and women. That is why the Twelve, Paul, and many another were sent. The Church is mission, and the mission is service. This is not pious poetry but essential ecclesiology. The primary thrust of the Church is summed up in the impassioned confession of St. Paul to the Christians of Corinth: "I will most gladly spend and be spent for you" (2 Cor 12:15).

II

This leads rigorously to my second main point: this mission is a mission of the whole Church, not only of priests and foreign missionaries.

You see, the Church is not a Platonic idea serenely suspended in mid-air; the Church is people. And this people is not simply—or even primarily—pope and prelates and priests. The Church is what the early Christians saw so clearly: the Church is "the 'we' of Christians." *We* are the Church, all of us, we in community. *We* are sent. Sent when? Cardinal Suenens put it startlingly: the greatest day in the life of a pope is not his coronation but his baptism, the day of his mission "to live the Christian life in obedience to the gospel."[3] Where are we sent? Like Christ, into "the world," to every being born of woman. Sent why? Like Christ, "to preach good news to the poor, to proclaim release to those in chains, sight to the blind, to set at liberty the oppressed" (Lk 4:18).

The point is, the people of God is not divided into "two species of Christians," cleric and lay. The Church is a totality, a oneness, in which the basic relationship is equality in the Spirit. All Christians are consecrated, by God's call and their baptism, to form a holy people, a priestly kingdom, a spiritual temple, to render to God a spiritual worship and to announce God's "wonderful deeds" (cf. 1 Pet 2:9–10; 1 Cor 3:16–17). By baptism, therefore, each Christian is incorporated not simply into Christ and the Church, but into the missionary apostolate of Christ's Church. Each Christian is "sent" on mission. This is not to deny or depreciate the special ministry of the ordained priest. It rather restores a long-needed balance: it recalls the common priesthood of all Christians, which is prior in nature to any distinction of ministerial functions, shapes all the baptized to Christ. Each Christian shares inescapably in the priesthood of Christ; each Christian's life is a sacrifice to God; each Christian is minister; each Christian is on mission.

In this fundamental common mission inseparable from baptism, there is, as St. Paul insisted, "neither Jew nor Greek" (no ethnic difference), "neither slave nor free" (no social difference), "neither male nor female" (no sexual difference). Here indeed we are "all one in Christ Jesus" (Gal 3:28).

The thrust of all this can be frightening: each of you is a missionary. Oh, not to Bengal or Bukidnon, but where you are and wherever you go. Your mission fields are the corridors and streets you walk each day, the subways you sway in and the homes you inhabit. Sin and war, hunger and hate—these are in the hearts and hands, in the stomachs and on the lips, of people you pass each day, work with and play with, eat with and drink with, dance with and teach. To all of these you are by baptism agents and signs of the reconciling Christ: agents empowered to represent Christ, signs commissioned to re-present him. It is his life, his love, his forgiveness you have a mission to mediate; and you can mediate it because he works in you to will and to do.

And do not say that you are too weak because so human. Intrinsic to your reconciling mission is that, like Christ, you are so fearfully human. In the comforting language of the Epistle to the Hebrews, you "can deal gently with the ignorant and wayward" because you yourself are "beset with weakness." You are "bound to offer sacrifice for [your] own sins as well as for those of the people." Like Jesus, you too, "in the days of [your] flesh," must offer up "prayers and supplications, with loud cries and tears, to him who [is] able to save [you] from death." Like Jesus, you too will learn "obedience through what [you suffer]" and will become a "source of eternal salvation" to those to whom you minister (Heb 5:2–9).

III

Which brings me to my third point, the cutting edge of this address: What has mission to do with frustration—the mission of the Church with the frustration of the Christian? What does your being "sent" say to a burning Christian complaint, "This is not the Church I knew, the Church in which I grew"?

First, a Church on mission is a Church in change. Why? Because the Church is sent not to some immobile, rigid "world," but to pulsing persons with more colors and cultures, more smells and mind-sets, more yearnings and burnings, more hates and loves than a single finite mind can possibly wrestle with. And in coming to grips with Jewish culture and Greek genius and invading barbarians, in touching mandarins and Moros, WASPS and the Sioux, in its effort to make Christ a real presence to your own children, the Church does not come armed with a catechism and an encyclical. It comes with two paradoxical weapons: the power of God and the weakness of men. The power of God brings ceaseless life to the Church (doctrinal, moral, liturgical), but the weakness of men (your weakness and mine) means that mission will forever involve sin and schism, conflict and confusion, frustration and failure.

Second, as missionaries, you and I dare not see the Church through rose-tinted glasses; for then we will not really recognize the Church. With rose-tinted glasses we might find it hard to recognize the Church unfailingly in the decade since Vatican II closed. The thrilling vision of the Council, to refashion the Church on every level in the image of Christ, has not always been matched by remarkable results. Much good, of course. And yet, many of our people are dreadfully confused, many reformers have simply given up the struggle. Thousands of clergy and religious, many of them my dear friends, have found their vocations empty of meaning or too painful to endure. Churches are emptying, schools closing; Church law is openly defied, Catholics create their own morality, and the pope, to many a Catholic, is a figurehead, just another guy who simply isn't with it.

Frustration indeed; for many, a sort of martyrdom. But the missionary response to frustration, the missionary reaction to martyrdom, is not surrender or despair, not cynicism or sarcasm, not a nostalgia for "the good old days." This is not yet the kingdom; this is the Church. And you are not in heaven; you are on mission. And salvation is still not the work of man; it is the work of God. And so, to all those Catholics, to any of you, who may be weeping over Vatican II, bemoaning a new modernism, holding wakes over dying schools and dead rosaries, I say: "Lift up your eyes! Raise your gaze! Look beyond your kitchen window, out over the world, where two out of every five human beings go to bed hungry each night, where far more than that hunger for the Christ who warms your heart. Take courage from the missionaries you support, the missionaries you love—men who rival Francis for frustration. They do not water gardens of Eden. They touch the rotting lips of lepers, and not too long ago they looked into the hate-filled eyes of Japanese captors. In some places they are permitted to make men human, are forbidden to turn them Christian. Some still hack their way through jungles, others brave waves from island to island.

They take years to build a church, only to see a typhoon devastate it in seconds. These are names, living and dead, that have become dear to you: Hurley and Cervini, Delaney and Halligan, Feeney and Walter, Neylon and Kennally, Costigan and Masterson, Fullam and Cullen, McNulty and McManus and McCoy.[4] The list is endless, as endless as their frustrations, as endless as their hope in Christ."

Dear friends in Christ: I too have known frustration. Oh, not a frustration like Francis'; not even frustration such as yours. But frustration all the same. For it is a sort of martyrdom to be a theologian, to make my life a ceaseless struggle to grasp and express the ways of God with man, and to be mocked by Catholic columnists, charged with heresy, asked why I don't get out of the Church since I'm really out already. It was a sort of martyrdom when, to be true to myself, I had to disagree publicly on a delicate moral issue not with another theologian but with the Vicar of Christ on earth. It was a sort of martyrdom to watch Woodstock destroyed, the place that housed my heart for thirty-five years, the place my head still tells me should still stand. It is a sort of martyrdom to see our Catholic people so confused, so rebellious; our young so alienated from Church structure, so indifferent; Christians lusting for one another's blood in Belfast; Catholics at war over Communion in the hand and the kiss of peace. It is a sort of martyrdom to watch so many of my Jesuit brothers leave my company, our Company, forever. It is a sort of martyrdom to live the priesthood of Christ so unchristly, to look into so many despairing eyes and watch them turn away sadly, because I do not reflect to them the compassion of Christ. It is a sort of martyrdom to come to the late afternoon of life and realize how different I am from the way people see me, how sinful, how desperately far from God.

It is a sort of martyrdom, but let me tell you one lesson I have learned from the missionary Christ, from the missionary Church, from your own Jesuit missionaries: a Church on mission is a Church in hope. The trouble with Catholic hope is that so often it is not Christian, not hope at all. So many rest their hope in pope, in pastor or priest; they hope a Roman document will tear the wolves from our sheepfold; they hope the altar will be turned round again, an organ blare forth Bach again, Roman collars restore the image of a clergy not of this world.

No, my friends, in the Christian vision, hope is because God is. What I admire and love in you is that your hope is *Christian* hope: you hope for God . . . from God. That is how you have brought hope to so many hearts you never see, from Cagayan to Ponape, from Tokyo to Cebu. The human face of the Church is a wrinkled face (as wrinkled as mine), soiled by sin (our sin): we are not yet utterly redeemed. And still you can lift up your hearts, because God is really present: not only in the Waldorf but in Davao. In large measure, God is there because you are here. Here with your very human frustrations, but more importantly, here with your very divine hope.

Not too long ago I told the Jesuit Guild how passionately I love this Company of Jesus, your sons and my brothers, how under God it is largely because of them that I remain happily a Jesuit. Let me add tonight how impassioned is my love for this Church with all its spots and wrinkles, this Church which is on mission, this Church which is one and the same in New York City and Quezon City, this Church which is you. My fearfully human frustrations are transmuted into hope largely because I find on your faces the face of Christ. You must have hours of anguish in this Church on pilgrimage, and still here you are, missionaries to your own missionaries, because you know that what is impossible to men is possible to God. You are a people of irrepressible hope, and so I can say of you what the Frenchman Paul Claudel said of Francis Xavier: "He did what he was told to do—not everything, but all he was able to do."[5] Largely because of you, our missions are missions of hope. And largely because of you, I live a man of hope—and, with God's grace, I hope to die in hope.

25
ECUMENISM 1970 STYLE
To those who want Christians to be one

In 1969 many of us who were actively engaged in the struggle for Christian unity were sensing what a perceptive Methodist theologian, Albert Outler, called the "ecumenical slump." Inspired by Pope John XXIII, the Roman Catholic Church had altered its closed stance, had thrust itself into the movement with unexpected vigor. A decade of unprecedented activity on several levels—papal, episcopal, theological, grass-roots—seemed to carry unlimited promise for the oneness of the churches. But as the sixties drew to a close, a number of committed ecumenists were worried. In both camps, Roman and non-Roman, they espied three tall obstacles: suspicion, impatience, and inertia.

In this context I was invited to preach on June 20, 1969, to a congregation of varied religious hues gathered in the Harvard University Memorial Church. I was then professor of patristic theology at Woodstock College in Maryland, but I suspect that the invitation was more closely linked to my ecumenical involvements: I was then a member of the Baltimore Archdiocesan Commission for Christian Unity and a member of the Lutheran-Roman Catholic Dialogue.

I felt it was imperative to face the three-pronged challenge directly, admit what might be understandable and valid in that challenge, insist nevertheless that to abandon the quest for unity was not a Christian option, and end by opening our perspectives beyond the churches, to the human person.

A decade ago the ecumenical movement, the search for Christian unity, rocketed into a new orbit. What had been primarily a Protestant movement became more globally Christian. The Roman Catholic Church, fired by John XXIII, was incredibly open: to contrition, to conversation, to some form of "conversion," to a recognition of the fact that the unity for which Christ prayed has not been achieved within the unity that is Catholic. Today, a decade later, after amazing advances in understanding and love, a fresh crisis, a new era, faces the total Christian community. At this moment the movement toward Christian unity confronts three powerful enemies: suspicion, impatience, and inertia.

First, suspicion. On both sides, Protestant and Catholic, there are those who suspect that ecumenism is a subtle sellout. For some Catholics, what the past decade has witnessed is a progressive Protestantizing of Catholicism. Dogma is toppling, from indulgences through infallibility to one-true-Church. The liturgy is more and more Protestant, from the wooden table through hillbilly music to the "real absence" of Christ. Traditional devotion is under assault, from the Rosary through the Way of the Cross to the Sacred Heart. Soon we shall have no saint save Luther.

For some Protestants, Protestantism can only suffer from the ecumenical movement, can only lose through compromise what the Reformers lived and died for: protest against idolatry in every shape, against all that displaces the one Mediator, against pope and priest, Mary and merit, law and works. One thing only they want from Romanism: unconditional surrender. For the Catholic Church is still the great harlot of the Apocalypse, and they will not rest satisfied till the angel announces again: "Fallen, fallen is Babylon the great, she who made all nations drink the wine of her impure passion" (Rev 14:8).

A second enemy to ecumenism is impatience. On both sides, Catholic and Protestant, there are those who complain bitterly that the ecumenical movement is dragging its heels. They are angry over failure to move where movement is obviously demanded. Why not offer Communion to anyone who believes that Christ is really present? Why not exchange pulpits? Why not share our sacraments when we are so ready to share our hearts? Why argue about creed and cult, about ministry and authority? In a word, why should doctrine limit our love? If this be ecumenism, a plague on both your houses!

A third enemy to ecumenism is inertia. The honeymoon is over; the original glow has dimmed; the passion that pervaded the beginnings of Catholic-Protestant relations is difficult to sustain. After all, the task is so vast, and we have not the time. Organization is a must, and we cannot stand any more structures. The laity is ill equipped for dialogue, and the clergy on the whole is hardly more competent. And it is so hard to wax enthusiastic about religious unity when the world is coming apart, when human beings are locked in a death struggle in the rice fields of Vietnam and on the streets of Detroit.

In the face of this three-edged challenge, what is the ecumenical response? I shall make three points. First, the challenge is not utterly without foundation, not utterly divorced from reality. Second, despite the challenge, the Christian has no choice, no option: the movement toward unity must go on. Third, the unity Christians seek can no longer be limited to the churches; its perspective must henceforth be man.

I

First, the three-edged challenge (suspicion, impatience, inertia) is not utterly without foundation, not utterly divorced from reality. I am not conceding that ecumenism is a sellout, subtle or
massive. For if conversion is unlikely, compromise is impossible;
we shall not become one by sacrificing what is sacred to us. I am
simply conceding that the third "c" in Gustave Weigel's vision—
convergence—is a perilous adventure. It means that we draw increasingly closer to one another by recognizing where we really
differ from one another. But this can only be achieved by a process
that runs incredible risks. It calls for self-reflection—which means
that the Church is prepared to reappraise critically (as Paul VI insisted) her doctrine, her mission, her very self; that I am ready to
admit my vision is myopic, my faith defective, what I hold about
God and man may be false, may call for refinement, for revision,
for recantation. Convergence calls for dialogue—which means I
come to my brothers and sisters not to debate but to discuss, not
so much to talk as to listen, in the conviction that the Spirit is
speaking through each of the churches. Convergence calls for contrition—which means I agonize within for all the damnable injustice my religious community has inflicted in the name of God, agonize over my contribution to disunity. Convergence calls for
prayer, not only *for* one another but *with* one another. Convergence calls for openness to the future, in the spirit of Vatican II's
unparalleled summons: "This most sacred Synod urgently desires
that the initiatives of the sons of the Catholic Church, joined with
those of the separated brethren, go forward without obstructing
the ways of divine Providence and without prejudging the future
inspiration of the Holy Spirit."[1] And, most demanding and difficult
of all, convergence calls for love—which means I open myself to
another, I become, in the image of Christ, a man or woman for others; this is now my life, my personhood, my Christian existence.

If this be the way to oneness, do you wonder that there is on
the one hand suspicion, on the other impatience? If your commitment to Christ within the community of Catholicism has been deep
and decades long, if your life within the Church has been a glorious experience of the unchanging and the abiding and the secure,
is there not something unnerving about reappraisal, dialogue, contrition, common prayer, openness—yes, even love? If your Protestant heritage is precious to you, if built into that heritage is a conviction that Catholicism is at bottom a betrayal of the gospel

incapable of reformation on principle, is there not something suspicious about Rome's new look? And if, Protestant or Catholic, you are young, keenly conscious of Christianity's unchristian past, in anguish over Christ crucified in his black and his poor, concerned over the "now" in man's distress, how can you fail to be impatient with convergence, with the slow and the gradual? Why not wash your hands of this Roman-Reform "bit," this intermural narcissism? Why fiddle in the sanctuary when the world is ablaze?

II

These questions lead directly to my second affirmation: despite the challenge, the Christian has no choice, no option; the movement toward unity must go on. The mandate stems from Christ and may not be refused. It echoes from the prayer of Christ for the Church universal the night before he died (Jn 17:20–23):

> I do not pray for these only [the disciples], but also for those who believe in me through their word, that they may all be one; even as thou, Father, art in me, and I in thee, that they also may be [one] in us, so that the world may believe that thou hast sent me. The glory which thou hast given me I have given to them, that they may be one even as we are one, I in them and thou in me, that they may become perfectly one, so that the world may know that thou hast sent me and hast loved them even as thou hast loved me.

From the prayer of Christ two ideas emerge. In the first place, those who believe are to be one. Not loosely one, not amorphously one, but "perfectly one"—so perfect a unity that it images the oneness between God the Father and His only Son. What precise form ought this oneness to take if it is to be genuinely Christian, responsive to the prayer of Christ? Here we are torn by uncertainty: we do not know the nature of the unity we seek. But this much we do know: the unity for which Christ prayed is not our present disunity. Oh I know, there are powerful bonds that link us. Vatican II pointed to them: loving belief in God the Father and Christ the Savior; union with Christ through baptism; Scripture as a norm of faith and of action; the sanctifying power of the Spirit; in some instances, the Eucharist and devotion to the Mother of God; and so on and so forth. And still we are dreadfully divided—not on incidental issues but at the very core of our Christian existence: Who is Christ? Where is he to be found? Where is his community? How is he to be worshiped? What does it mean to be a Christian? Questions so basic and so divisive that out of them has been spawned a hate that is of Satan.

No, the disciples of Christ have not become one as the Father and His Christ are one. Since this is so, the Christian has no choice: the movement toward unity must go on. And more intensively than ever, on the level of love as well as truth; for if love without truth is dangerously sentimental, truth without love is coldly unchristian.

From the prayer of Christ a second idea emerges, an idea fundamental to interchurch ecumenism. The reason why the churches, Protestant, Catholic, and Orthodox, can never cease seeking for unity is not something selfish: united we stand, divided we fall. It is not (what may well be true) that only a tightly-knit Christianity can withstand the contemporary assault on religion and its structures. The reason lies deeper, in the urgent words of Christ: "I pray . . . that they may become perfectly one, so that the world may know that thou hast sent me and hast loved them even as thou hast loved me."

In a word, Christian oneness is a witness. To the extent that those who confess Christ are united in understanding and linked in love, the world outside will recognize two crucial Christian mysteries: Christ was sent by God, and we are loved by God. The tragedy is, history bears out the words of Christ—in reverse. We have come a long, sad journey from the first century, when pagans exclaimed in breathless accents "See how these Christians love one another," to the twentieth century, when all over the world men dismiss us with mocking laughter: "See how these Christians hate one another." We have simply not given the world the individual and corporate witness for which the Son of God asked during the supper of his love. This is why Vatican II, in its Decree on Ecumenism, called for a common Christian profession of faith, a witness to our common hope, a co-operation even in social matters; for such cooperation "among all Christians vividly expresses that bond which already unites them, and it sets in clearer relief the features of Christ the Servant."[2]

III

So then, the primary purpose of interchurch unity is witness: witness to the world that God's love has come to us in Christ. This leads directly to my third affirmation: the unity Christians seek can no longer be limited to the churches; its perspective must henceforth be man. Here my springboard is a moving paragraph in which Avery Dulles has voiced his concern over an ecumenism in danger of overemphasizing the past, an ecumenism of interest to only an elite because it does not take its stand in the midst of living men:

> From many quarters ... one hears the call for a new ecumenism—one less committed to historical theological controversies and more in touch with contemporary secular man; one less turned in upon itself, more open to the world and its concerns. The great decisions affecting man's future are being made in the sphere of the secular, and Christianity does not seem to be there. A cry to all the churches rises up from the heart of modern man: "Come to us where we are. Help us to make the passage into the coming technocratic age without falling into the despair and brutality of a new paganism. Teach us sincere respect and affection for our fellow men. If the charity of the Good Samaritan burns in your hearts, show that you share our desires and aspirations. In our struggle to build the city of man, we need the support which your faith and hope alone can give. If you remain comfortably in your churches and cloisters, we are much afraid that God will become a stranger to modern life. Christianity, secluded in a world of its own, will turn into a mere relic to be cherished by a few pious souls."[3]

The underlying insight is this: "ecumenical" properly refers not only to the movement toward unity of the churches, but also to the inescapable Christian task of bringing the gospel to the whole world. There is ecumenism as unity, and there is ecumenism as mission, "an outreach to, concern for, and involvement in the secular order."[4] And this outreach, this concern, this involvement must, I submit, operate on at least two levels: dialogue and service.

On the level of dialogue, the Christian must listen to what the Spirit is saying outside the formal structures of institutional Christianity. The fact is, the grace of God is active, the Spirit is at work, in persons and situations that have no tangible commitment to Christ. The Christian, then, must listen to the Spirit speaking in the arts—from an unbeliever's *Man for All Seasons* to Samuel Beckett's "Two times anything equals zero." The Christian must listen to the Spirit as He speaks through philosophy—through personalism and existentialism, through process philosophy and linguistic analysis. The Christian must listen to the Spirit as He speaks through the university—through every discipline that touches the human person. The Christian must listen to the Spirit as He speaks through the Jews; for, in the inflexible affirmation of St. Paul,

"God has not rejected His people whom He foreknew" (Rom 11:2). The Christian must listen to the Spirit as He speaks through living man—man as he cries to us that he cannot discover God in creation or abstraction, as he stands mute and unresponsive before an immutable God whose love does not break through the miasma of evil, as he insists that, if he is to find God at all, he must somehow find Him in man.

On the level of service, the churches have a common task: as communities and as individuals, we must bring the compassionate Christ, the servant Christ, to a sick and suffering society. The meeting place of God and man is not only the altar rail. Often it is a stinking slum in Washington or a rat-plagued tenement in Harlem, a street in Selma or a jail in Jackson, a vineyard in Delano or a decaying schoolhouse in Appalachia. In point of fact, we shall not *bring* Christ there; he *is* there—wherever man is. But man will not *know* Christ is there, will not see his face, unless we are there, unless he sees the face of Christ in our face.

In his address opening the second session of Vatican II on September 29, 1963, Pope Paul VI addressed himself to the fourth aim of the Council: "the Church will build a bridge to the contemporary world." He made it clear that "the Church looks at the world with profound understanding, with the sincere intention not of conquering it but of serving it." He listed categories of human beings on whom the Church looks with particular solicitude: "the poor, the needy, the afflicted, the hungry, the suffering and sorrowing." He stressed that the Church looks to "men of culture and learning . . . to defend their liberty," to "the workers" and their "mission to create a new world," to "the leaders of nations" and their power to "make of humanity a single city," to "the new generation of youth desirous of living and expressing themselves," to "the new peoples now coming to self-awareness, independence, and civil organization." To all without exception he proclaimed Christianity's "good news of salvation and hope." Here, my brothers and sisters in Christ, here is ecumenism as mission; here is the field of your service.

This is not to reduce the Church or the ecumenical movement to just another secular social-service agency. Karl Rahner met this problem head on in some remarks at the St. Louis University Divinity School on October 12, 1967:

> . . . today more than ever the churches bear a gigantic responsibility in our society for bringing about justice, peace, and a life

of dignity and equality for all men. The churches cannot withdraw to the sacristy. They cannot promote merely a private and individualistic interiority, and be concerned only with the private and other-worldly salvation of the individual. But the churches can fulfill this responsibility and task in the world and for the world [only] if they remain truly Christian, and do not degenerate into a vague humanism. The radical obligation to love one's neighbor in the social and political sphere remains vital and effective only if one believes in God, his justice, his eternal life; only if one prays; only if the Lord's death is preached until he comes to judge the living and the dead.[5]

My dear brothers and sisters in Christ: I have set before you what I see to be "ecumenism 1970 style." It recognizes that the Christian has no choice but to work toward Christian oneness. At the same time it is agonizingly aware that the unity Christians seek cannot be limited to the churches: its perspective must be man. We must live what that remarkable rabbi, Abraham Joshua Heschel, wrote several years ago:

> To meet a human being is a major challenge to mind and heart. I must recall what I normally forget. A person is not just a specimen of the species called *homo sapiens*. He is all of humanity in one, and whenever one man is hurt we are all injured. The human is a disclosure of the divine, and all men are one in God's care for man. Many things on earth are precious, some are holy, humanity is holy of holies.
> To meet a human being is an opportunity to sense the image of God, *the presence* of God. According to a rabbinical interpretation, the Lord said to Moses: "Wherever you see the trace of man there I stand before you. . . ."[6]

Tonight a new era opens to man: the first footstep on the moon. We are about to complete the crash program of a decade— involving thousands of workers, 24 billion dollars, international cooperation. And all this time, x number of human beings are starving in the United States, 36,000 Americans have been killed in Vietnam, our cities are jungles. And so tonight, when the first man walks on the moon, my joy will be tempered, my excitement dulled. For I shall be thinking of the human beings who walk this earth without hope. I shall see a hungry child staring at me with eyes that do not understand, a soldier with no arms and no legs, a white man and a black man lusting for each other's blood.

My brothers and sisters, here lies ecumenism—1970 style.

26
ISRAEL: A LIGHT TO THE GENTILES?
To our ancestors in faith

It was a "first" on both sides. The Reform Synagogue in White Plains, New York, had never before welcomed a Catholic priest to its holy place; and I, for my part, had never entered a synagogue, much less to speak therein. At that time, February 21, 1964, Catholic-Jewish relations were just beginning to improve. Pope Paul VI had visited Israel seven weeks before, but twenty months were to elapse before Vatican II issued its Declaration on the Relationship of the Church to Non-Christian Religions, the springboard for a profound effort to heal the wounds of centuries.

I was there to give a message that would be my own and still a word from the Catholic community. The task was extraordinarily hard, for we were more than strangers: I represented an institution that to many of my listeners was hostile to Judaism, bore a large responsibility for the traditional plight of the wandering Jew and the ghetto Jew. We were severed by Jesus, by our histories, in our day-to-day living. I could hardly ask my listeners to "forget it"; to the Jew, as Elie Wiesel put it, "whoever forgets becomes the executioner's accomplice."

I decided to make a small beginning toward reconciliation by focusing on the famous Suffering Servant passage in Isaiah. I had read that for the last eight centuries most Jewish interpreters had seen in the Servant the Jewish people, had seen in his sufferings not only the agony of the Captivity but the sufferings of the whole Jewish people. I wanted to suggest the redemptive power of Jewish suffering—for them and for me. It was, at best, a magnificent failure. From certain reactions, then and later, especially from the young, I was forced to conclude that a theology of redemptive suffering makes little or no sense if your history includes (among much else) the Holocaust. It was a disturbing experience that has served me well in Jewish-Christian dialogue: not only are my eyes more open to the complexities of our historical and theological problems; my heart has expanded in love and compassion for living, loving people "of [whose] race is the Christ" (Rom 9:5).

This is a historic moment. It is not spectacular: it does not rival the entrance into Israel of Pope Paul, the first pontiff since Peter to walk among the olive trees and cypresses of that lovely land. But the underlying significance is the same. A Catholic priest walks reverently into the holy place of the Jewish community, with a message of love. This is historic—hands clasped over centuries; and, please God, it will not end with this night, with this message.

I

The problem is: What is the message to be? After nineteen hundred years, what is the message to be? For we are dreadfully divided. We are divided in doctrine, we are severed by history, we are divorced in day-to-day living.

In doctrine, a single word divides us: Jesus. Good man or God-man? The Christ or a pale prophet? Holy One of God or misguided rebel? It is the anguished question of John the Baptist from a prison cell: "Art thou he who is to come, or shall we look for another?" (Mt 11:3). Or, shall we look for no one?

History severs you from us: every Jewish ghetto ever structured by Christians; every forced baptism; every Crusade to liberate the Holy Places; every Good Friday pogrom; every forced exodus like 1492; every portrait of Shylock exacting his pound of flesh; every accusation of deicide; every Dachau and every Auschwitz; every death for conscience' sake; every back turned or shoulder shrugged; every sneer or slap or curse.

And we are divorced in day-to-day living: by a Sunday-closing law; by a Supreme Court decision on prayer in public schools; by a Jesuit editorial warning "our Jewish friends" against anti-Semitism; by the reaction of Christians to the Eichmann trial; by Christmas in Grand Central Station; by a play on Broadway about a "political" pope and gas chambers. And beneath all this is the basic problem of an American society whose spirit, principles, and conduct are allegedly Christian—so much so that an articulate Jew has written:

> It is not that Christianity is abhorrent to the Jew . . . ; it is rather that the Jew is simply not Christian, that he believes that *he*, not the Christian, has a truer view of God and man. If then the Jew must choose between a society which is Christian and one which is religiously neutral, he will obviously prefer the latter. If, however, this is not the choice, if American society is rather, as some Christian thinkers argue, an essentially Christian society . . . then Jews might, it seems to me, prefer a return to the ghetto which, however socially isolated, was spiritually free.[1]

We are, therefore, frightfully divided: in doctrine, in history, in daily living. In this context, what is the Catholic message to be? Much could be said. I could say: the contemporary Catholic with a sense of history looks back with shame and sorrow upon much of the Christian past—and this would be true. Too often in history men who call themselves Christians have ceased to be not simply Christian but human, have failed to grasp what a fictional Jew phrased so realistically:

> Hath not a Jew eyes? hath not a Jew hands, organs, dimensions, senses, affections, passions? fed with the same food, hurt with the same weapons, subject to the same diseases, heal'd by the same means, warm'd and cool'd by the same winter and summer, as a Christian is? If you prick us, do we not bleed? if you tickle us, do we not laugh? if you poison us, do we not die? . . .[2]

I could say: though there is much that divides us, there is much that unites us—and this too would be true. The Catholic cannot but revere the "Guiding Principles of Reform Judaism," can only rejoice when he reads:

> 1. [Judaism's] message is universal, aiming at the union and perfection of mankind under the sovereignty of God. . . . Judaism welcomes all truth, whether written in the pages of scripture or deciphered from the records of nature.
>
> 2. The heart of Judaism and its chief contribution to religion is the doctrine of the One, living God, who rules the world through law and love. In Him all existence has its creative source and mankind its ideal of conduct. Though transcending time and space, He is the indwelling Presence of the world. We worship Him as the Lord of the universe and as our merciful Father.
>
> 3. Judaism affirms that man is created in the Divine image. His spirit is immortal. He is an active co-worker with God. As a child of God, he is endowed with moral freedom and is charged with the responsibility of overcoming evil and striving after ideal ends.[3]

In the light of all this, a Catholic sermon from a Jewish pulpit might well be a message of repentance and of reverence: repentance for your past, reverence for your present; a Catholic contrition for our part in your sufferings, a Catholic recognition of your deep devotion to God and to man. Nevertheless, I shall focus on your future. I shall try to show how, as I see it, the anguish of your past and the godliness of your present can be integrated into a meaningful future, into a mission that is genuinely Messianic, a mission that will make of Israel "a light to the Gentiles" (Lk 2:32).

II

In the biblical book traditionally called Isaiah, there is a long section, beginning with chapter 40, which modern scholars call the Book of the Consolation of Israel. Within that section there is a remarkable passage (52:13—53:12) which deals with the Suffering Servant. Now I am aware that over the centuries Jewish interpreters have found this a puzzling passage. I know that, for some of them, the Servant is the righteous worshiper of God; for others, some sort of Messiah; for still others, an individual figure like Jeremiah or Hezekiah or Nehemiah, Job or Josiah. But seemingly from the twelfth century on, the more common view has seen in the Servant the Jewish people as a whole, or at least the righteous element among them; and in the suffering of the Servant, not only the agony of the Captivity, but all the sufferings of the Jewish people to the time of the particular rabbi discussing the text. It is in this light that I would read to you the inspired passage on the Suffering Servant:

Who could have believed what we heard?
And the might of the Lord—to whom has it been revealed?
For he grew up like a sapling before us,
Like a root out of dry ground;
He had no form or charm, that we should look upon him,
No beauty, that we should admire him.
He was despised, and avoided by men,
A man of sorrows, and acquainted with pain;
And like one from whom men hide their faces,
He was despised, and we esteemed him not.

Yet it was our pains that he bore,
Our sorrows that he carried;
While we accounted him stricken,
Smitten by God, and afflicted.
He was wounded for our transgressions,
He was crushed for our iniquities;
The chastisement of our welfare was upon him,
And through his stripes we were healed.
All we like sheep had gone astray,
We had turned everyone to his own way;
And the Lord made to light upon him
The guilt of us all.

When he was oppressed, he humbled himself,

And opened not his mouth;
Like a sheep that is led to the slaughter,
Or like a ewe that is dumb before her shearers,
He opened not his mouth.
Through violence in judgment was he taken away,
And who gave thought to his fate—
How he was cut off from the land of the living,
For our transgressions was stricken to death?
They made his grave with the wicked,
His tomb with evildoers;
Although he had done no violence,
Nor was any deceit in his mouth.

Yet the Lord saw fit to crush him with pain,
So that, although he makes himself a guilt-offering,
He shall see posterity, shall prolong his life,
And the pleasure of the Lord shall prosper in his hand.
The fruit of his suffering shall he see,
In knowing himself righteous he shall be satisfied;
My servant shall bring righteousness to many,
And he shall himself bear their guilt.
Therefore will I divide him a portion with the great,
And with the strong shall he share the spoil;
Because he poured out his lifeblood to the utmost,
And was numbered with the transgressors,
And himself bore the sin of many,
And made intercession for the transgressors.

(Isa 53:1–12; Chicago)

My dear friends: What confronts us in this sacred passage is the role of suffering in the life of God's servant. You see, for a human being, suffering can be many things. It can be a sheer fact of human existence, to be endured in stoic fashion, without fear or tear. Or it can be a meaningless thing, against which I cry to heaven in protest. Or it can seem divine rejection, God's curse on my sinfulness. Or it can be the source of resentment, of bitterness, of hatred, of revenge.

For the believing Jew, however, suffering can never be a mere fact of life, never without meaning, never God's rejection of His people; above all, it dare not be the seedbed of hate, of division. And precisely here, as I see it, lie the peril in your past and the possibilities in your future. The peril is that the sufferings of your past, from Babylon to Dachau, may drive you further and further from the non-Jewish world. And this would be tragic: tragic for us, who are not quite whole without you; and tragic for you, who have pro-

claimed to the world: "We regard it as our historic task to co-operate with all men in the establishment of the kingdom of God, of
universal brotherhood, justice, truth and peace on earth. This is
our Messianic goal."[4]

The possibilities in your future stem from a deeper insight
into suffering. For if Isaiah speaks to Israel at all, in your own tradition he speaks to *you*; and if the prophet speaks to you, his meaning
is that your suffering is not sheer punishment for a sinful past, is
not mere education for a sinless future. Its ultimate design is redemption, for you and for me. I mean, it is intended to bring you,
and me through you, closer to God.

> My servant shall bring righteousness to many . . .
> Because he poured out his lifeblood to the utmost,
> And was numbered with the transgressors,
> And himself bore the sin of many,
> And made intercession for the transgressors.
>   (Isa 53:11–12)

How, concretely, can the Jewish attitude to suffering affect the
redemption of Catholics? In two ways. First, by example. I do not
mean the example of passivity: naked endurance need not be godly
at all. I do not exclude protest: remonstrance is called for whether
a single Jew is tortured or six million. I mean the example of a people whose suffering has increased not their isolation but their love,
whose blood is a prayer not for revenge but for forgiveness, whose
oppression makes them weep for all the oppressed—a people
whose pain has brought them closer to God and to men. The example of such a suffering servant will inspire the Catholic to compassion and love, to forgiveness of men and oneness with God.

There is a second way in which Jewish suffering can touch
Christian redemption. It is not easy to understand, because it is
hidden in the mystery that is God. But this much can be said, and
this much Isaiah reveals: God does accept the suffering of His servants, to bring salvation to others. In the establishment of God's
kingdom, on earth and within me, I cannot say to you, "You have
no effect on me"; and you dare not say to me, "You are no concern
of mine." Your suffering, yesterday and today and tomorrow, offered to God on the altar of your flesh, can bring God to my heart,
God's love to my life. The pain of a suffering servant may enable
me to observe the two great commandments of the law: to love
God above all else, with my whole heart, and to love my fellow
man, every man, you, as I love myself.

For all this, and much more, I extend to you my warm gratitude, my deep love, and the blessing which God Himself phrased for you centuries ago:

> The Lord said to Moses,
> "Say to Aaron and his sons, 'This is the way that
>   you are to bless the Israelites; say to them,
> The Lord bless you, and guard you;
> The Lord make His face to shine upon you,
>   and be gracious unto you;
> The Lord lift up His countenance upon you,
>   and make you prosper!' "
>
>   (Num 6:22–26)

27

FREE? IN PRISON?
To women in chains

It was a unique challenge. Four women were to graduate with the equivalent of a high-school diploma. To graduate, but not to leave the institution. They were prisoners in a women's reformatory in Maryland, committed on a variety of charges. One I remember in particular, a face striking in its bone structure; she had shot an abusive husband to death.

The audience, too, was unusual: in the main, several hundred female convicts. The crimes? Armed robbery, murder, prostitution—you name it. The ages? Fifteen and up. Intelligence? Feeble-minded to genius. Each in a shapeless uniform, the color beyond my recalling, save that it was depressingly drab. Marching into the auditorium single file, under the eye of expressionless guards. Looking at me and my Roman collar, some curious, most just bored.

Up the center aisle walked the "graduates"—in cap and gown (God bless that sensitive lady superintendent!), to the strains of "Pomp and Circumstance." Four women, stepping forward to clutch a precious piece of paper, stepping back to . . . a cell. What could a theology professor say to them, say to the "captive audience"?

Not a homily, you may object. Right on! Bars instead of stained-glass windows; guards for ushers; a community not of faith, hope, and love, but of cynicism, despair, and hate. But if we are to preach "release to captives" (Lk 4:18), I suggest we must often go where they are, where they are held captive. And when we get where they are, when we reach this shapeless mass, what liberating word do we have for them? What would you have preached?

Last October I spoke to the men at the Maryland Penitentiary, the Maryland Jail. It was the feast of their patron saint, St. Dismas, the thief who was crucified at the right hand of Christ on Calvary, the thief who heard Christ whisper: "This day you will be with me in paradise." That morning I asked one of the prisoners what in prison life he found hardest to take. He was a very sensible young fellow, intelligent, and he answered: "Father, for the most part it's not too bad. They're quite kind to me here: I'm learning a trade; I have friends; I have some time to myself; even the food could be worse. But the one thing I don't have is the one thing I want: I don't have freedom; I'm not free."

If I were to ask you the same question—what is the hardest

thing to take here?—I suspect your answer would be pretty much the same. Most of it you can take; most of it you can endure; what is difficult to take, difficult to endure, is the most important thing of all: you are not free. You do what you are told to do; you do it when you are told to do it; you do it where you are told to do it. From the moment you rise to the moment you lie down again, you do what the State of Maryland wants you to do. You cannot call your life your own. You are not free.

The point I shall make this afternoon is this: there is a part of your life that is utterly free, a part of your life that no state can take from you, no power can force. In that aspect of everyday living you do as you please; in every waking hour you are as free as president or pope, you are as free as I. There is a part of your life no human being can enter, unless you say yes. I mean: your mind, your thoughts.

I

You see, what I think is not determined by where I am. Just because I am kneeling in church does not mean that my thoughts are fixed on God. So too for you. The state can put you behind bars for stealing; it cannot compel you to believe that stealing is sin. It can put you in total darkness; it cannot extinguish the light in your mind. It can make you *say* "I'm sorry"; it cannot make you *think* it. It can keep you here for a lifetime; it cannot make you like it. I can talk to you till sundown with all the warmth of my soul; and you— you can close your mind to every word. Why? Because your mind is your own. God *will* not force it, and man *can* not. There is only one way to destroy that freedom—and that would be to destroy *you*.

It is a remarkable gift, this power to know, this power to think. Why can it not be taken from you by force? Because it is one of the qualities which make you a human being, which make you so very much like God. Do you remember the words of Scripture when it describes the sixth day of creation? "And God created man to His own image; to the image of God He created him; male and female He created them." What does this mean? It means that every human being bears a striking likeness to his Lord. It means that, no matter who you are, no matter what your blood or skin or accent, you come into this world sharing two of God's precious perfections: you have the power to know, and you have the power to love.

It is the power to know that interests me now. You are like God in that you have intelligence, you have the power to know. Not as a plant knows where the sun is; that is a figure of speech. Not as a dog knows where an enemy lurks; that is a question of seeing and hearing and touching and tasting and smelling. No; of all earth's creatures, you alone can think. You alone can put 2 and 2 together and get 4. You alone can fashion the formula for an H-bomb. Only you can appreciate a sonata, a cantata, or a fugue. Only you can think of God; only you can know God.

II

So then: you have the power to think; this power makes you somewhat like God; this power no human being can take from you. This is where your freedom lies—you are master of your mind. But the big question is: what are you going to think about? This is the big question, because this is what separates the big people from the little, the women from the girls, the good from the bad, the wise from the foolish. It all depends upon what is going on inside of you, in that mind of yours which nobody else can touch.

On broad lines, there are two ways you can think. You can, if you wish, make all your thinking center around yourself. You can pity yourself for the pitiful situation you are in. You can blame others—mother, father, relatives, friends, enemies, society, a cop, a stoolie—for what they have done to you or have not done. You can hate, with a hatred bitter as bile. You can plot revenge, lick your lips in devilish anticipation of what will happen when you get out. You can think lustful thoughts, all the more frustrating because you can do so little about them. You can be selfish and catty and angry; you can be mean and obscene. And all you will achieve is this: you will be small, foolish, ignorant, inhuman, unloved and unlovable.

Or you can do just the opposite. You can fill your mind with what is true, what is beautiful, and what is good. By reading and thinking, by talking and listening—yes, by praying too—you can open your mind like a ripening bud to truth and beauty and goodness. Instead of imprisoning your mind in Jessup, you can let it roam over the world, to Europe and Asia and Africa, even to those Communist-controlled lands where men and women are far less fortunate than you, because unlike you they have no hope. You can fill your mind with history, with the story of man and what he has done, because this is *your* story. You can learn how to *do* things: to make and create. You can grace your mind with art and music and literature. You can even think about God; at least, don't close your mind to Him, for He loves you very dearly, and He wants so very much to live in you. Do this, and you will achieve a remarkable change, a transformation; you will be a different person: you will be much wiser, much more mature, .much more human, much more lovable.

III

And that, I suggest, is what makes this occasion, this graduation, such a striking thing. Had they wanted to, these young women might well have imprisoned their minds as well as their bodies in Jessup. They could have been content with the little they knew; they could have closed their minds to the outside world, to truth and beauty and goodness, could have closed their minds to everything except their own small selves. Had they done so, they would this day be tragic women, because they would be women without hope. And a human without hope is not quite human; a woman without hope is not quite womanly.

But this they have not done. They have used their minds as God intends minds to be used. They have opened their minds—opened them to a little more truth, a little more beauty, a little more goodness. And so they are this day a little more divine, because they are a little more like the God who *is* Truth, who *is* Beauty, who *is* Goodness. And they are a great deal more human, because their minds are so much more free. More divine, more human; no wonder their hope is high.

My dear young women: I am unbelievably moved by what you have achieved—far more moved than I have ever been at a graduation outside these walls. Outside, young women are free—so free that most of them resist knowledge. Here, only your mind is free—and you have opened it to knowledge. That is why my hope for your future is so high: high hope that, when you are utterly free, you will use your freedom to know what is true, to love what is good, to do what is right. God bless you, and keep you ever in His care!

28
TRUTH, JUSTICE, LOVE—AND FREEDOM
To architects of a new social order

Not a homily or sermon, but an address whose focal thesis, I am convinced, ought to be preached. Truth, justice, and love—so central in the Christian tradition—are insufficient service to humankind if the man or woman they serve is not free.

The occasion was a May 1971 Seminar on Reconstructing the Social Order and the World of Work, sponsored by Temple University's School of Business and the Association for Social Economics, at the Albert M. Greenfield Conference Center in Chestnut Hill, Pa. Convened on the eightieth anniversary of Rerum novarum, *the fortieth of* Quadragesimo anno, *and the tenth of* Mater et magistra, *the seminar explored progress in this century, described the condition of the workingman, and fashioned guidelines to help promote a social order with truth and justice.*

Influential people participated: e.g., Leon Ter-Davtian of the Organization for Economic Co-operation and Development (Paris); James D. Hodgson, Secretary of Labor; Dean Seymour L. Wolfbein of Temple's School of Business Administration; Donald McGannon, president of Westinghouse Broadcasting Company; Walter Maggiolo of the Federal Mediation and Conciliation Service.

At the closing luncheon, I tried to show how the three traditional Catholic principles of social order—truth, justice, and love—had finally been rounded out with a fourth principle indispensable in our time. And the Church must accent not only the inner core of freedom but the external conditions that make it possible to act in freedom.

My task today is uncommonly difficult. This seminar has brought together architects of a new social order; it is understandable that you should be asked, with your considerable competences, to create a new world of work. What passes understanding is that the same seminar should link your lunch with my theology, that a silver-thatched theologian reeking of royal octavo should be asked to close this conference on the high note that has characterized its course.

I shall not mimic your technical expertise; you would soon ferret out the phony in me. I shall do what comes much more naturally: I shall take the experience of the Church—my Church—in one living area and touch it to your concerns—if only to keep you from repeating our mistake.

My thesis is simply this: In its efforts to construct a liveable, viable social order, the Church did well to stress three facets of human living: truth, justice, and love. Where the Church failed was in its failure to recognize that truth, justice, and love are not enough, are not really there, if the man they serve is not free. Let me explain my thesis by moving swiftly and relentlessly from truth, through justice and love, to freedom.

I

A rich word in the Catholic lexicon is "truth." I grew up with it—at home, in school, yes even with the Jesuits! There was strong stress on making sure that what I thought and what I said were conformed to what is. Our philosophy, our whole way of life, was built around truth: learning how to move from the world of sense (see, hear, touch, taste, smell) to the world of understanding. How to use the verb "to be," how to affirm what is, the relationship between a subject and an object.

And it was frightfully important. There was all the difference in the world between "God is" and "God is not," between "man is flesh and spirit" and "man is a chemical compound," between "America is a democracy" and "America is a tyranny," between "murder is wrong" and "murder is getting caught." That monosyllable "is" was the most significant single word in our vocabulary.

And truth was frightfully important for the social order. The Catholic social movement dared not build on a lie, not even on error. That is why Leo XIII had to reject the solution of socialism so attractive to the working class; why Pius XI condemned the thesis that the economic order and the moral are alien one to the other; why Pius XII reminded Italian civil servants that work done with God and for God is prayer; why John XXIII insisted that fat nations have a responsibility to the lean. What the popes saw with admirable lucidity was that Catholic social principles had to treasure truth because they had to respect reality: on the one hand, the nature of things; on the other, changing conditions of man's social existence.

Yes, we did well to make truth central to our lives. It may well be that we overdid it, that our truth was so abstract as at times to seem unreal, so cold as to lack compassion, so objective as to hang suspended in mid-air, divorced from history and from people. But on the whole the emphasis was good, its results were fruitful. Without it, the social encyclicals could never have been framed—*Rerum novarum, Quadragesimo anno, Mater et magistra, Pacem in terris.* Without it, you will never fashion a viable social order; for to be severed from the true is to be severed from the real.

II

A second rich word in the Catholic lexicon is "justice." Again, I grew up with it—at home, in school, yes even with the Jesuits! There was strong stress on giving to every human being, to individuals and communities, what was their due. Our ethics, our moral philosophy, focused on justice: learning how to move from the childish world of "mine" ("gimme") to the mature world of "mine and thine," of rights and duties.

As with truth, so with justice—it was frightfully important. Without what St. Thomas Aquinas called "the strong and firm will to give to each his due,"[1] life could only be warfare—ruthless, relentless, pitiless. Without it, there could be no government and no laws, no measures for the common good, no fair distribution of burdens and privileges.

And so justice was frightfully important for the social order. Past ages of privileged classes—even more, ages of individualism—ignored a perspective of justice that the twentieth century came to prize: social justice. From the time of Pius XI's *Quadragesimo anno* (1931), social justice became recognized as a new and important subspecies of justice. Its chief concern was not so much legal rights and duties; its chief concern was natural rights. And natural rights of many communities: the economic community, where the worker should be paid as a member of a family; the domestic community, where the child has a right to a wholesome family and genuinely human growth; the political community, where the state must safeguard the right to life and work, to equality and security; the community of nations, where no country can say to another "I have no need of you," and no country can say to another "I have no duty toward you."

We did well to stress justice. It may be that we overdid it, that we were open to overkill, that we stressed duties at the expense of rights, that we played up the Greek notion of justice and played down the biblical, did not insist enough that justice among men is a Christian virtue only if it is an extension of the grateful justice we owe to God; we did not see that justice *demands* love. But on the whole the emphasis was good, its results were fruitful. America is the richer for the Catholic emphasis on law and order, on the larger family that is the family of man, on doing not so much your "thing" as your duty. Without such stress, you will never fashion a viable social order: for to refuse what is due is not only to reject order; it is to refuse to be social.

III

A third rich word in the Catholic lexicon is "love." Again, I grew up with it—at home (where its expression was largely in terms of justice: my brother and I got, in generous portions, everything we had coming to us), in school (where its expression was largely in terms of truth: to know the truth is the first step toward loving it), yes even with the Jesuits! There was strong stress on the two great commandments: love God with your whole being, love your fellow man as you love yourself. Our theology focused on love; for our theology was summed up by John Courtney Murray in two sentences which Thomas Aquinas borrowed from the sixth century. (1) Love is a centripetal force. That is, love makes for oneness; the lover produces another self. (2) Love is a centrifugal force. That is, love carries the lover outside himself; the lover becomes self-less.

As with truth and justice, so with love—it was frightfully important. Unless we give, not simply of our goods but of our selves, not simply what we have but what we are, life becomes a computer: truth is a system, and justice a blindfolded lady with scales and a sword.

And love was frightfully important for the social order. For family, for state, for society, for the world community. We knew that living together without loving could only turn a marriage barren. We sensed that law without love might well lead the unloved to lawlessness. We read that unless we loved, the poor would never forgive us for the bread we gave them. And through sweat and blood and tears we came to see that our "one world" is not really one just because satellites beam one picture to Europe and America, just because atomic annihilation is one push button away; that Vietnamization without love could scorch not only the earth but the hearts of those we wanted to help.

We did well to stress love's urgency. It may be that our rhetoric surpassed our performance. It took us too long to grasp that Gospel love is not an excess of love, is as much a duty as Greek justice. In practice so many of us limited our love—to our own color, to our own country, to our own creed: a white American Catholic love. We have not solved the age-old dilemma, how to kill your enemy and still claim you love him. But on the whole the emphasis was good, its results were fruitful. If today's unbeliever is not tempted to repeat with his first-century counterpart "Look how these Christians love," still the Church's love has softened the furrowed face of man, transmuted despair into hope. Without a love accent, you will never fashion a viable social order; for only if you love will you respect diversity, all that is original in another, in man or nation. Only if you love will you be human.

IV

Truth, justice, love—by all odds we should have created a viable social order. We have not. In the century since Leo XIII, the "mother and teacher" (*mater et magistra*) should have achieved a measure of "peace on earth" (*pacem in terris*). She has not. Oh I know, some situations have improved: the workingman is better off than he was in 1891; the citizen is (in much of the Western world), participant in, not merely subject to, the processes of government; the nations are more sensitive to international community than ever before in history (ping-pong players of the world, unite!). But by and large, man is dissatisfied, angry, perched on the edge of revolution. Where? Not only in the emerging nations of Africa, but in the sophisticated Americas. Not only in the America to the south of us, but in the America you and I walk each day. Why? Because all too many human beings go to bed each night inhumanly hungry; because all too many human beings are compelled to lust for the blood of other human beings; because all too many human beings are refused a human existence for the simple reason that they are black.

Oh I know, the Church is only one factor in the social process, hampered and harassed, at times denied any role in public life— from the France of 1880 to the Poland of 1970. Many reasons must conspire to explain it adequately. I submit, however, that one formidable factor has rarely been highlighted enough. It was only with John XXIII that the Church put on the same level with truth, justice, and love a fourth principle of social order to structure our philosophy of society and state. I mean . . . freedom.

Now "freedom" has a rich history within Catholic thought. It has long been part of my philosophical and theological baggage: the free disobedience of the first man that originated our sinful schizophrenia; the free obedience of Christ that makes the children of God genuinely free; the psychological freedom, the inner yes or no, that makes me human; the free commitment to Christ that makes me Christian—all this and so much more.

The problem is, our accent has been on the inner core of freedom. Little accent on the external conditions that make it possible for a person to *be* free, to *live* freely, to *act* in freedom. Why, it took the Church till 1965 to catch up with the nineteenth century, to declare officially that religious freedom is a human right, that "the very dignity of the human person" demands that "in matters religious no one is to be forced to act in a manner contrary to his own beliefs, nor is anyone to be restrained from acting in accordance with his own beliefs."[2] Similarly, the Church has been dreadfully reluctant to state publicly that man must be allowed to seize more and more the reins of his own destiny, directing it toward a society where he will be free of every kind of slavery. Oh, not in general terms—the abstract principles flood our documents. Reluctant rather to speak out for freedom in concrete cases. In Latin America, for example, where seven out of every ten persons live in grinding poverty, it is only recently (and not totally) that the Church has begun to emerge from its ghetto situation, shake off the ambiguous protection of the moneyed and the powerful, break with the unjust order to which it is bound in a thousand conscious or unconscious ways, denounce the institutionalized violence that has kept a continent in chains, speak not so much of "development" as of "liberation." And in Latin America, to speak of liberation is to risk revolution.

In our own country, the Church's record of caution and *status quo*, our historic reluctance to leave the rarefied atmosphere of principle and point an accusing finger at situations and institutions that enslave—this has created in the popular mind the image of a power structure that does not care, that does not weep when human flesh bleeds and starves and dies. George Higgins and Frank Quinn, James Groppi and Dan Berrigan, yes indeed—these *individuals* say something to the poor and the oppressed; but "the Church"? Forget it!

I shall never forget the annual meeting of the Catholic Theological Society of America in 1968. I was president—but that is not quite why the meeting is unforgettable. Not far from the hotel where we were meeting stood two symbols of our impotence. The twin symbols were Resurrection City and the Pentagon. That very day the Poor People were marching on Washington. Naked feet and swollen bellies, they were crying out for one thing: bread with dignity. The scandal was, the Poor People's March had nothing to do with the Catholic vision of man. They did not know we theologians existed; if they had known, they would not have cared. For we did not have an effective theology of wealth, effective because not only intelligent but passionate. In their minds Catholic theology had consecrated two values: the sacredness of property and the glory of following the naked Christ naked. And in their concrete circumstances these values could only tighten their chains.

The second symbol was the Pentagon. That very day several hundred human beings (men, women, children) were to die in Vietnam—blown to bits, burned to a crisp, knifed in the dark. The scandal was, life in Southeast Asia, death in a rice paddy, had nothing to do with the Catholic vision of man. The warmakers (I do not use the word pejoratively) did not know we existed; if they had known, they would not have cared. For we did not have an effective theology of war, effective because not only intelligent but passionate. In their minds Catholic theology had consecrated two values: patriotism and obedience. And at that moment these values had no power to make men free, only to make them kill.

Where the Church has failed is in its failure to recognize that in the building of a social order truth, justice, and love are not enough if the man they serve is not free. In fact, truth, justice, and love are not really there if the man they serve is not free. Free not in that he can do whatever he wants. Free rather because he can in some real sense decide his destiny, has something to say about the food he eats and the air he breathes and the house he sleeps in and the bus he rides on and the work he sweats at and the school his children go to and the war he fights in and the toilet he urinates in. Free because he *feels* human, because each waking day is not a burden too heavy to endure. Unless such freedom is the rule, is the common climate of our social order, the Catholic Church cannot say that our society is constructed on truth, on justice, on love.

Much of what I have said about freedom is now history. You cannot change history, but you can refuse to repeat it. The tragedy would be for America to imitate the Catholic myopia. And the danger is indeed a present danger. Not because you are hostile to freedom. Rather because in any era of profound change, in any revolution, you can so concentrate on the surface manifestations of a movement as to miss the valid dynamisms at work beneath the surface. This happened to the Catholic Church in the nineteenth and early-twentieth centuries. Only a few individuals were perceptive enough to do a work of discrimination, to discern the signs of the times, in order to discover, beneath the transitory historical forms assumed by each new movement, the legitimate work of growth and progress going on in the depths. Only a few saw, beneath the violent separation of Church and state, the valid effort of civil society to differentiate itself from the religious community. Only a few saw, beneath the heresy called Modernism, the valid movement away from the mentality of classicism (truth somewhere out there, apart from history and people) to historical consciousness (truth ever in the quicksilver grasp of a human person). Only a few saw, beneath the cloak of anticlericalism, the heart's true yearning for freedom.

Something of the same sort can happen today—is happening today. You can, with countless of your countrymen, focus on speed and shoulder-length hair, on campus violence and Panther bombs, on draft-file burnings and Kissinger kidnapings, and blind yourselves to the radical rebellion they symbolize. I mean the widespread rejection of a society less willing to risk property than the lives of its children, a political system where the people are not sufficiently free and the government is not limited enough, an economic set-up that makes Americans the slaves of their own prosperity.

This is not the time for definitive value judgments. Or perhaps for one only. As I read the signs of the times, one in particular is overriding. From Warsaw and Vietnam, from Biafra and Brazil, from the rat-infested tenements of Harlem and the rotting schoolhouses in Appalachia, from a campus like Columbia and even from Women's Lib, one cry of the heart drowns out all others: set us free! You can debate on details; you can disagree on situations and individuals, on Mayday in Washington and Betty Friedan. You dare not dispute the dynamism deep down. To be human today, you must be free.

Is there risk here? Of course. But no greater risk than in the search for truth, in the quest for justice, in the yearning for love. In each of these areas, society, like individuals, is awfully vulnerable, exposed to heartbreak, to bloodshed, to disaster. But from the willingness to risk, to give to others the freedom you demand for yourselves, may well be born a social order beloved of God and of His human images.

29
FREEDOM '76
To the free, on what freedom is for

In 1976, Americans of all faiths and no faith celebrated the bicentennial of freedom. Believers of every persuasion rejoiced in a religious freedom that has grown through two bittersweet centuries. On July 31, feast of St. Ignatius Loyola, hundreds of lay Catholics gathered with scores of Jesuits in Old Saint Joseph's Church, Willings Alley, Philadelphia, to recall with thanksgiving that on this day in 1734 the Governor and Council, gathered in the same State House where the Declaration of Independence was to be signed forty-two years later, confirmed with their tacit approval the privilege which Philadelphia Catholics enjoyed to celebrate the Eucharist in their small chapel on Walnut Street dedicated to St. Joseph. The "Popish Chapell" that fathered the church in which they were this day worshiping had been part and parcel of the struggle for religious freedom. It was fitting that the faithful who filled the impressive present-day edifice were joined for the liturgy of thanksgiving by a powerful leader in the effort to link faith and justice, Father Pedro Arrupe, Superior General of the Society of Jesus.

In the context of the bicentennial it would have been excessively narrow to focus on Old Saint Joseph's Church and its role in the fashioning of American freedom. It seemed more important to lift our eyes and hearts to a broader reality, to a fundamental Christian truth. To be freed from some enslavement is only a beginning: we have all been "freed from" so as to be "free for." For what, for whom? For "the other," for those who are still enslaved. To this end, the liturgical readings, Galatians 5:1, 13–15, and Luke 4:16–21, were strikingly appropriate.

"My brothers and sisters, you were called to freedom. Only do not use your freedom as an opportunity for the flesh, but through love be servants of one another" (Gal 5:13).

In the past twenty-five years, many key words have bombarded Christian ears, have dominated human discourse. I think of . . . charism, collegiality, community, conscience, dissent, ecumenism, experience, identity, integrity, peace, people of God, reconciliation, reform. These are key words, crux words, in two senses: (1) they are crucial words for human and Christian living; (2) they are dreadfully difficult to define. Rarely has vocabulary been so arbitrary. It is Humpty Dumpty reincarnate: "When *I* use a word, it means just what I choose it to mean—neither more nor less."

Today one key word outstrips the rest in its importance and its looseness. I mean the word "freedom." It is indeed important. This whole year is a celebration of American freedom. At the same time, blacks still cry in the streets that neither Abraham Lincoln in 1863 nor the Supreme Court in 1964 really set them free. In 1965, Vatican II declared religious freedom a demand of reason and the gospel. And at the close of the Council, Paul VI asked the rulers of the world: "What does the Church ask of you?" He answered his own question: "Nothing but freedom." In the Third World, nation after nation has won freedom in blood; but peoples from Hungary to South Africa are crying for the same freedom—in vain. Women over the world are organizing for freedom. Within Catholicism, male and female are struggling for what they see as Christian freedom: clergy are clamoring for due process, and women are no longer content to wash the linens of today's Church and the diapers of tomorrow's Church.

But, like those other words, freedom is not easy to define; it is used with lamentable looseness; so often it means what I choose it to mean. Now a pulpit is not the place to philosophize; a homily ought not fashion definitions. And still I see two facets of freedom as frightfully important to explore: what we are freed *from* and what we are freed *for*. And so I shall ask three questions: (1) What have we been, or what are we being, freed *from*? (2) What are we freed *for*? (3) What does this say to us as citizens and as Christians?

I

First, it is relatively simple to say what any of us have been freed *from*, what we are striving to be freed *from*. It is always some form of oppression, of slavery, of tyranny. When the colonies rebelled against Britain, they felt they were rebelling against enslavement—what they saw as British abuses of American rights and liberties: from the threat posed by a standing army and laws regulating shipping, to providing beer for British troops and paying taxes for tea.

The "Popish Chapell" that fathered this church in which you sit is a splendid example of struggle for freedom *from* threatening tyranny. Long before the War of Independence, Jesuits had to struggle for their right to worship on this spot, had to declare: "We are, and of right ought to be, free and independent of any civil law restricting or debarring our right to religious liberty."

When blacks in this country rebelled in Birmingham, linked

arms in Selma, marched on Washington, they were marching for freedom *from* a social system, a system that enslaved, a "land of the free" that condemned a whole race to ghettos and the back of a bus, forced it to study in shacks and work in toilets, forbade it our sidewalks and our pews, barred it from hotels and restaurants, from movie houses and rest rooms—not because they were ignorant or dirty or penniless—only because they were black.

Women's Lib is a freedom *from*: from bonds that tie woman in traditional ways to man—in industry and sacristy, in boardroom and bedroom, on every level that subserves subservience, woman's domination by man. It is a refusal to act as a male-dominated society, a male-dominated Church, expects woman to act. Many a woman will no longer be imprisoned within four domestic walls. She wants to be freed from illiteracy, from forced marriage, from unequal salaries, from second-class citizenship.

And what Christianity is all about is freedom. The Son of God took our flesh to free it. "The Spirit of the Lord has anointed me. . . . He has sent me to proclaim release to the captives . . . to set at liberty the oppressed" (Lk 4:18). Freedom from what? From every form of enslavement; from all that keeps a child of God from being properly human, genuinely divine; from all that bars me from oneness with God, with myself, with you, with the earth; from all that makes me either enslaved or enslaver. In a word, freedom from sin: from original sin and personal sin and social sin—from the sin of Adam, from the sin that rises from my own heart, from the sin that surges up from unjust social, economic, and political structures. This is why God walked our earth; this is why the Church circles our globe.

II

But to be freed *from* slavery is only a beginning. Whether it be thousands of Israelites freed from Pharaoh or thirteen colonies freed from George III, whether it be America's blacks freed from white chains or the world's women freed from male supremacy, whether it be the Church freed from political pressure or the Christian freed from enslaving sin—freedom *from* is not the end, it is a beginning. All have been freed *for* something.

But for what? Not simply for self-fulfilment. Oh yes, freedom should fulfil; for freedom creates a context where an individual can grow as a person, an institution can flower to become more itself. But self-fulfilment can be perilously selfish. The danger in liberation movements is that *I* may become the center of the universe. The way *I* see things, what *I* want and need, this becomes all-important. And this is what makes for polarization, for hostility and hate. I do not care what *you* want, what *you* need; *your* vision of the universe, of reality—why, I couldn't care less.

No, my brothers and sisters, the Christian context of freedom, the human context of liberation, is not I but the other: the Other with a large O and the other with a small o. St. Paul's paradox is strong and clear: "You were called to freedom. . . . Be servants!" You need to be free so that you may serve. Serve God: live to the full your free covenant with your Creator. Serve man: give yourself fully to your brothers and sisters.

All around you is a human family with its hungers. Hungry for food: 460 million are starving; America's own poor roll up to 60 million. Hungry for freedom: whole nations have been raped, and there are still countries where to be black is to be not beautiful but bastard. Hungry for peace: in Northern Ireland, in the Middle East, in our city jungles. Over the globe, social, economic, political oppression makes it hard to live humanly, a life in union with God.

These millions ask for justice—what is due them as human persons. And while we theologians must debate about how precisely you relate the search for justice to the mission of the Church, no Christian dare say that the Church can stand apart from the effort to free the human person for human living. With the Roman Synod of 1974 we must affirm: "the Church . . . believes firmly that the promotion of human rights is required by the gospel and is central to her ministry."

This is not some newfangled theory of salvation.[1] It stands in splendid consonance with the Old Testament and the New. The God of Israel ceaselessly tells His people that He is weary of burnt offerings, solemn assemblies, the melody of harps. He does not want rivers of oil, their feasts, even their first-born. He asks for their steadfast love *and that they execute justice* (cf. Isa 1:11–18; 42:1–4; Hos 2:18–20; 6:6; Amos 5:18–25; Mi 6:6–8; Jer 7:5–7.

But the justice God asked was not simply what people had a strict right to demand. Justice was a whole web of relationships that stemmed from Israel's covenant with God. They were to father the fatherless and feed the stranger, not because the orphan and the outsider deserved it, but because this was the way *God* had acted with *them* (cf. Deut 10:18–19). In freeing the oppressed, they were mirroring the loving God who had delivered *them* from oppression. In loving the loveless, the unloved, the unlovable, they were imag-

ing the God who wooed Israel back despite her infidelities, betrothed her to Himself forever (cf. Hos 2:14–23). For Israel, the
practice of justice was an expression of steadfast love, a demand of
steadfast love—God's love and their own love. Not to execute justice was not to worship God.

This is the tradition that sparks the ministry of Jesus (cf. Mt
12:17–21; 23:23). In harmony with Hosea, he wants not sacrifice
but compassion (cf. Mk 9:13; 12:7). And the just man, the just
woman, is not primarily someone who gives to another what that
other *deserves*. The just man, the just woman, has covenanted with
God; this covenant demands that we treat other human persons as
God wants them treated in His covenant plan, treat friend and enemy as He treats them. And He "makes His sun rise on the evil and
on the good, sends rain on the just and on the unjust" (Mt 5:45).

The early Christians seem to have grasped that. If *anyone* is
hungry or athirst, naked or a stranger, sick or in prison, it is always
Christ who clamors for bread or water, Christ who cries to be
clothed or welcomed, Christ whom you visit (cf. Mt 25:31–46). And
the first Letter of John is uncompromising: "If anyone has the
world's goods and sees his brother in need, yet closes his heart
against him, how does God's love abide in him?" (1 Jn 3:17).

III

My third point, briefly: what does this say to us as citizens and
as Christians? What St. Paul said to the Galatians: "You were called
to freedom; . . . be servants of one another." If you want to know
how free you are, ask yourself a single question: how much of your
life is service? Are your eyes fixed narcissistically on your small self
or agonizingly on parched minds without number and wasted bodies beyond counting? You are not God's people to save your individual souls. Your existence as a Christian community, your existence as Jesuits, is justified to the extent that it makes possible an
apostolate you cannot achieve in isolation. An apostolate to a thousand hells: to hunger and hate, ignorance and fear; to countless human persons who share so much of Christ's crucifixion and so little
of his resurrection; to so many who look to your communities, the
Christian community and the Jesuit community, as a sacrament, a
living sign that God is alive, that God is here, that God loves. Disregard that service, to do each your own "thing," and your community will deserve to die. Jesuit Order or Catholic Church, it will
deserve to die.

This is not a throwback to slavery. There is a profound difference between slavery and service. St. Paul summed it up in a word: "through *love* be servants of one another." These are your brothers and sisters—from the skin-and-bones starving in Calcutta, through the blasted bodies in the Middle East, to the unloved child on your own street.

But there's the rub: "my brothers and sisters." Is this the way I see the hungry—as if someone I love were starving? Isn't it ironic that so many who have no God save man feel more anguish for the hungry than so many whose God-given commandment is to love others as they love themselves, to feed the hungry Christ under pain of damnation? The Bread of Life that is the Eucharist should make me solidary with all who need bread to live; but too often the Eucharist feeds no one but me.

Christian freedom demands of me a Eucharistic spirituality, where the Christ of Holy Thursday not only feeds me. He does with me today what he did that night with the bread: he takes me, and he blesses me, and he breaks me, and he gives me. The broken bread—then as now, Christ or I—the broken bread is a force for freedom; but then as now, Christ or I, the bread must be broken. Otherwise it cannot be given—especially to those who are themselves broken.

"My brothers and sisters, you were called to freedom. Only do not use your freedom as an opportunity for the flesh, but through love be servants of one another."

30
DO WE DESERVE PEACE?
To those who war over peace

In the fall of 1969 the war in Vietnam was still raging. But increasingly the conflict was dividing Americans at home. Many still felt that we belonged there, that our motives were reasonably pure and our hands reasonably clean, that Communism had to be checked and American honor was at stake, that to pull out of Southeast Asia at that juncture would be a betrayal of freedom and of our friends in the free world. Others were equally adamant at the other extreme: the war in Vietnam was immoral, either because no war could be justified or because this particular conflict did not satisfy the conditions for a just war. And more and more decent folk were simply confused.

In this context a number of seminarians in the New York City area organized a special Mass for Peace. It was celebrated in St. Patrick's Cathedral late in the afternoon of November 13, 1969. Given the divisions described above, what might a homilist say if he is to speak to the issues courageously and in a Christian spirit, while avoiding partisan politics and crabbed confrontation—especially if he himself is still struggling to make peace between violence and the gospel, if he is torn between Paul VI's cry to the United Nations "No more war!" and the cry for freedom from millions of peasant lips, if he is just beginning to see a little light in the tunnel?

"Do We Deserve Peace?" is a quiet but almost desperate meditation, a colloquy with God, that perhaps says more about the homilist than it does about peace.

"When Jesus drew near
and saw the city,
he wept over it,
saying:
'Would that even today
you knew the things
that make for peace!
But now they are hid from your eyes.' "
(Lk 20:41–42)

I

Lord, we come before you a motley lot. We are wonderfully and dreadfully different. Some of us are violent in our convictions;

181

others could not hurt a fly. Some of us have years behind us; the lives of others lie ahead. Some of us are knowledgeable, others quite ignorant. Some of us are happy people; others have forgotten how to laugh. Some of us have money; others must pinch and squeeze, beg and borrow. Most of us are white; only a few, I'm afraid, are black or yellow or brown. Some of us are settled, have it made; others are restless, trying to make it. Some of us have killed; others have seen death only on TV.

Some of us are awfully sure—about the war, about its morality or immorality, about ROTC and Dow Chemical, about American idealism or imperialism, about napalm and defoliation; others are confused, uncertain, torn this way and that, even anxious about our own uncertainty. Some of us think your Church is "out of it," a slave to the *status quo*, hidebound and a straddler; others feel she has gone too far too fast, runs after the latest fashion, is even heretical. Some of us have tasks that excite us; others go through motions from 9 to 5. Some of us have stored up hate in our hearts; others thrill with love. Some of us are neat and clean; others could not care less for middle-class hygiene. Some of us have come to terms with society; others have fled it or vowed to destroy it. Most of us are here because we still believe in you; some surely have come from curiosity, or custom, or even despair. A few of us may even be "effete snobs."[1]

Lord, we *are* a motley lot, aren't we?

II

Only one thing unites us at this moment, Lord: we all want peace. We are *all* convinced that war is hell. We *all* feel that there is something tragically wrong when the governments of the world spend 120 billion dollars a year to kill, to threaten, to deter, to keep peace. When a B-52 sets fire to fifty square miles so that nothing therein can live. When homes of the innocent are converted into incinerators. When the ratio of civilian-to-military casualties is 3 or 5 to 1. When three million refugees water the roads and rice paddies with their tears. When human beings are tortured by other "human" beings.

We *all* weep for it, Lord—even those of us who feel that it cannot be otherwise, that it is not Christian, is not human, but must be. Even those who are soldiers or sailors or marines—who are trained to kill and to destroy—even they are nauseated at what they must do.

We all want life, Lord, and not death. We know the love and the anguish and the pain and the joy that goes into fashioning a single child. Many of us have shared with you the creation of life. We sense how precious each life is to you. And so we weep for each life that is snuffed out. We cannot rejoice when a headline proclaims that *only* 200 Americans were killed this week; we cannot be glad when 5,000 Viet Cong are flushed out and massacred. For these are not statistics, Lord; these are persons. And when even one shrieks to heaven with his flesh in flames—friend or enemy—we all weep, we are all ashamed, we all want peace.

III

We all want peace, Lord. The problem is, we are not agreed on how to get peace; we do not know "the things that make for peace." Oh yes, we have our convictions. There are those of us who "know" that the first step to peace is for us to get out, leave Southeast Asia. There are those who "know" that only all-out war will bring peace. And there are those silent millions somewhere inbetween who don't want us to stay and don't see how we can go. And there are *all* of us who sense that, even if Southeast Asia is pacified, there is still the Middle East, there is Czechoslovakia, there are Libya and Bolivia, there is the whole vast continent of Africa.

We do not know, save superficially, "the things that make for peace." For some reason—perhaps for our sins—"they are hid from [our] eyes." If, as your prophet proclaimed, "peace is the fruit of righteousness" (Isa 32:17), and if, as your Council taught, "peace is likewise the fruit of love,"[2] then war is the fruit of unrighteousness, of hate. But I dare not lay that unrighteousness, that hate, solely at the feet of the enemy, only in the heart of the politician—in Hanoi or Washington or Saigon. If I am as honest as I want my neighbor to be, I must look within, to see if the seeds of war are planted in my heart.

IV

And as we look, Lord, we must be distressed. Our love for human beings, we were told by your Son, our love would be the sacrament, the visible sign, that he is among us. This is how the world would recognize him. And the world does not see him, because the world does not see him in our love. Whole cities could live on the garbage from our dumps, on the clothes we wear once, on the luxuries we have made necessities. Black and white are threatened with bloody combat because we have been as color-conscious as our unbelieving neighbors. For so many of us, a court of law is more effective than the Sermon on the Mount. There is no evidence that we Catholics drink less, lust less, hate less than the men and women who never eat the flesh of your Christ or drink his blood. I am afraid we are what St. Paul called the pagans of his time: we are "faithless, ruthless, pitiless" (Rom 1:31).

For all its own tyranny, what does Hanoi find in America, in us, to shake it, to make it marvel and cry "Look how they love"? The seeds of war are within us, from the jealousy of Cain to the hate in my own heart, from the commerce that makes a jungle of the world to the ghettos we have structured for the Jew and the black, from the dishonesty of the little clerk to the tyranny of the big cleric.

A horrifying thought has just struck me, Lord: perhaps we do not *deserve* peace. Perhaps war is the logical fruit of our unrighteousness, of our personal hate, of our lack of love. It may be that what is happening in Southeast Asia began in our hearts, in my heart, not too long ago. No wonder your Son weeps over *our* city, saying: "Would that even today you knew the things that make for peace! But now they are hid from your eyes."

V

When we first came to you this evening, Lord, I think we came for a miracle, for your special intervention in the world, for a breakthrough that would change the heart of Hanoi, inspire our president, make the lamb and the lion lie down in Paris. I rather think now it is a different miracle we are asking. Just as you do not make wars, Lord, so neither do you end them. We make them, Lord, and so we have to end them. With your grace, of course; but unless *we* do it, it will not be done.

The miracle we ask, each of us, is a conversion. Change *us*, Lord. If we are unshakable on Vietnam, keep us from being unloving. If we are uncertain, let it not make us cowards. Take bitterness from us, even if we have cause to be bitter. Take hate from us, for we have never just cause for hatred. If we have bled, let the blood we shed be redemptive like your Son's. If we have grown fat—by our own honest industry or over the bodies of others—scourge us till we cry out. Each of us knows what it is within us that makes for war. Prick all our hearts with a sense of guilt; for we have sinned, Lord, all of us—we have sinned against peace.

VI

We are a motley lot, Lord; but do not let difference destroy love. Two days ago, in our Woodstock College community, two young guests threw from our dining room a large bowl of fruit, because it included some grapes, and the grapes might be from California. A young friend, also a guest, was asked by a Jesuit in the community if *he* had done this. He replied: "In the sense that the hands that did this were the hands of my brother, yes, I did it." He was pressed: "But aren't we your brothers too?" His answer, slow and serious: "I'm afraid I must say no."

Dear Lord, if this is the way we are, I weep, for we do not deserve peace. If we can love (as indeed we should) a hostile soldier on the other side of the Pacific, call him brother, can we not open our hearts to the human being next to us, despite our deep divisions?

That is why, Lord, in much hope and some fear, I am asking the men and women in front of me to take a first step toward peace. I am asking each to clasp the hand of the person next to him or her, the person on each side—whoever that person is, whatever he or she looks like—without even looking. I want them, by this act of faith and trust and love, to cry out to you that we do want peace, that we want to begin it here and now, that we see in each human being a brother or sister and the image of your Christ, that our hearts are open to them as never before, that we are ashamed and weep for our crimes against them. And I am asking them to sit like that, hands clasped, for one minute—all of us . . . for one minute . . . at peace.

31
STEWARDS OF GOD'S DAPPLED GRACE
To those who must ask for money

I feel I can call this talk a "near homily," because it would not be out of place within the liturgy. The actual setting was the Philadelphia Sheraton Hotel on the evening of April 14, 1977. The Archdiocese of Philadelphia was formally opening its 20th Annual Catholic Charities Appeal, and the Grand Ballroom was jammed with laity and clergy.

The problem I decided to face was twofold. First, what lies theologically behind Christian giving? Granted that the gospel enjoins us to give freely what we have freely received—and, if possible, do it cheerfully—the deeper question remains: why? Second, what is it we are to give? In the context of an appeal for money, the immediate realistic response is . . . money. Naked money, however, is not quite Christian enough, not human enough—not when people are at stake, people who need us not only to take care of them but to care. What might such caring be in the concrete?

Once more I realized how indispensable and how exciting it is, in the fashioning of a homily or near homily, to fuse the biblical word, Christian experience, and prayerful reflection on both. After that, all you have to do is what the sportswriter Red Smith said when asked how he came to compose such consistently fine columns: "You sit at a typewriter until little drops of blood appear on your forehead."

It has not been easy deciding what to say to you. I dare not tell you how to solicit funds; for I am not a practical man: a fuse is something I blow, a hammer is a threat to my thumbs. I had best stick to what I do best. I am a theologian; and, at its simplest, a theologian tries to research systematically, understand profoundly, and express intelligibly what God has said and is now saying to us. And it struck me that in your Charities Appeal there is a highly important idea God would like you to grasp, important for those who beg, important for those who give. The idea is summed up in a thrilling verse from the first Letter of Peter: all Christians should employ (literally, "deacon") the many-splendored charisms they have from God for the advantage of one another, "as good stewards of God's dappled grace" (1 Pet 4:10).

Good stewards of God's dappled grace—that is my theme tonight. And I shall unfold it in three stages, by asking three questions. (1) In the Christian vision, what does it mean to be a steward? (2) As the New Testament would have it, what makes a steward a good steward? (3) In the context of your attractive theme—"How do you measure a person?"—what is it that the human person asks of the Christian steward today, asks especially of you?

I

First then, in the Christian vision, what does it mean to be a steward? I make no pretensions tonight of offering you *the* theology of Christian stewardship. The subject is too vast: to be a steward is to be a Christian. And theology is not exhausted by one man or one address: the best of Burghardt is not necessarily the cream of Catholicism. What I shall sketch is one approach, one framework within which to fit the rich, scattered fragments of your own stewardship.

To be a steward is to manage what is someone else's. That is the first meaning of the word in, say, the American Heritage Dictionary: "one who manages another's property, finances, or other affairs." And that is the profoundly suggestive biblical meaning as well. Everything I administer as a Christian really belongs to someone else. The frightening facet of this idea is that the "someone else" is not president or pope; the "someone else" is God.

That is all too obvious in the area of the Spirit, of the supernatural. When I preach, I do indeed use my words, but it is *God's* word I proclaim. When I pour life into a fresh-born child, it is *God's* life I minister. When I murmur "I absolve you," it is *God's* forgiveness I communicate. It is to *His* supper that I invite the faithful. I have no power over the marriage covenant, only a very fallible insight into whether the covenant is there, whether it is *God* who has joined these two together.

Lay or cleric, we are signs and agents of the reconciling Christ. "All this," St. Paul insisted, "is from God, who through Christ reconciled us to Himself" (2 Cor 5:18). It is the reconciling power of Christ that operates through us. To heal the ruptures that sever men and women from God, from the images of God, and from the things of God, we bring to bear not the weakness and ignorance of man but the power and wisdom of God. We have not chosen Christ; he has chosen us. It is his life, his love, his reconciliation we mediate; and we mediate it only because he works in us to will and to do.

Very simply: I do not own the grace of God. Oh yes, it filters through my fragile fingers; but it never becomes my grace, the grace of man; it is always and everywhere the grace of God.

But is there not something the Christian does own, something of which you are not sheerly steward? The fruit of your toil, what flows from your initiative and your sweat, the money you have amassed and the power you have purchased, your ideas and your computer, is this not your very own? Only in a limited sense. I do not deny the right to private property, but private property is not an absolute. It is subordinate to core personal rights: the right to life, to human dignity, to bodily integrity. As for America, so for Americans—we are not entitled to keep or consume everything we can produce or purchase. It is through the things of earth, from water to atomic energy,. that a man or woman becomes human or inhuman; it is largely by their use of God's creation that our brothers and sisters are saved or damned. And so it is frightening that at least a billion human persons fall asleep hungry each night, frightening that, despite the dollars pouring into Latin America, the rich get richer and the poor get poorer. Each man, each woman, each child have a strict right to as much of this earth's resources as they need to live a human existence in union with God.

This means, paradoxically, that I cannot simply do what I will with what is my own. Paradoxically, what I own I hold in trust. I can be, I will be, called to account for the use I make of all I have. As a Christian, I can never be completely comfortable as long as one brother or sister cries in vain for bread or justice or love. As a Christian, I must tear from my lips those horrible half-truths, "Charity begins at home," "Let the shiftless shift for themselves," "They are only getting what they deserve," "Give them an inch and they will take a mile," "Why should I give to others what has cost me sweat and blood and tears to achieve?" As a Christian, I may not squander what is my own, even clutch it possessively, in disregard of my brothers and sisters.

As a Christian, therefore, I can draw no hard and fast line between what belongs to God (redemption, grace, church, sacraments) and what belongs to me (private property). A line yes, but not hard and fast. Ultimately, all things are God's: not only divine grace but the world's energy, the fish of the sea and the birds of the air, earth's loam and my life, my time and talent and treasure. Whatever I touch, whatever comes within my grasp, I hold in trust from God for man. In all that I do, in all that I have, I am a steward: I manage what is someone else's. I manage what is God's.

II

My second question: as the New Testament would have it, what makes a steward a good steward? The primary characteristic of a Christian steward is the adjective St. Paul demands of a steward: that he (or she) "be found *pistos*, faithful" (1 Cor 4:2). It is the same adjective you find in Luke, where the Lord says: "Who then is the faithful . . . steward whom his master will set over his household, to give them their portion of food at the proper time?" (Lk 12:42).

The first meaning given to *pistos* in New Testament lexicons, the meaning that attaches to it when it modifies steward in Paul and in Luke, is "faithful" in a somewhat passive sense: the steward should be reliable, dependable, trustworthy, should inspire trust or faith. In this sense Christian stewards are like their Master, like the God whom the New Testament calls *pistos*, the One in whom we can have complete confidence. The Pauline letters echo and re-echo it: "God is faithful, by whom you were called into the fellowship of His Son" (1 Cor 1:9). "God is faithful, and He will not let you be tempted beyond your strength" (1 Cor 10:13). "As surely as God is faithful . . ." (2 Cor 1:18). "He who calls you is faithful, and He will do it" (1 Thess 5:24). "Let us hold fast the confession of our hope without wavering, for He who promised is faithful" (Heb 10:23). You find the same insistence in 1 Peter: "Let those who suffer according to God's will . . . entrust their souls to a faithful Creator" (1 Pet 4:19). And you find it in the first Letter of John: "If we confess our sins, He is faithful and just, and will forgive our sins and cleanse us from all unrighteousness" (1 Jn 1:9).

Impressively in this connection, the Pauline letters speak of Christ in the same way they speak of God: "The Lord is faithful; he will strengthen you and guard you from evil" (2 Thess 3:3). "If we are faithless, [Christ Jesus] remains faithful; for he cannot deny himself" (2 Tim 2:13).

Here are the models of our fidelity, here is the challenge to our faithfulness: a God absolutely true to His promises, a Christ faithful even unto death. And here lies my examination of conscience; as a steward of "God's dappled grace," how reliable am I, how trustworthy? Not in some vague, gossamer fashion. Can God depend on me to serve Him as my one Master? Can God's human images rely on me to minister God's life to them with a loving fidelity that even crucifixion cannot kill? And can God's creation, the nonhuman, look with confidence to me to shape it and use it only for God's greater glory, the salvation of the human person, and nature's own redemption?

A second New Testament meaning of *pistos* is more active. It is not explicitly applied to a Christian steward, but it is surely taken for granted. To be *pistos* is to be faith-full, full of faith. It denotes the authentic believer—in the Lord, in Christ, in God. And it is this second, more active meaning that, for a steward, explains the first, more passive meaning: Christian stewards are faithful because they are faith-full. You can be trusted completely because you have entrusted yourself completely: you are totally committed—to God, to God's people, to God's creation. For faith is not primarily the yes of an intellect to a proposition. Faith is, in the first instance, the yes of a person to a Person. Heinrich Fries once put it splendidly:

> Faith is an act of decision, a decision for a person, a recognition and acceptance of him, which takes place in freedom, love, openness, and familiarity. . . . It is an act of the person which engages the whole man—understanding, will, and heart—and is brought to full realization in the fulfilment of the following specification of faith: "I myself, entirely myself, yield myself to you."[1]

Here again lies a neuralgic examination of conscience: as a steward of "God's dappled grace," how faith-full am I? I do not mean, is my Christian existence free of all doubt? I mean, is my Christian existence a ceaseless struggle to whisper an increasingly total yes to God, to the images of God, to the things of God? Not to one or other, but to all three. For only if you can say a festive yes to all of the real, only then will you see, with Teilhard de Chardin, how "God is as out-stretched and tangible as the atmosphere in which we are bathed."[2] The divine milieu, Teilhard insisted, is not only the mystical Body of Christ; it is also the cosmic Body of Christ; here it is that creative union takes place.[3]

III

So far, two facets of stewardship: (1) As Christian stewards, you manage what is someone else's: you manage what is God's. And if your existence is completely Christian, then whatever comes within your grasp you hold in trust from God for man. (2) The one quality which more than any other ought to characterize your calling as stewards is fidelity. In imitation of God and His Christ, you must be absolutely true to your promises, faithful to God, to God's images, to God's creation—even unto death. And you will be faithful if you are faith-full: totally committed to God, to the people of God, to the things of God. My third question: in the context of your theme, what especially does the human person ask of the Christian steward today?

The immediate answer is . . . money. Children orphaned or abused or retarded or delinquent; the cancer-ridden and the age-ridden; infirm priests, brothers, and sisters; unwed mothers; the deaf and the mute; black and white tensions; Catholic and Jewish conflicts—all these and more call for money, call for $4.4 million. But if you realize that all of these projects are people, are persons, then I submit that what they ask of you is more basic than money. It is a gift that money will facilitate (hence the Charities Appeal); but money alone cannot guarantee it. What this little world of persons asks of you above all else is . . . understanding.

I am not talking about understanding in the sense of sheer knowledge or intelligence. I mean that understanding which involves a special kind of personal relationship, marked by an innerness that comes through to another as empathy. I mean an understanding so intimate that someone else's thoughts, motives, feelings come through to me as if they were my own. It is this quality Jesus possessed pre-eminently; it is this quality your archdiocese must recapture if you are to be good stewards, if the money you ask and the money you give is ultimately to touch a person.

But how can we begin to translate into flesh-and-blood reality a whole world's hunger for this kind of understanding? No single address can fashion a solution; I shall simply suggest five facets of understanding that may spark your own reflections.[4]

First, I must relearn the *value* of *each* human person. There is a serious problem here. Things happen on such a vast scale in our time that an individual is lost in the crowd. More than 22,000 are killed in Guatemala's earthquakes; 56,500 U.S. troops die in Vietnam; 460 million men, women, and children are starving right now; in 13 institutions of your archdiocese last year, "899 children received 328,397 days of care." There are no faces here, only ciphers. All the more reason why I must recapture the vision of a remarkable rabbi, Abraham Joshua Heschel. In an article aptly titled "No Religion Is an Island," Heschel wrote:

> To meet a human being is a major challenge to mind and heart.
> I must recall what I normally forget. A person is not just a speci-

men of the species called *homo sapiens*. He is all of humanity in one, and whenever one man is hurt we are all injured. The human is a disclosure of the divine, and all men are one in God's care for man. Many things on earth are precious, some are holy, humanity is holy of holies. To meet a human being is an opportunity to sense the image of God, *the presence* of God. According to a rabbinical interpretation, the Lord said to Moses: "Wherever you see the trace of man there I stand before you. . . ."[5]

In this my mind-set: wherever I touch a human person, I sense a divine presence?

Second, I must sense my *solidarity* with all that is human. It will not be easy. Skim any day's paper. What makes the headlines? Not human solidarity but dividing lines: the Golan Heights and the barriers of Belfast, poverty levels and unemployment rates, color lines and party lines—all those marks that spell difference. The way you and I define ourselves often stresses our differences: we are smarter or richer, better tanned or better dressed, in a more important job or having more fun, than he or she or they. But if I want to understand, I must base my self-definition not on being different but on being the same: the common experience of being human.

This awareness of sameness, of solidarity, once struck Thomas Merton so forcefully that he has confessed: "This sense of liberation from an illusory difference was such a relief and such a joy to me that I almost laughed out loud. . . . 'Thank God, thank God, that I *am* like other men, that I am only a man among others. . . .' It is a glorious destination to be member of the human race."[6]

Third, I must learn to *listen*. Listening is an arduous art. You see, most conversations are not conversations at all. Either they are monologues: I wait patiently until you have finished—since civility demands it—and then I say exactly what I would have said if you had not spoken. Or they are debates: I do indeed listen, but only for that inept word or false phrase at which I proceed to intercept and destroy. No, to listen is to give yourself totally, for that moment or that day, to another, to put yourself into the other's mind, yes the other's heart. It means that you hear not naked words but a human person.

Fourth, to understand others, I must understand their *history*. That is true of a nation, and it is true of a person. In a *Newsweek* column on the uses and abuses of history, Meg Greenfield made an astute observation: "I have heard every political and technical explanation there is for the failure of our 10-year-long adventure in

Southeast Asia. But I think there is one that takes precedence over them all. Quite simply, we didn't know who the Vietnamese were."[7]

To understand a people, to understand a person, it will help if I know where they come from and where they've been. Oh yes, it is quite possible to look into another's eyes and instantly understand; but it is also possible to look into another's eyes and misunderstand. We are all too prone to pigeonhole whole peoples: "India is lazy and Italy is dirty, the Russians are barbarians and the Spaniards are fascists, the Germans are power-hungry and the Scandinavians are sex-crazy, the Jews own most of our banks and the Arabs are a menace to the Middle East, the English are oppressors of the Irish and the Puerto Ricans are juvenile and senile delinquents." And we are so quick to turn away from persons we do not like. There are so many men and women and children who would be much more lovable if someone loved them; but we shall not love them if we do not try to understand them, if we do not try to discover where they come from and where they've been.

A fifth and final facet: I must accept my own *brokenness*. Not in sheer resignation, because I can do naught else; rather as a positive asset, a help to understanding. I do not come to others—to unwanted child or unwed mother, to cancerous flesh or ravaged mind—I do not come to others fearless and tearless, unscarred and unshaken. Like Christ, I am a *wounded* healer. I too am vulnerable; I too must confront the brutal condition of my mortality; ultimately I too must stand alone before an abyss; I too must murmur "I believe, Lord; help my unbelief!" In ministering to another, therefore, in trying to care, I am not simply removing a fear, alleviating an anxiety, cauterizing some human cancer. No, we are ministering to each other, deepening our different pains to a level, a Calvary, where, in Henri Nouwen's words, "they can be shared as different manifestations of our similar dread-full condition."

To relearn the value of each human person, to sense our solidarity with all that is human, to learn to listen, to discover where others come from and where they've been, to accept our own brokenness—here is one road to understanding. This is what the broken of your archdiocese have a right to expect from you who are "stewards of God's dappled grace." They yearn not only for your money, but for you; they ask not only Catholic Charities, but Catholic charity, Catholic love. As stewards, you are not your own, you do not belong to your isolated selves. You are God's and you belong to your brothers and sisters. Indeed give to the broken, but in the giving, above all give yourselves . . . your broken selves.

32
TO FILMS, WITH LOVE
To all the arts in one art

An unusual place for me: the Lotos Club in Manhattan. Un-usual people too: film producers and directors, neon-light figures like Warren Beatty and Maureen O'Sullivan. The occasion: the Second Annual Joint Award Reception of the Broadcasting and Film Commission of the National Council of Churches and the Na-tional Catholic Office for Motion Pictures.

On that March evening in '68 the butterflies that plague my stomach before every talk were more than ordinarily active. I was prepared, yes; my manuscript would fill the six minutes doled to me. The unsettling problem was whether my effort to link theology and the film would speak meaningfully to about two hundred men and women who lived life almost in a different world from mine, on a distant planet called Hollywood. Nor were my nerves soothed by the prelude to the awards and to my talk: ninety minutes of loud liba-tions to Melpomene, Thalia, and Terpsichore.

I need not have worried. It was one of those rare moments when, for reasons not instantly apparent, a speaker strikes fire. A week later, in its issue of March 13, Variety (not my customary outlet) printed the address under the title "A Jesuit Valentine to Films," with this prefatory sentence: "After the speech, two members of the audience—one a priest, one a film-company publicist—were overheard making almost identical remarks: 'They should have him speak at the Academy Awards ceremonies; he'd make them under-stand that they were doing something important.'"

The obvious question is, why am I here? Despite the Roman collar, I am not here as protector of the public morality. Therefore I am not here either to celebrate your new morality, or to castigate your alleged immorality, or to proclaim another Catholic category: un-objectionable for discriminating Jesuits.

What mask, then, do I wear? The mask of a theologian. I am here as one who lives with symbols (word, sacrament, Church), who plays with mystery (spirit and matter, divine and human, God and man). And, as a theologian, I am here to thank you for tackling more powerfully and profoundly than I the common task that is ours: human experience and its meaning—"What's it all about?"

The point is, the American film has come of age. I can say this without condescension, because it is not at all clear that American theology has come of age. But you have. In a short span you have turned from mascara to mystery, to the gut aspects of human existence, to the agony and ecstasy of being alive. You plumb the depths of our agonizing monosyllables: what it means to love, to hate, to bleed, to cry; what it feels like to be poor, to be free, to be black, to be dead. On the lips of a *Pawnbroker* you epitomize despair: "Everything I loved was taken away from me, and I did not die." And at the close of *Two for the Road* you give a new dimension to two ugly words: with unbelievable sensitivity you reveal the hope as well as the hell in "bitch" and "bastard."

But it is not simply with words that you have come of age. What makes you so unparalleled an expression of experience is that you are now consciously all the arts in one art: you alone are sculpture and architecture, painting and poetry, music and the dance, dramatic art. The consequence is, in your temple I am rarely a spectator: I do not look on from afar, aloof, down a Buckley nose. Like it or not, know it or not, I am caught up in your experience. Your colors shade my mood. I swelter and choke *In the Heat of the Night*; I bleed for freedom in *The Battle of Algiers*. You capture not merely my mind but my bones and my blood, my very pith and marrow. Electronic, instantaneous, massive—you hold me prisoner.

Even more importantly: on your screen I live not a naked experience, but your interpretation of that experience. Your lens looking on man from above is not your lens focusing on man from below. Your *Gospel according to Matthew* is as much a commentary on God as your *Bonnie and Clyde* is a vision of man. That lens is frighteningly human: now it is cold and ruthless, now it is warm and tender. That lens can be startlingly honest: it can rip open the lie in a human heart, the sham in a loveless society. And, of course, that lens can be discouragingly dishonest: it can be as shallow and as sightless as the eye that directs it.

I suppose what I am saying is that to come of age is to become responsible. And yet, no theologian can spell out responsibility for you; that way disaster lies, moral and artistic. A theologian would have advised an unbeliever not to try his hand at *A Man for All Seasons*. All I can demand is that you be true to what is most genuinely human in you; that you deepen and expand this newborn quest, this plunge into mystery, into man and God; that you realize, with a certain fear and trembling, that because of you I am different.

This evening I am happy, because I can unofficially welcome you to the fraternity of theologians: those who live with symbols and play with mystery. This evening I am envious, because so often your experience and your expression of mystery are richer and more powerful than mine. This evening I am grateful, because through your vision and your artistry I and so many of my colleagues on Cloud 9 are more human—perhaps even a bit divine.

33

WHAT MARY IS. . . .
To those who wonder where our Lady has gone

The homily to come was preached in a ticklish situation—a context not contemplated when I said yes to the invitation. The date: December 3, 1967. The occasion: a dedication. The west apse of the National Shrine of the Immaculate Conception in northeast Washington, D.C.—an apse honoring our Lady through five Jesuit saints—had been built with $800,000 in donations from the Society of Jesus and from those the Society serves.

Shortly before the Mass began in the upper church, twelve Jesuit seminarians picketed the edifice to protest the expenditure. In their view, the apse, the basilica, made no sense. With millions of stomachs bloated from hunger, bodies bloodied on battlefields, injustice rampant over the earth, this dedication was seen as a scandal. Two Jesuit provincial superiors attending the ceremony urged the protesters to cease and desist (many of them had come from the Woodstock College seminary outside of Baltimore), but the point had been made, and it was duly reported the next day in the news. It is this context that colors my opening remarks.

The focus of my homily, however, was not the appropriateness of an expensive apse but the significance of a singular woman. At a time when devotion to the Mother of Christ was on a steep decline, I was compelled to ask a critical question: is there something about our Lady that transcends times and cultures, that should make her a living, loved reality for every Christian?

Today's happening is not universally popular. Not everyone is pleased that we have a west apse in honor of Mary Immaculate completed through a gift of the Society of Jesus and the people the Jesuits serve. Not even all Jesuits are happy: not happy with the emphasis on Mary rather than on Jesus, not happy with mosaics and statues and windows that, like the ointment of Bethany's Mary, could have been "sold and [the money] given to the poor" (Jn 12:5).

There is a twin problem here: a shrine and a woman. The shrine I shall not argue, but it must be mentioned, for the problem will not disappear for the dreaming thereof. On the one hand, there is a passionate conviction that basilicas and marble columns are an anachronism, an affront to the poor, a medieval display of pomp and popery the while stomachs are empty and bodies bleed on battlefields. There is a gathering murmur that challenges the Catholic hierarchy to echo the decision of Episcopal Bishop Donegan of New York: "The Cathedral [of St. John the Divine] will for the immediate future remain as it now stands, unfinished. While the present agonies in our cities prevail, while the barriers of hate, prejudice, injustice, and inequality, which keep men apart and embitter life, exist in our land, this unfinished Cathedral shall be the prophetic symbol that our society is still as rough-hewn, ragged, broken, and incomplete as the building itself."

On the other hand, a counterfeeling crosses the land. There is an ageless tradition that man does not live on bread alone. There is a warm conviction that room remains for structures which sweep the soul to God. There is a feeling that if an unfinished cathedral points a prophetic finger at the present, at man's inhumanity to man, a perfected shrine may well point to the future, symbolize man's hope for man, the while it reminds the worshiper it is not stones we must fit together but the community of men. I have even heard a harsh reminder that the disciple who denounced the extravagance of Mary's ointment was called Judas, and that he was rebuked by Jesus for his blindness.

The shrine I shall not argue—not from cowardice but from uncertainty. I shall focus on the second problem, the problem of the Woman. This problem begins where we are: I mean, in a shrine built in Mary's honor, near five chapels that spell out the Joyful Mysteries, hard by five Jesuit saints whose devotion to the Mother of God was quite remarkable, beneath a many-splendored mosaic of the Woman Clothed with the Sun. The problem, at its most simple, is: what meaning has this Marian apse for the contemporary Christian? I shall try to answer the question through three stages.

I

The first stage: the Jesuit apse dare not be a mere memorial. Lovely as it is, it cannot be sheer tribute to the past, to the affection of an Alphonsus or an Aloysius, a nostalgic yearning for a way of life that is dead. Like it or not, this is 1967. New generations are growing—boys and girls for whom hippie beads are more meaningful than rosary beads, Jesuits who do not care to come "to Jesus through Mary," Catholics who are "turned off" by an immaculate conception, a virginal motherhood, a body-and-soul assumption. They do not disbelieve; they simply do not care.

Challenging, yes; frightening, perhaps; but not necessarily unchristian. For the contemporary crisis compels the Catholic community to ask itself again and again: what is the profound significance of our Lady, and how does it relate to our situation? What is it beneath Mary's unique conception, underlying her unparalleled motherhood, at the root of her unexampled resurrection, what is it that makes this peerless lady a reality in 1967? What must a Catholic preserve in his Marian vision and veneration, even if he discards lifeless beads and living rosaries, the May devotion and the vigil light, all the symbols that were second nature only yesterday? What is it about Mary that is a dynamic lesson for every Christian, for man and woman, for young and old, for cleric and lay, for conservative and liberal, for East and West, for 67 and 1967 and 2067? Is there anything like that?

I submit that there is; and this brings me to the second stage in our search.

II

Central to a Catholic vision of Mary is an exciting affirmation: our Lady is type or figure of the Church. The point is this. The Mother of Christ did not and does not exist in splendid isolation, raised by her prerogatives above the common herd. Quite the contrary: Mary's meaning for the Christian lies in this, that in her God has realized first and perfectly His design for the whole Church and for each individual Christian. In a word: what Mary is, that we are destined to be.

When we are talking about Mary, therefore, we are ultimately saying something about ourselves, we are proclaiming the Christian idea of man. She is the perfect Christian, for she is the perfectly redeemed. In her life and person she expresses to perfection what it means to believe, to love and be loved, to be graced, to be saved. In her we see in living flesh the meaning and inner thrust of the Church. She is redemption's finest hour.

You see, to be a Christian is to receive God's gift of Himself in grace-given freedom; to accept without reservation the salvation of God bodied forth in Jesus; to be totally committed to one's unique function in the task of redemption; to radiate one's own graced life in selfless service for the salvation of others. In a word: to be Christian is to commit ourselves to Christ and our Christ-committed selves to others.

And this is our Lady, to perfection. The crucial hour is the Annunciation. That first Angelus, so simply told by St. Luke, veils

Christianity's essence: I mean the love-laden response of a human being to divine disclosure, to God's invitation. The Incarnation is more than a living reaction of Mary's body to the activity of the Spirit; in St. Augustine's fine phrase: "It was by faith she gave him birth, it was by faith she conceived him." "Be it done unto me according to thy word" is the perfection of Christian faith. A remarkable yes. Remarkable because the answer did not come easily: "she was greatly troubled" (Lk 1:29). Remarkable because she could have said no: there was no force save love. Remarkable because it was a total yes: her whole self, to whatever God wanted. Remarkable because it rested on God's word alone: not knowing all that God's call implied, only that it was God who called.

That instant realized in Mary the mystery of the Church to come: the union of God and man in the Body of Christ. At the decisive moment in salvation's story, a human being's total yes brought God to her and to the world, linked God and man within her, linked God to man everywhere and forever. This is why Vatican II could call Mary model of the Church in faith, in love, in perfect union with Christ. For the task of the believing Church is to continue through space and time Mary's murmured yes. The community of the redeemed has for vocation to co-operate in redemption by loving faith, and so to bring Christ to birth in the human frame. What Mary is, that we are destined to be.

This vision of Mary-figure-of-the-Church pervades each of her prerogatives. Not only in her childbearing, but from the first instant of her earth-bound existence to the very last, in talking about Mary we are saying something about ourselves. The Immaculate Conception that dominates this shrine reveals our redemption, for the love it bespeaks speaks not merely of Mary but of man. Her first human moment declares dramatically that love begins above, that oneness with God starts with God: God gives the beginning, takes the initiative in all salvation. It is a striking reminder that redemption stems from God's mercy and not our own deserving—not even Mary's. It reveals God's incomparable love for a human being, and in this one human being His love for all—not because we are lovable of ourselves, but because His love makes us lovable. Mary's first moment is proof that God is faithful to His promises—a promise that the same love which enveloped her will be ours, the same God will be ours, the grace that is not a thing but a Person.

As for Mary's last moment on earth, what we affirm of her we hope for ourselves. I mean the perfection of redemption, when flesh as well as spirit will be transformed, and the whole man will confront his Creator in eternal ecstasy of knowledge and love. This perfection of humanity redeemed, the risen Christian endlessly one with the risen Christ, finds its first realization in the Mother of God, in Mary assumed into heaven, body and soul. What she is, that we are destined to be.

III

A third and final stage: Mary is more than a model. Oh yes, it is remarkable enough that in her fiat we see our own Christian existence. But her unique yes is not simply something to admire, nor did it cease when the angel left her. Her yes did something, and it does something. At the midpoint of history, her yes brought God to birth on earth; it does not cease to link God and man. For the Amen she said to all God willed, this Amen has entered with her into eternity. She still says Amen to the whole ordered plan of redemption; her consent is an eternal yes; and so in some mystery-laden way she continues to share in the redemptive work of her Son.

I admit, it is dreadfully difficult to express what we call the mediation of Mary, how in blood-and-bone reality she can mediate grace without doing violence to the one Mediator. But the fact remains, all of us are in a genuine sense mediators between God and man. God needs men; such is His design for redemption. "No man," says Thomas Merton, "enters heaven all by himself." We reach God through a community, through one another. Yes, we are called individually, we are loved as persons. "Nevertheless, unique individuals as we are, we are loved by God only because we belong to all others and because they belong to us" (Karl Rahner). All are mediators for all. And in this task of mediation she who gave and gives a unique Amen to Christ has a unique role to play. We do not reach God without her. How, then, can we live without her?

My dear brothers and sisters in Christ: I cannot say whether this shrine as a total structure symbolizes something quite Catholic or images something rather unchristian. But I do know that the Woman of the Apocalypse as translated so perceptively in the west apse represents magnificently the Catholic vision of our Lady. She is at once an individual, the Mother of Christ, and a collectivity, the People of God. And the two come together: what she is, God's People is destined to be.

Redemption is a master plan, divinely conceived, divinely executed. It finds its first, its ideal, its perfect realization in a single human being: Mary redeemed. It finds its ultimate realization in a community of human beings: humanity redeemed. What the Mother of God is, that the Church is destined to be. And what the Church is, that is already discoverable in God's Mother. When Léon Bloy saw the lesson of the Immaculate Conception in this, that redemption was successful at its very outset, because it produced a Mary, he spoke more truly than he knew. For Mary is not simply redeemed; she is humanity redeemed.

This vision of Mary makes for authentic devotion. In attachment to the immaculate Virgin Mother of God in glory, we are not simply bent low before mystery—mystery that is meaningless as far as contemporary living is concerned. We are not lost in wonder at an immaculate conception which can never be ours; at a wedding of perpetual virginity and physical motherhood unique in history; at a glorious resurrection not preluded, like ours, by the corruption of the tomb.

Our devotion to our Lady is the fruit not so much of mystery as of insight. In her we encounter in human form the plan of God for man. In this one woman we see what the community of believers is and is destined to be. In her life and person we glimpse in its perfection the role in which God casts every human being. What He asks of you and me is active receptivity—that, when we hear the word of God, we welcome it, and Him, within. For on this depends our holiness, our oneness with God, our redemption—the openness, the freedom, the utterness with which we can respond: "Be it done unto me according to thy word."

HUMAN AND
CHRISTIAN DYING

34
I DO
A Christian theology of death

This talk on death, originally given on April 1, 1973 over a network (NBC) radio program (Guideline), is uncommonly meaningful to me—perhaps because when I wrote it I was a near sexagenarian and was beginning to believe (and fear) with the Psalmist that "the years of our life are threescore and ten" (Ps 90:10).

Two factors in particular persuaded me to address this topic. First, I have never looked forward to dying. Despite a long ascetical training and almost a half century in religious life, I have never shared the yearning of the saints to move into eternity. In fact, I am quite unenthusiastic about leaving this life. Second, much Christian preaching on death I have found dissatisfying—orthodox enough, but not quite on target. (To be honest, I have managed to miss the mark myself.) There is the usual distinction between this life as preparation and the next life as goal; sometimes a contrast between the misery of the here and the happiness of the hereafter; sometimes an effort to console by insisting that the loss is sheerly ours, does not touch the departed. In particular, death is seen as inevitable: it simply happens to you.

I am not sure that my opening remarks, on death's brutality, ought to be incorporated into a funeral homily. Two other themes that occur later, however, ought to be impressed on those who mourn. One can be consoling: what our Lord meant when he insisted that a true believer will never die. The other should be challenging: death for a Christian ought to be a personal yes—"I do."

Last year a respected medical doctor wrote in a respected medical journal: "In my opinion death is an insult; the stupidest, ugliest thing that can happen to a human being."[1]

In its bald brevity the sentence is startling. The instinctive Christian reaction is to deny it outright. But the longer I look at it, the more tempered is my reaction. That sentence has forced me to face up to three profound questions: (1) What does it mean for a human being to die? (2) What did it mean for Christ to die? (3) What should it mean for a Christian to die?

I

First then, what does it mean for a human being to die? Two years ago the Catholic philosopher Vincent E. Smith penned some profoundly personal reflections on the death of his wife. He called it "Toward a Theology of Death or . . . What Really Happened to Virginia?" One passage is particularly pertinent here:

> . . . Death is not the mere flight of a ghost-like soul from a machine-like body that remains a human body after the death. Nor is the death of a human being a merely biological event. A cow or a chicken is in some sense replaceable when it dies. But in the death of a person, there is a loss of something absolutely unique. When an animal dies, there is the loss of an "it," in the language of Martin Buber; when a human being dies, an "I" is lost to the world and a "thou" to the survivors. . . .[2]

There, for me, lies death's tragedy—yes, if you will, death's "insult." A unique I, an irreplaceable thou, is destroyed. I who lift my eyes to the stars and only yesterday looked down on snow-capped Alps . . . I who catch with my ears the rapture of Beethoven's Mass in D and once throbbed to the music of my mother's voice . . . I who breathe the smog of New York, whose nostrils twitch to the odor of Veal Scallopini . . . I who cradle the Christ on my tongue and whose lips thrill to a kiss . . . I who run my fingers lazily through water and gently caress the face of a friend . . . I whose mind ranges over centuries and continents, to share Plato's world of ideas and Gandhi's passion for peace . . . I who laugh and love, worry and weep, dance and dream, sing and sin, preach and pray: this "I" will be lost to the world, this "thou" lost to those who survive me.

This "I" God will not replace, cannot replace. I am not just *some*one; I am *this* one. And for good or evil—for good *and* evil—I touch, I change, I transform a whole little world. Men and women, human persons—this black man, that cancerous woman, those little children next door—they are better or worse, more human or less human, divine or animal, in some measure because I am who I am. And when I die, this warm, pulsating flame of human living and loving will die with me.

Little wonder I don't care to die; little wonder I don't want to die.

II

My second question: what did it mean for Christ to die? Theologians are still groping to grasp it. For *his* death, too, was unique. Not only the way your death and mine will be unique, because an unrepeatable "I" will die. The "I" that died on Calvary was not only an unrepeatable *man*; the "I" was *God*-man. It meant that he suffered not less but more: more exquisitely and more brutally, with an awareness, a sensitivity, that no other person could parallel, no mere man rival.

But what did it *mean* for this God-man to die? To begin with, four Gospel facts: he knew he would die; he had to die; he was ready to die; and he wanted to die.

He knew he would die. To the scribes and Pharisees who asked for a sign, he promised a sign: "As Jonah was three days and three nights in the belly of the whale, so will the Son of Man be three days and three nights in the heart of the earth" (Mt 12:40). And to his disciples: "The Passover is coming, and the Son of Man will be delivered up to be crucified" (Mt 26:2). He knew he would die.

And he had to die. Not long before that dread death his soul was troubled. "What shall I say? Father, save me from this hour? No, for this purpose I have come to this hour" (Jn 12:27). And after his rising, to the two discouraged disciples on the road to Emmaus: "Was it not necessary that the Christ should suffer these things?" (Lk 24:26). He had to die.

And he was ready to die. "The Son of Man came," he insisted, "to give his life as a ransom for many" (Mk 10:45). And in Gethsemane, his "soul sorrowful even to death" (Mk 14:34), his whole being in rebellion against the impending Passion, he could still pray to his Father: "If this [cup] cannot pass unless I drink it, thy will be done" (Mt 26:42). He was ready to die.

And he wanted to die. "There is a baptism," he cried, "a baptism I must needs be baptized with, and how impatient, how oppressed am I until it be accomplished!" (Lk 12:50). That is why, at the Last Supper, "he took bread, broke it, gave it to his disciples" with the words that summed up his existence: "This is my body, which is given for you" (Lk 22:19). He wanted to die.

But why? Because with his death, death would cease to be "the enemy." Oh, I do not mean that with Calvary, on Calvary, death became easy; it did not. I mean that on Calvary Christ gave death a new look, fresh meaning. What that new meaning is can be said quite simply, and it can be plumbed more profoundly.

Quite simply, from the death of Christ life was born. Not only for him—for us. "Amen, amen, I say to you, unless a grain of wheat falls into the earth and dies, it remains alone; but if it dies, it bears much fruit" (Jn 12:24). God had decided that the oneness between man and God which had been ruptured in Paradise would be re-established on Calvary, that divine love would recapture man's heart through crucifixion—not the crucifixion of man, but the crucifixion of God! "When I am lifted up from the earth, I will draw all men to myself" (Jn 12:32). That is why, for me, the most rapturous words in the Gospel are the short words our Lord spoke to his apostles the night before he died—pregnant words that sum up Christian existence: "I live, and you will live" (Jn 14:19). More accurately: "I have life, and [so] you will have life."

With these words, "I have life, and so you will have life," we can plumb more profoundly the meaning of Calvary; for here, if anywhere, is the core, the pith, the marrow of John's Gospel. It is Jesus who has life; in fact, Jesus *is* life: "I am *the* life" (Jn 11:25). That is why the first Letter of John opens as it does, an ecstatic affirmation of him who is life: "That which was from the beginning, which we have heard, which we have seen with our eyes, which we have looked upon and touched with our hands . . . the word of life—the life was made manifest, and we saw it, and testify to it, and proclaim to you the eternal life which was with the Father and was made manifest to us" (1 Jn 1:1–2).

Jesus not only *has* life, he *is* life—because the Holy Spirit, that Spirit who gives life, is his Spirit; and this Spirit, this life, this Spirit of life, he gives to us. In John's vision, Jesus never really dies; for, in John's vision, a man dies only if and when the Spirit of life leaves him. That is why Jesus consoled a mourning Martha as he did. He was not satisfied with her belief in *another* life, her conviction that her dead brother Lazarus would "rise again in the resurrection at the last day" (Jn 11:24). No, "whoever lives and believes in me shall never die" (Jn 11:26). Shall *never* die. He is life, his life becomes our life, and that life need never leave us. That is why Jesus could say of himself: "This is [I am] the bread which comes down from heaven, that a man may eat of it and not die" (Jn 6:50).

In a word, the death of Christ is the death of death. "The ruler of this world is coming," he trumpeted at the Last Supper, "[but] he has no power over me" (Jn 14:30). At the very moment he "bowed his head and gave up his spirit" (Jn 19:30), he was gloriously alive, because the Spirit of life, the Holy Spirit, was still and forever his Spirit, his life.

III

That much said, my third question is basically answered: what should it mean for a Christian to die? It should mean for a Christian what it meant for Christ. Oh yes, an "I" is lost to the world and a "thou" to the survivors. That was true even of Christ. Surely Peter hurt and Mary wept; and over the centuries countless Christians have mourned the "real absence" of Christ, have yearned to meet his eyes, to hear the music and thunder of his voice. Death is indeed death.

But more importantly, death is life. Not only shall I not die altogether, totally, utterly; that is so frightfully negative. Death is that unique point between time and timelessness when the Spirit of Christ, the Spirit of life, can finally take complete possession of me, permanent possession, without my earth-bound resistance, reservation, reluctance. Death is that extraordinary experience when the Christ who *is* life fashions me finally to his life, in his image.

You see, you and I are more or less human to the extent that the life you and I live is penetrated by, instinct with, the life of Christ. He is the perfect man, the utterly human. That is why in the second century Bishop Irenaeus of Lyons, in an inspired moment, affirmed that the first man fashioned on earth was framed on the model of Christ to come. Not our traditional way of looking at Jesus: he was fully human because he was so much like the first human. Quite the opposite: Adam, or whoever, was genuinely human, perfectly human, because he was created in the image of Christ. The marks of humanity are flesh, soul, *and* Holy Spirit. This, for Irenaeus, is what it means to be alive, to be human, to be man or woman: throbbing flesh, pulsating soul, both quickened by the Spirit of Christ.[3]

With St. Paul, then, the Christian should be able to say: "For me, life is Christ, and [therefore] death is gain" (Phil 1:21). But this conviction compels a new attitude. I dare not be "resigned" to death: that is insufficiently Christian; I am still looking on death as "the enemy." In contrast, the German theologian Karl Rahner insists that death should be an act I personally perform, not an experience I endure. Death is a yes, an "I do."[4] When Jesus cried with a loud voice "Father, into your hands I commit my spirit" (Lk 23:46), it was not sheer acceptance, surrender to the inevitable. That death cry was a death-defying cry. It was not negation but affirmation. And what Christ was affirming was, simply, life: "I have life." And this is precisely what a Christian proclaims with his last breath: "I have life." Only with this attitude can death be an act I personally perform. *I die.*

Don't misunderstand me: I am not asking you to be enthusiastic about death. Even the Son of God did not quite scale those heights. I suspect I shall never really want to die. Not because my faith is infirm. Rather because there is so much life, God's life, right here—in myself, in you. The authentic Christian tension is not between life and death, but between life and life. Paul felt it: "Which I shall choose I cannot tell. I am hard pressed between the two. My desire is to depart and to be with Christ, for that is far better. But to remain in the flesh is more necessary on your account" (Phil 1:22–24). Ignatius Loyola felt it. If given a choice—on the one hand, die now and be surely saved; on the other, stay alive, do a signal service for the Lord, but no assurance of salvation—he would choose this way: "I would beg him to leave me here until I had done it, and I would not think twice of the peril to me or the assurance of my salvation."[5]

Not enthusiasm but readiness; not surrender but a love-laden yes. Not many years ago a sixteen-year-old girl, Janet Sullivan, lay dying in a Phoenix hospital. A dear friend was that remarkable Carmelite William McNamara. The last time he saw her he must have looked dreadfully upset. As he tells it, "she looked up into my worried and harried face and said: 'Father, don't be afraid.' " Such, at its most profound, is the Christian theology of death: "Don't be afraid." It is most profound when a child can say it to an adult, a girl to a priest, when it is the dying who can say it to the living: "Don't be afraid."

35
A MIND, A MANNER, A MAN
Elegy for John Courtney Murray

Here is surely the most difficult of my homilies. It was late on an August afternoon in 1967 when word came to us at Woodstock College in rural Maryland that John Courtney Murray had died in a taxicab on Long Island. The shock on Woodstock's corridors echoed through much of the country: a voice immeasurably effective for human and Christian freedom had been stilled. But for so many who not only admired the mind but loved the man, the grief was far more personal. I, for one, had lost my dearest friend. After the death of Gustave Weigel only three and a half years before, this was a dreadful blow to absorb.

Asked to preach the funeral sermon at St. Ignatius Loyola Church in New York City, I was initially of two minds. I could hardly say no, but there were problems. A theoretical problem: how do you measure up to such a task? A psychological problem: how do you preach about your best friend without tears? A practical problem: if it ordinarily takes you forty hours to compose a ten-minute homily, how do you fashion a fitting tribute in a day and a half? No time for mulling, for research, for data, for rewriting. . . .

Once I had said yes, the creative experience was unforgettable. From the moment I sat down at the typewriter, ideas and memories simply deluged me. It was as if John Murray were there with me. The result: a homily which, many thought, did capture the mind, the manner, and the man—a homily which another remarkable man, Robert F. Kennedy, inserted into the Congressional Record.

How does one recapture sixty-three years? How do you bring to life a man who taught with distinction in the Ivy League and on the banks of the Patapsco; who served country and Church in Washington and Rome; who graced the platform of so many American campuses and was honored with degrees by nineteen; who researched theology and law, philosophy and war; who was consulted "from the top" on the humanities and national defense, on Christian unity and the new atheism, on democratic institutions and social justice; whose name is synonymous with Catholic intellectualism and the freedom of man; whose mind could soar to outer space without leaving our shabby earth; whose life was a living symbol of faith, of hope, of love?

How does one recapture John Courtney Murray? No one really recaptures him for another. Each man or woman whose life he touched, each one of you, has his or her own Murray-for-remembrance. As for me, leafing through the last third of those sixty-three years, I remember a mind, a manner, a man.

I

I remember a mind. Few men have wedded such broad knowledge with such deep insight. Few scholars can rival Father Murray's possession of a total tradition and his ability to tune it in on the contemporary experience. For, whether immersed in Trinitarian theology or the rights of man, he reflected the concerns of one of his heroes, the first remarkable Christian thinker, the third-century Origen. He realized with a rare perceptiveness that for a man to grow into an intelligent Christianity, intelligence itself must grow in him. And so his own intellectual life reproduced the four stages he found in Origen.

First, recognition of the rights of reason, awareness of the thrilling fact that the Word did not become flesh to destroy what was human but to perfect it. Second, the acquisition of knowledge, a sweepingly vast knowledge, the sheer materials for his contemplation, for his ultimate vision of the real. Third, the indispensable task that is Christian criticism: to confront the old with the new, to link the highest flights of reason to God's self-disclosure, to communicate the insight of Clement of Alexandria that Father Murray loved so dearly: "There is but one river of truth, but many streams fall into it on this side and on that." And fourth, an intelligent love: love of truth wherever it is to be found, and a burning yearning to include all the scattered fragments of discovered truth under the one God and His Christ.

The results, as you know, were quite astonishing. Not in an ivory tower, but in the blood and bone of human living. Unborn millions will never know how much their freedom is tied to this man whose pen was a powerful protest, a dramatic march, against injustice and inequality, whose research sparked and terminated in the ringing affirmation of an ecumenical council: "The right to religious freedom has its foundation" not in the Church, not in society or state, not even in objective truth, but "in the very dignity of the human person." Unborn millions will never know how much the civilized dialogue they take for granted between Christian and Christian, between Christian and Jew, between Christian and unbeliever, was made possible by this man whose life was a civilized conversation. Untold Catholics will never sense that they live so gracefully in this dear land because John Murray showed so persuasively that the American proposition is quite congenial to the Catholic reality.

II

With the mind went the manner. What John Murray said or did, he said or did with "style." I mean, the how was perfectly proportioned to the what. There was a Murray style. It stemmed, I think, from a singular feeling for the sacredness of words, the sacredness of things, the sacredness of persons. How fresh syllables sounded when *his* rich voice proclaimed them—even when he changed the church-state issue into the "eclesiastico-political problematic." How fascinating a problem proved as *he* probed surgeon-like for its heart—from the Law and the Prophets he plumbed so profoundly to the latest experience of contemporary man. How dear human beings became while *he* fathomed the four bases on which a people must be built: truth, justice, love, and freedom.

Each of you has his or her private memory of the Murray manner. How your heart leaped when he smiled at you; how your thoughts took wing when he lectured to you; how good the "little people" felt when *he* spoke to *you.* How natural it all sounded when *he* ordered a "beefeater Martini desperately dry." How uplifted you felt when he left you with "Courage, Walter! It's far more important than intelligence." How the atmosphere changed when he entered a room: it was warm, electric, somehow bigger. How he spoke first and softly to *you*—not because you were colored, but because you were his friend, or because you were a stranger—or because you were human. For, as his Jewish secretary put it, all you had to be was a human being and he respected you, even loved you.

Each of you has his or her memory of the Murray manner. How aloof he seemed, when he was really only shy—terribly shy. How sensitive to your hurt, how careful not to wound—with his paradoxical belief, "A gentleman is never rude save intentionally." How courteous he was, especially if you were young, just beginning, fumbling for the answer or even for the question. How gentle he was, as only the strong tested by fire can be gentle. How firm and outgoing his handclasp—his whole self given for this moment to you only. How open he was, to men and ideas, as only "the man who lives with wisdom" can be open. How stubborn and unbending, once the demands of truth or justice or love or freedom were transparent.

How rhythmic he was, on the public platform and the private links. How serene, in delicate dialogue and mid the threat of a world's destruction. How priestly in every gesture, a mediator between God and man—not only at the altar (so warm and majestic) but in the day-to-day encounter with the learned and the illiterate, with the powerful and the impotent, with those for whom God is a living reality and those for whom God is dead. How delighted he could be with the paradoxes of life—as when the Unitarians honored this professional Trinitarian. How the laughter lit his eyes when he recalled that during the Rome discussions on religious freedom "Michael Cardinal Browne proved more unsinkable than his famous Irish cousin Molly." And how confident he looked as he predicted that the postconciliar experience of the Church would parallel the experience of the bishops in council: we will begin with a good deal of uncertainty and confusion, must therefore pass through a period of crisis and tension, but can expect to end with a certain measure of light and of joy.

III

The captivating thing is, the manner was the man. As the mind was the man. Here was no pose, no sheerly academic exercise. Here was a man. In his professional, academic, intellectual life, he lived the famous paragraph of Aquinas: "There are two ways of desiring knowledge. One way is to desire it as a perfection of oneself; and that is the way philosophers desire it. The other way of desiring knowledge is to desire it not simply as a perfection of oneself, but because through this knowledge the one we love becomes present to us; and that is the way saints desire it." Through Father Murray's knowledge, the persons he loved, a triune God and a host of men and women, became present to him.

The mind and the manner were the man. A man of warm affections and deep loves. In love with God, in love with man, in love with life. It is this that explains his joy in human living: at his desk or at an altar, on the lecture platform or in the home of a friend. It is this, I think, that explains his agony in the period of suspicion— agony not because he had been rebuked, not because the underground was active again, but because he knew then what most Catholics know only now, that he was right; because he knew that human beings would go on suffering needlessly, unjustly, as long as the Church did not say flatly and unequivocally what she in fact says now: religious freedom is a human right.

John Courtney Murray was the embodiment of the Christian humanist, in whom an aristocracy of the mind was wedded to a democracy of love. Whoever we are—Christian or non-Christian, believer or atheist—this tall man has made it quite difficult for any of us who loved him to ever again be small, to ever again make the world and human persons revolve around our selfish selves. We have been privileged indeed: we have known and loved the Christian man, "the man who lives with wisdom."

Dear friends of Father Murray: On his questionnaire for Woodstock's forthcoming evaluation by the Middle States Association and the American Association of Theological Schools, Father Murray listed the two lines of research in which he was currently engaged: (1) the problem of contemporary atheism; (2) a Trinitarian conception of the state of grace. In his mind the two areas were not segregated. For the twin poles of his life were man and God—the heady synthesis of his beloved Aquinas: God in His secret life, man as he comes forth from God, and man as he returns to God through Christ.

Through Christ, this man of God, this man of men, has returned to God. It should be an intriguing return, especially if, as I suspect, there is a Jesuit named Weigel waiting in the wings. For sheer knowledge and love, the dialogue, or trialogue, may well be unique.

36

HOW ABSURD OF GOD
On the sudden departure of John Paul I

It was traumatic—not only for cardinals but for the Catholic world. Five weeks before, the College of Cardinals had chosen a successor to Pope Paul VI. On September 28, 1978, John Paul I was dead. He was such an obviously good man, profoundly pastoral, with an engaging smile, ready to walk in the ways of John XXIII and Paul VI. And before he could do more than touch the world with a promise, he was taken from us.

Many of us asked, understandably, "why?" At Washington's National Cathedral, Jesuit theologian Avery Dulles asked, unexpectedly, "why not?" Still, the suddenness of it did raise questions we could hardly hope to answer—questions about divine providence, about the ways of God with man, with this man presumably Spirit-selected to shepherd the flock of Christ.

At the gracious request of the Apostolic Delegate to the United States, Archbishop Jean Jadot, I preached the homily at the Pontifical Requiem Mass which he celebrated on October 5 at St. Matthew's Cathedral in Washington, D.C. The usual approach, a eulogy, did not seem in order: there was really not much to eulogize; John Paul's time with us had been all too brief. Nor did it seem appropriate or promising to ponder why death struck so swiftly. One question proved particularly appealing: for all our witlessness, our dulness in the face of tragedy, is there not a Christian lesson to be learned from those thirty-four days?

My brothers and sisters: Friday morning you and I were confronted once again with absurdity. Yes, absurdity. Another man had died. No, not just another man. He had been pope—for thirty-four days. We knew him not; but he smiled, and a smile creased the drawn face of humanity. He asked a little boy if he wanted to be in fifth grade all his life, and we *all* laughed "no." He assured the sick, "Know that the pope understands and loves you," and suddenly their hurt softened. He welcomed with warmth non-Roman representatives to his installing, and a Church of Scotland minister went up and confessedly "cuddled" him. He denied we are "in a rotten and dishonest society. There are still many good people, so many honest people. Violence cannot do anything, but love can"—and we wanted to believe him. Praying for peace and Camp David, he noted that God is not only father but "even more so mother, who . . . wants only to be good to us," and our spirits soared. He promised "no miracle solutions," only that he would serve us. . . . How absurd of God: to show us the face of humanity at its best, and then to take John Paul in his sleep; to lift a lowly man from nowhere to raise our hopes, and then to return him hastily to the dust.

It *is* absurd, in the sense that it seems to make no sense. That "God's ways are not our ways" is obvious, yet not very enlightening. But if it is unclear what God Himself is trying to tell us, it is still worth probing the apparently absurd for what we can take from it. I suggest two readings, twin interpretations, of those thirty-four days.

First, in one man and one month John Paul revealed to us the importance of being not earnest but *human*. I am speaking of all of us, but I mean especially those whose frightening task is to lead others. Someone defined a leader as one who can move minds and hearts—not force them but move them. "No one can come to me," Jesus warned, "unless the Father who sent me draws him" (Jn 6:44). Draws him not by chains but, as St. Augustine saw, by the bonds of love. John Paul drew us, because his words, his hands, his smile were woven of love. Not solutions, only service—which is the only "miracle" most of us have to offer.

In a world dominated by power, John Paul proved that love is not powerless. His love touched peasant and diplomat, the keen and the dull, the hale and the halt, the young and the aging, those who love and some who are bitter as bile. He touched them because love was the man, and the man was love. And so he spoke to a child with the same affection and respect he showed his Curia or our Vice President. For him, the Mideast was indeed a place, but more importantly it was pulsing people. He sensed, I think, that war, like peace, rarely begins in councils of state; the seeds of war are in our hearts; they flower in our homes and on our streets; war, like peace, stares out of our eyes.

John Paul breathed a thrilling truth: however powerless you feel, however bare of miracle solutions, you can touch another person, you may even move an acre of God's world, if you will only reach out, very simply, in love. Little wonder that, when John Paul died, at his bedside lay . . . *The Imitation of Christ*.

Second, those thirty-four days tell us how little *time* there is for any of us. There is so much to be done, so many need our love, and there is so little time. I cannot promise myself tomorrow. Only today. Not even that. Only this moment am I alive—alive to live and to love, to work and to dance, to play and to pray, to laugh and to weep. Oh yes, a resurrection beckons beyond (today's Gospel guarantees that), but tomorrow's resurrection will not raise today's world from its despair, will not fill this hungry stomach. We cannot wait for tomorrow; for tomorrow war may blaze on the hot sands of Sinai; tomorrow may be too late for love; tomorrow I or the other may be dead.

It is the importance of the "now" in human living. Not that each moment should be a frantic search for God and goodness, for holiness in word and work, even for peace; that way madness lies. Simply a sensible awareness that God and His images are here and now: in *this* political crisis, in *this* social injustice, in *this* starving child, in *this* homeless stranger, in *this* confrontation with evil. Simply the command of the Psalmist to the chosen people: "O that *today* you would hearken to [the Lord's] voice!" (Ps 95:7). Today; for salvation is now, reconciliation is now, love is now, life is now. Not that tomorrow can take care of itself, but that today God speaks and today you must respond. It is today's reading from Romans: "None of us lives as his own master and none of us dies as his own master. While we live we are responsible to the Lord, and when we die we die as his servants. Both in life and in death we are the Lord's" (Rom 14:7–8).

My brothers and sisters: John Paul offered his last Mass last Thursday. The Responsorial Psalm he said at that Mass was so prophetic it makes me shiver. It begins with a word peculiarly pertinent to him, and it ends with a word gently hortatory for us:

> [Lord,] you turn man back to dust,
> saying, "Return, O children of men."
> For a thousand years in your sight
> are as yesterday,
> now that it is past,
> or as a watch of the night.
> You make an end of [men] in their sleep;
> the next morning they are like the changing grass. . . .
> Teach us to number our days aright,
> that we may gain wisdom of heart. . . .
> And may the gracious care of the Lord our God be ours;
> [Lord,] prosper the work of our hands.
>
> (Ps 90:3–17)

NOTES

1. Cf. *Oedipus the King*, lines 1528–30.
2. Cf. *On the Crown* 169 ff.
3. Cf. *Republic* 7, 1 ff.
4. Plato, *Apology* 42.
5. *Iliad* 1, 34.
6. *Fourth Eclogue*, lines 5–6.
7. *Odes* 1, 17.
8. *Odes* 1, 11.
9. *Odes* 1, 37.
10. *The Life of Henry the Fifth*, Act 4, Scene 1.
11. *The Tragedy of Romeo and Juliet*, Act 2, Scene 2.
12. *The Tragedy of Hamlet, Prince of Denmark*, Act 3, Scene 1.
13. *The Merchant of Venice*, Act 3, Scene 1.
14. Gerard Manley Hopkins, "The Blessed Virgin Compared to the Air We Breathe," in W. H. Gardner and N. H. MacKenzie, eds., *The Poems of Gerard Manley Hopkins* (4th ed.; New York: Oxford University Press, 1970) 93–97.
15. Edmond Rostand, *Cyrano de Bergerac*, tr. Brian Hooker (New York: Random House, n.d.) 304–5.
16. John L. McKenzie, "The Word of God in the Old Testament," *Theological Studies* 21 (1960) 205.
17. Ibid. 206.
18. For the different modes of Christ's presence in liturgical celebrations, see chapter 1-E in the Instruction *Eucharisticum mysterium* of the Sacred Congregation of Rites, May 25, 1967 (translation in Austin Flannery, O.P., ed., *Vatican Council II: The Conciliar and Post Conciliar Documents* [Northport, N.Y.: Costello, 1975] 109). Note especially the final sentence: Christ's presence under the species of the Eucharist "is called 'real' not in an exclusive sense, as if the other kinds of presence were not real, but *par excellence*." The words are taken from Paul VI's Encyclical *Mysterium fidei* (*AAS* 57 [1965] 764).
19. For simplicity's sake, I shall concentrate on the homily within the Mass; what I say can be applied *mutatis mutandis* to other liturgical events, e.g., a communal-penance service.
20. *Inter oecumenici* (= Sacra Congregatio Rituum, *Instructio ad executionem Constitutionis de sacra liturgia recte ordinandam*, Sept. 26, 1964) 3, no. 54 (*Normae exsequutivae Concilii oecumenici Vaticani II [1963–1969]*, ed. Florentius Romita [Naples: D'Auria, 1971] 58). This definition has been incorporated into the "General Instruction on the Roman Missal" in the Roman Missal of 1970, no. 41.
21. Constitution on the Sacred Liturgy, no. 35.
22. Ibid.
23. Dogmatic Constitution on Divine Revelation, no. 10.
24. For the homilist's consolation, the acts of Vatican II reveal a concern not to require of the homilist "a mere exegesis of the scriptural section of the liturgy but, connected freely with the text of one of the lessons or even of another detail in the word or rite of the liturgy itself, [the homily] should rather offer instruction for the religious and moral life of the faithful. . . . During the two festival circles of the Church's year it would be devoted more to the facts of salvation and their consequences, but outside these circles it would be all the more open for all the

219

questions of the moral order of life. In all cases it should in some way, as mysta-gogical sermon, lead the faithful inwardly into the service, be in harmony with it and facilitate its inner celebration, rather than stand independently beside it" (Josef Andreas Jungmann, "Constitution on the Sacred Liturgy," in Herbert Vorgrimler, ed., *Commentary on the Documents of Vatican II* 1 [New York: Herder and Herder, 1967] 38).

25. *Humani generis* (Denzinger-Schönmetzer [ed. 32] 3886 [2314]).
26. John Gallen, "Liturgical Reform: Product or Prayer?" *Worship* 47 (1973) 606.
27. Cf. Walter J. Burghardt, S.J., "A Theologian's Challenge to Liturgy," *Theological Studies* 35 (1974) 244.
28. Jungmann, loc. cit. See also *Inter oecumenici* 3, no. 55: If there is a set program of homilies for certain times, it should still preserve an intimate nexus with the more important times and feasts of the liturgical year or with the mystery of the redemption; "for the homily is part of the liturgy of the day."
29. Yves Congar, O.P., "Sacramental Worship and Preaching," in *The Renewal of Preaching: Theory and Practice* (= Concilium 33; New York: Paulist, 1968) 51–63.
30. Ibid. 54.
31. Cf. ibid. 55–56.
32. Ibid. 56.
33. Constitution on the Sacred Liturgy, no. 59.
34. Cf. Congar, "Sacramental Worship and Preaching" 58–59. See also Vatican II, Decree on the Ministry and Life of Priests, no. 4: "In the Christian community itself, especially among those who seem to understand or believe little of what they practice, the preaching of the word is required for the very administration of the sacraments; for these are sacraments of faith, and faith is born of the word and nourished by it."
35. Congar, "Sacramental Worship and Preaching" 60.
36. Ibid. 62.
37. Joseph P. Fitzpatrick, S.J., "Justice as a Problem of Culture," in *Studies in the International Apostolate of Jesuits* 5, no. 2 (December 1976) 18–19.
38. For a useful treatment of the problem of translation, see Karl Rahner, S.J., "Demythologization and the Sermon," in *The Renewal of Preaching* (n. 29 above) 20–38.
39. Ibid. 21.
40. Ibid. 25.
41. *National Catholic Reporter*, Sept. 15, 1972, p. 2.
42. Otto Semmelroth, S.J., *The Preaching Word: On the Theology of Proclamation* (New York: Herder and Herder, 1965) 200. See the whole section "Preaching as a Communication Which Summons," 179–202.
43. Rod McKuen, *Listen to the Warm* (New York: Random House, 1969) 112.

Homily 1

1. Joseph Plunkett, "I See His Blood upon the Rose," in *The Oxford Book of Irish Verse: XVIIth Century—XXth Century* (Oxford: Clarendon, 1958) 208.
2. Gerard Manley Hopkins, "S. Thomae Aquinatis Rythmus ad SS. Sacramentum," in W. H. Gardner and N. H. MacKenzie, eds., *The Poems of Gerard Manley Hopkins* (4th ed.; New York: Oxford University Press, 1970) 211.
3. Teilhard de Chardin, *The Divine Milieu* (New York: Harper, 1960) 110.
4. Ibid.
5. Gerard Manley Hopkins, "God's Grandeur," in *Poems* (n. 2 above) 66.
6. Constitution on the Church in the Modern World, no. 22.
7. *The Divine Milieu* 116–17.
8. Cf. Pierre Fransen, "Towards a Psychology of Divine Grace," *Cross Currents* 8 (1958) 229–30; Jean Mouroux, *The Christian Experience* (New York: Sheed and Ward, 1954) 38.

Homily 3

1. Schalom Ben-Chorin, as quoted by Hans Küng, *The Church* (New York: Sheed and Ward, 1968) 149.

Homily 4

1. Abraham J. Heschel, *The Prophets* (New York: Harper & Row, 1962) 181.
2. W. H. Auden, "After Christmas: A Passage from a Christmas Oratorio," *Harper's* 188, no. 1124 (January 1944) 154–55.

Homily 5

1. *Hamlet, Prince of Denmark*, Act 3, Scene 1.
2. I have profited much from the treatment by R. A. F. MacKenzie, S.J., "Job," in *The Jerome Biblical Commentary* 1 (Englewood Cliffs, N.J.: Prentice-Hall, c1968) 510–33.
3. Ibid. 533.
4. *Webster's New International Dictionary of the English Language* (2nd ed. unabridged; Springfield, Mass.: Merriam, 1958) 2727.
5. John L. McKenzie, S.J., *Dictionary of the Bible* (Milwaukee: Bruce, c1965) 441–42.

Homily 6

1. Basil the Great, *The Long Rules*, q. 17 (tr. M. Monica Wagner, C.S.C., in *Fathers of the Church* 9 [New York: Fathers of the Church, Inc., 1950] 271–72).
2. See Jean Leclercq, *Le défi de la vie contemplative* (Gembloux: Duculot, 1970) 360–61, 367–68.
3. See the provocative essay by Thomas H. Clancy, S.J., "Feeling Bad about Feeling Good," in *Studies in the Spirituality of Jesuits* 9, no. 1 (January 1979).
4. This reference to Christ as clown was inspired by a pantomime that preceded my homily. See Harvey Cox, *The Feast of Fools: A Theological Essay on Festivity and Fantasy* (New York: Harper & Row, 1969), especially 139–57 on "Christ the Harlequin."
5. Ignatius Loyola, Rules of Modesty (where "modesty" has to do with human and Christian decorum applied to the life of a Jesuit).
6. Eugene O'Neill, *Lazarus Laughed*, Act 1, Scene 1; in *The Plays of Eugene O'Neill* (New York: Random House, 1955) 280.

Homily 7

1. When I wrote this homily in 1967, the English version of Hans Urs von Balthasar's *Glaubhaft ist nur Liebe* (Einsiedeln: Johannes Verlag, 1963) had not yet appeared. When it did appear two years later, the title, unfortunately, read simply *Love Alone* (New York: Herder and Herder, 1969).
2. Constitution on the Church in the Modern World, no. 1.

Homily 8

1. *The Paschal Mystery: Ancient Liturgies and Patristic Texts*, ed. A. Hamman, O.F.M. (Staten Island, N.Y.: Alba, c1969) 9.

2. Raymond E. Brown, S.S., *The Gospel according to John (xiii–xxi)* (Anchor Bible 29A; Garden City, N.Y.: Doubleday, 1970) 569.
3. *Didache* 9, 4.

Homily 9

1. In preparing this homily, I was richly informed and profoundly stimulated by two cassettes produced by the National Catholic Reporter Publishing Company (P.O. 281, Kansas City, Mo. 64141): John Gallen's "The Shape of Easter in the Liturgy" and John Grabner's "Passion Sunday."
2. On this aspect of Advent, see the homily "What Are You Waiting For?" (Homily 3 above).
3. On this aspect of Lent, see the homily "For Your Penance, Look Redeemed" (Homily 6 above).
4. Taken from the Gallen cassette (n. 1 above).
5. See my article "A Theologian's Challenge to Liturgy," *Theological Studies* 35 (1974) 233–48, especially 240–44.

Homily 10

1. For what follows on the biblical notion of truth, I am much indebted to Ignace de la Potterie, S.J., "Truth," in X. Léon-Dufour, ed., *Dictionary of Biblical Theology* (2nd ed.; New York: Seabury, 1973) 618–21, and to R. Bultmann, "alētheia," in G. Kittel, *Theological Dictionary of the New Testament* 1 (Grand Rapids: Eerdmans, 1964) 232–47.

Homily 12

1. Piet Smulders, *The Design of Teilhard de Chardin: An Essay in Theological Reflection* (Westminster, Md.: Newman, 1967) 176–77.

Homily 14

1. Gerard Manley Hopkins, "God's Grandeur," in W. H. Gardner and N. H. MacKenzie, eds., *The Poems of Gerard Manley Hopkins* (4th ed.; New York: Oxford University Press, 1970) 66.
2. Hans Urs von Balthasar, *Love Alone* (New York: Herder and Herder, 1969). My translation, *Only Love Is Believable*, recaptures more accurately the original German title *Glaubhaft ist nur Liebe*.

Homily 15

1. Bull *Ineffabilis Deus* (Denzinger-Schönmetzer [32nd ed.; Freiburg: Herder, 1963] 2803 [1641].
2. For a more detailed exposition of this Mariological theme, see Homily 33 in this volume entitled "What Mary Is. . . ."
3. Daniel J. Levinson *et al.*, *The Seasons of a Man's Life* (New York: Knopf, 1978) 21.
4. See John Courtney Murray, "The Danger of the Vows," *Woodstock Letters* 96 (1967) 421–27. The text of this famous conference, given to the Woodstock College Jesuit community on Feb. 21, 1947, was reconstructed after his death (1967) from two of Fr. Murray's personal copies, one with his own handwritten emendations, together with a number of slightly varying mimeographed copies. Ft. Murray was reluctant to publish the conference without updating it in the spirit of Vatican II; he never found the opportunity.

5. Ibid. 426.
6. Ibid. 427.
7. Ibid.
8. Ibid.
9. William Shakespeare, *The Merry Wives of Windsor*, Act 2, Scene 2.
10. See, e.g., 1 Cor 1:18–31.

Homily 16

1. See Raymond E. Brown, S.S., *Priest and Bishop: Biblical Reflections* (New York: Paulist, c1970) 21–45.
2. Nikos Kazantzakis, *Report to Greco* (New York: Simon & Schuster, 1965) 511.
3. Margery Williams, *The Velveteen Rabbit or How Toys Become Real* (Garden City: Doubleday, no date) 17.

Homily 17

1. For more detailed information and specific texts, cf. Gerhard Kittel, *Theological Dictionary of the New Testament* 7 (ed. Gerhard Friedrich, tr. Geoffrey W. Bromiley; Grand Rapids: Eerdmans, 1971) 465–526; André Barucq and Pierre Grelot, "Wisdom," in Xavier Léon-Dufour, ed., *Dictionary of the Bible* (2nd ed.; New York: Seabury, 1973) 657–61.
2. This is a local allusion to a minor scandal involving a Member of Congress and friend.
3. St. Jerome, *Letter 52*, no. 5.

Homily 18

1. The full Gospel reading was John 17:6, 15–20. For the interpretation of the difficult verse 19 ("And it is for them that I consecrate myself, in order that they too may be consecrated in truth"), specifically the meaning of "consecration," see Raymond E. Brown, S.S., *The Gospel according to John (xiii–xxi)* (Garden City, N.Y.: Doubleday, 1970) 766–77.
2. This model is more in harmony historically with a Protestant view of ministry, especially the Barthian.

Homily 19

1. Rod McKuen, *Listen to the Warm* (New York: Random House, 1969) 112.
2. Eugene O'Neill, *Lazarus Laughed*, Act 1, Scene 1; in *The Plays of Eugene O'Neill* (New York: Random House, 1955) 280.

Homily 20

1. Acts 4:8–12; 1 Jn 3:1–2; Jn 10:14–18.

Homily 21

1. For some very pertinent texts, see Isaiah 1:11–18 and 42:1–4; Hosea 2:18–20 and 6:6; Amos 5:18–25; Micah 6:6–8; Jeremiah 7:5–7.
2. This is an idea dear to a remarkable theologian and spiritual writer of the fourth

century, St. Gregory of Nyssa, as expressed eloquently by Roger Leys, *L'Image de Dieu chez Grégoire de Nysse* (Brussels: L'Edition Universelle, 1951) 139–40.

Homily 22

1. For rhetorical reasons I have decided to retain the translation "man alive," rather than introduce the less "sexist" but clumsy expression "human person alive." On the whole, especially in recent years, I have tried to be sensitive to legitimate demands in this area.
2. Augustine, *Confessions* 3, 1.
3. Augustine, *Commentary on John* 26, 4.

Homily 24

1. *Monumenta Xaveriana* 1, 509–12; translation in James Brodrick, S.J., *The Origin of the Jesuits* (New York: Longmans, Green, 1940) 133–34.
2. Constitution on the Church, no. 4.
3. Léon-Joseph Suenens, *Coresponsibility in the Church* (New York: Herder and Herder, 1968) 31.
4. These are modern Jesuit missionaries from the East Coast, whose names were well known to many, if not most, in the audience.
5. Paul Claudel, "Saint Francis Xavier," in *Coronal* (New York: Pantheon, 1943) 190.

Homily 25

1. *Decree on Ecumenism*, no. 24 (tr. *The Documents of Vatican II*, ed. Abbott-Gallagher [New York: America Press, 1966] 365).
2. Ibid., no. 12.
3. From a sermon at the National Shrine of the Immaculate Conception, Washington, D.C., Jan. 22, 1966; quoted in *Catholic Mind* 64, no. 1203 (May 1966) 31–32.
4. Robert McAfee Brown, "Ecumenism and the Secular Order," *Theology Digest* 15, no. 4 (Winter 1967) 262.
5. *Theology Digest* 15, no. 4 (Winter 1967) 273–74.
6. "No Religion Is an Island," *Union Seminary Quarterly Review* 21 (1965–66) 121.

Homily 26

1. Arthur A. Cohen, "Notes toward a Jewish Theology of Politics," *Commonweal* 77 (1962–63) 11.
2. William Shakespeare, *The Merchant of Venice*, Act 3, Scene 1.
3. From the "Guiding Principles of Reform Judaism," adopted in 1937 at the meeting of the Central Conference of American Rabbis in Columbus, Ohio: *Universal Jewish Encyclopedia* 6, 242.
4. Ibid.

Homily 28

1. *Sum. theol.* 2-2, q. 58, a. 1.
2. Vatican II, Declaration on Religious Freedom, no. 2.

Homily 29

1. I am quite aware that the four paragraphs to come are substantially to be found in Homily 21—in large measure, verbally. But for the homilist repetition is a constant temptation—not always overcome.

Homily 30

1. A reference to a caustic characterization of some adversaries by a high-ranking official in the Nixon administration around that time.
2. Vatican II, Constitution on the Church in the Modern World, no. 78.

Homily 31

1. Heinrich Fries, *Glauben-Wissen: Wege zu einer Lösung des Problems* (Berlin: Morus, 1960) 95.
2. Pierre Teilhard de Chardin, *The Divine Milieu: An Essay on the Interior Life* (New York: Harper, c1960) 14.
3. See ibid. 89 ff.
4. What follows is reproduced from my *Seven Hungers of the Human Family* (Washington, D.C.: United States Catholic Conference, 1976) 44–47.
5. Abraham Joshua Heschel, "No Religion Is an Island," *Union Seminary Quarterly Review* 21 (1965–66) 121.
6. Thomas Merton, *Confessions of a Guilty Bystander* (Garden City, N.Y.: Doubleday Image Books, 1956) 261.
7. Meg Greenfield, "Lest We Forget," *Newsweek*, Feb. 2, 1976, p. 76.

Homily 34

1. Emil J. Freireich, "The Best Medical Care for the 'Hopeless' Patient," *Medical Opinion*, February 1972, 51–55.
2. *Desert Call*, Spring 1971.
3. See, e.g., Irenaeus, *Proof of the Apostolic Preaching* 11; *Against Heresies* 5, 6, 1.
4. See, e.g., Karl Rahner, *On the Theology of Death* (Quaestiones disputatae 2; New York: Herder and Herder, 1961), and, more briefly, "Death," in *Sacramentum mundi* 2 (New York: Herder and Herder, 1968) 58–62.
5. Pedro de Rivadeneira, *Vida del bienaventurado Padre Ignacio de Loyola* (2nd ed.; Barcelona: Subirana, 1885) 501–2.

The Cultural Turn in U.S. History